MALE ORDER
Unwrapping Masculinity

Male Order

Unwrapping Masculinity

edited by Rowena Chapman and
Jonathan Rutherford

LAWRENCE & WISHART
LONDON

Lawrence & Wishart Limited
99A Wallis Road
London E9 5LN

First published 1988
Reprinted 1989, 1996

© Lawrence & Wishart, 1988

Each essay © the author, 1988

Photoset in North Wales by
Derek Doyle & Associates, Mold, Clwyd.
Printed and bound in Great Britain by
Redwood Books, Trowbridge.

Contents

Introduction:
Avoiding the bends

JONATHAN RUTHERFORD

In this new introduction to *Male Order* I want to focus on one significant development since 1988: the male reaction against women and liberal sexual politics.

A quick glance at contemporary youth culture would appear to contradict the idea of a male backlash. Dance culture and environmental politics have encouraged a coming together of the sexes after the gender conflicts of the 1970s and 1980s. To prove the point, the 1990s have recycled the 1960s aesthetic of unisex. Young men are lined up with young women in Calvin Klein adverts, wearing the same clothes, sharing the same fragrance. *Sky* magazine and *The Face* depict unisex images of wasted, anorexic white youth, hyping the mythologies of an outcast, disenchanted young. On the surface young men and women appear more at ease with each other. There are plenty who believe that the feminist battles for equality are now an unnecessary and divisive adjunct to a more egalitarian gender culture. But these images of young men and women joined together in a gender free androgyny evade the uncertainties and antagonisms which beset them. What unites young men and women is their disenfranchisement from the mainstream of political and economic life. What divides them is the differential effect

3

of uncertainty in their lives and their response to it.
Whatever the odds, increasing numbers of young women
express ambition and a desire to succeed. In contrast,
young men appear to be floundering. The old rules and
roles have changed and they can no longer expect an
allotted place in society. The legacy of feminism has been a
transformation in the attitudes and aspirations of young
women. Their expectations however, continue to be
thwarted by institutionalised and covert forms of
discrimination. To challenge and change these requires
political power and that means a willingness amongst men
to make common cause with women. It raises the question
of how men are going to respond. This is not just a
predicament of the sons. It has also visited the fathers.
The question applies to them both.

Men in Trouble

In the post-feminist era of the 1990s, there has been a
growing disaffection amongst middle class men with the
ideal of sexual equality. The massive expansion of
part-time jobs for women and the pattern of women
divorcing men have created a new wave of doubt and
uncertainty in men's private lives. Organisations like
'Families need Fathers', campaigning against the divorce
laws and for men's right to custody of their children had
already carved out a political space for a men's
anti-feminist politics during the 1980s. Middle-class men
began to experience a relative loss in their social prestige
and economic status. An era of economic insecurity has
been precipitated by globalisation, technology-driven job
losses and economic recession. Jobs and careers, once
clearly delineated functions, are being transformed into
contingent, flexible roles defined by sets of skills and
competences. Careers are being superseded by short term
contracts, freelancing, part-time work and piece-work at
home. For growing numbers in full time employment,
conditions of work are too insecure and idiosyncratic to be
called jobs. Throughout the golden age of post-war
consumer capitalism, full-time, tenured employment

underpinned the middle-class nuclear family and its twenty-five year mortgage. By the year 2000 it will have become a minority form of work.[1] The impact of this new work order on a generation of thirty and forty something men, who inherited their fathers' expectations of a career for life, threatens to undermine their role of head of household. At the same time it is destroying work as the principle source of their masculine self-esteem and personal integrity.

In 1996, insecurity at work, negative equity and falling salaries have propelled men into working longer hours. The recruitment agency Austin Knight reported two thirds of British workers working more than 40 hours a week and a quarter more than 50 hours. In a perverse mirroring of the stress and anxiety caused by overwork, a whole swathe of society suffers the hardships of no work. Paul Gregg of the LSE calculated that in 1979, 6 per cent of households had neither adult partner working. By 1989 the figure had risen to 16 per cent.[2] The Rowntree Foundation Inquiry into Income and Wealth reported that the numbers living on less than half of average incomes had trebled since 1978. The new work order has denied large sections of the adult population the prospects of meaningful employment and precipitated one third into a state of semi-permanent poverty and economic redundancy. The decline of traditional manual work, particularly skills in mining, shipbuilding, steel and engineering, has undermined numerous working-class communities and their cultures. Traditional working-class masculinities, without work and divested of the role of family breadwinner, have suffered a crisis of identity. While it was the fathers who suffered redundancy, it is their sons who are experiencing its longer term consequences.

The main governmental response to youth employment has been to expand and reform training and education provision. But growing evidence suggests that white, working class boys are at the bottom of the educational system.[3] Statistics released by the Department of Education in 1995 show that 37 per cent of boys are achieving five or more A-C GCSE grades, compared to 45.9 per cent of girls. A survey undertaken at Keele University between 1993 and 1994 of 7,000 young people found girls to be consistently more positive and better motivated than boys. A BBC *Panorama* programme on 16 October 1995 examined the contrasting fortunes of a group of young men and women who had attended the same comprehensive school in Darlington. Despite their similar IQ levels, the girls had out-performed the boys and were attending or preparing to go to university. Only one young man had an apprenticeship, the rest were unemployed or engaged in manual labour. One, who was packing fridges while his girlfriend left for university, was asked about their differing prospects. He didn't believe young women could succeed. 'They'll leave school. They'll go to university, get a job. They'll get a job where they went to university. They'll hate them and within two years they'll be back, because of all the pressures of work, because they've never done work in their lives.' His perception that manual labour was the only real work, was echoed by a young man who had been unemployed since leaving school: 'I'd rather have a job where I could use my hands, rather than just my mind. You feel like you've earned your money more – you come home and your shoulders are aching.' Chris Woodhead, the Chief Inspector of Schools wrote in *The Times* on 6 March 1996: 'The failure of boys, and in particular white working class boys, is one of the most disturbing problems we face within the whole education system ... Physics is the only subject in which boys now outperform girls.' Without an imaginable future within the mainstream economy these young men cling to the traditional masculinities. They are chauvinistic, archaic and rooted in the industrial revolution, but they have few other viable models of male working-class integrity and dignity.

The scorn for the feminised work of education and mental skills amongst many young working-class men suggests they have failed to recognise the technological revolution which is transforming the nature of men's work. But their self-deception is not caused by ignorance, but by a fear they will never match up to the social confidence, interpersonal skills and intellectual dexterity of the young women. Divested of hope and a productive role in society, unable to achieve adult independence and unwilling to contribute to the domestic economy of their mothers' homes, many young men have simply given up. Male redundancy has created cultures of prolonged adolescence in which young male identities remain locked into the locality of estate, shops and school. In their struggle to assert their independence, young men adopt a culture of risk-taking. Risk-taking is an integral part of an adolescent's struggle against parental authority, but if the transition to adulthood is delayed, risk-taking can become an end in itself. Violence, criminality, drug-taking and alcohol consumption become the means to gaining prestige for a masculine identity bereft of any social value or function. A Home Office report, *Young People and Crime*, based on 2,500 interviews, confirmed this prolongation of young men's anti-social adolescent behaviour. One half of the teenage boys and one third of the girls interviewed had been involved in crime. By their mid-twenties young women have grown out of crime, only 4 per cent admitting to committing a crime other than drug-taking. In contrast, the figure for men of a similar age was 31 per cent. Men were less likely to have left home, less likely to be in stable relationships and less likely to have secure employment.[4] The researchers found only a weak link between crime and social class. The pattern extends beyond areas of social deprivation. A report produced by the RAC in 1995 described young men as the most dangerous motorists, the most likely to commit deliberate violations such as speeding, 'undertaking' and jumping red lights, and the least ready to acknowledge they were doing wrong.

Kurt Cobain, morbid and suicidal, has been a symbol of 1990s youth culture. He stands in a long line of male icons – James Dean, Jack Kerouac, Sid Vicious – whose life on the edge has attracted the more romantic and morbid hankerings of adolescent hero worship. Their self-destruction and emotional isolation reflects a masculinity without the emotional wherewithal to maintain relationships and to live. They epitomise the spurious masculine autonomy created by society's injunction that young boys must separate from their mothers, deny their need for her and suppress their feelings. Boys attachment to their mothers remains unresolved, delaying emotional maturity and creating in many men a sometimes desperate and aggressive need to prove their manly independence. Ineptitude in interpersonal skills and emotional autarchy, which so often pass for appropriate masculine behaviour, leave men, particularly young men, ill-equipped to cope with social isolation and despair. In the UK in 1982, according to the Office of Population Censuses and Statistics, 320 men aged between 15 and 24 killed themselves. In 1992, the number was 500, an increase of 56 per cent. In 1990, coroners recorded 527 deaths of young men in this age range: the number of young women was 85.[5] The band Radiohead, in their song 'the bends', express the aimlessness of young men faced with uncertain futures.

> I'm just lying in a bar with my drip feed on
> talking to my
> girlfriend waiting for
> something to happen and i wish it was the
> sixties i wish i
> could be happy i wish i wish that something
> would happen.[6]

The wishful fantasy for the 1960s is for a time when there was hope in the future. Freud wrote about wishes in *The Interpretation of Dreams*: 'By picturing our wishes as fulfilled, dreams are after all leading us into the future.'[7] Dreams, wishes, desires, contain the idiom of our lives. They lead us into relationships with others and into ways of being with ourselves. They help to establish a sense of personal destiny and a belief in the ability to influence the course of one's life. The decline of traditional male roles, job insecurity, the boredom, poverty and sense of worthlessness created by redundancy, unemployment and

meaningless, badly paid work have placed many men on
the threshold of an inner feeling of emptiness in which
dreams, wishes and desire appear to be entirely lost. The
legacy of this pain is not just male self-destruction but
domestic violence and murdered women and children.

The rhetoric of anti-feminism

David Thomas, former editor of *Punch* and author of *Not
Guilty: In Defence of the Modern Man*, declared on BBC 2's
Fifth Column, in 1991: 'The anger that appears to be
building up between the sexes becomes more virulent with
every day that passes. And far from women taking the
blame ... the fact is that men are invariably portrayed as
the bad guys. Being a good man is like being a good Nazi.'[8]
Two years later he was writing in his book: 'The fact is,
people are in pain. And right now, the ones who wear
trousers and stand up to piss don't seem to count for much
when it comes to being healed' (p7). Such complaint has
little grounding in social and economic reality. In August
1993, The National Child Development Study, which had
been following the lives of 11,500 men and women born in
one week in March, 1958, presented a report to the annual
British Association meeting in Keele. It argued that
'Marital breakdowns are creating a new underclass of
women who are trapped in a downward economic spiral.'
It added; 'There are few signs that men had metamorphosed into the caring and labour-sharing breed that the
media was trumpeting in the early 1990s.'[9] In December,
the market research group Mintel published *Women 2000*,
a survey of 1500 men and women.[10] It came to similar
conclusions. Only one man in a hundred, it claimed, did
his 'fair share of the housework'. While two men in ten
said they took an equal share in the cooking, only one in
ten women thought they did. Over half of the women
interviewed had full-time jobs, but they were paid, on
average, 29 per cent less than men in comparable jobs and
were significantly less likely to have a company pension.
Only 20 per cent of the working women claimed their
male partners equally shared any single domestic task.

Mintel's consumer manager, Angela Hughes, told *The Guardian*: 'Men seem to set out with good intentions to share the domestic chores but the catalyst appears to be the arrival of children. At this stage, the man appears to abdicate responsibility for his share, regardless of whether his partner is working.'[11] The surveys indicate that the downturn in men's fortunes is unrelated to any tangible increase in female equality. If men are doing badly, women are doing worse.

The most publicised anti-feminist diatribe was published in 1992 by journalist Neil Lyndon. His book, *No More Sex War: The failures of feminism*, argued that the women's liberation movement had been 'fundamentally false in logic, thoroughly false in history and poisonous in effect.'[12] Lyndon's career as spokesman for a male backlash against feminism began with an article in the *Sunday Times Magazine* in 1991. 'It is hard to think', he declared, 'of one example of systemic and institutionalised discrimination against women in Britain today.' For Lyndon, society's neglect of the needs of men was epitomised in men's exclusion from their own homes and children: 'If our society is a patriarchy, why does it allow no statutory right to paternity leave?'[13] He argued that the liberation of women in the past twenty-five years had been a consequence of the new technologies of contraception and the right to abortion. Feminism had merely served to entrench gender stereotypes and promote antagonism and sex war between men and women. The effect of this revolution on his own life can be gauged by an article written by his wife, Deirdre Lyndon, which appeared in the *Daily Mail* on 21 September 1992 (reprinted in *The Guardian*, the following day). Her opening sentence – 'This is the book that killed my marriage' – summed up the consequence of what had become her husband's obsessive loathing of feminism: 'I kept urging Neil to temper his arguments … "It's not feminists you're attacking," I would say. "Surely it's only militant feminists?" But it became clear that it was indeed all feminists and that, to some extent, the war was indeed being waged on women.' Lyndon moved out of the family home and began a relationship with another woman who had been acting as his part-time secretary. In trying to understand her husband's 'politics of hatred', Deirdre Lyndon suggested he had moved out because 'he needed to shred all the strands of domesticity to write this book.' She added: 'In some ways I think Neil wants to strip women of motherhood.'

Deirdre Lyndon had put her finger on the primary target of the backlash against feminism: mothers and motherhood. The argument that a causal relation exists between absent fathers, lone mothers and social disorder has been a central tenet of the contemporary British right since the 1980s. In their introduction to *Family Portraits* (Social Affairs Unit 1986), a collection of right-wing essays on the family, Digby Anderson and Graham Dawson identified 'brands of feminism which are deeply hostile to the family, most especially to the role of fathers' (p11). Patricia Morgan's contribution develops this theme. Her essay, 'Feminist Attempts to Sack Father: A case of unfair dismissal', prefigured the anti-feminism of Thomas and Lyndon. She begins; 'If there is a war over the family', then one of its principal battle fronts is whether homes need fathers' (p38). She argues that the absence of fathers and exclusive feminine nurture condemn young males to a life of violent crime and underachievement at school. Her political crusade is to defend 'the home', and its 'cultural heritage and the middle class values' which it, and thus the family, is felt to harbour and transmit' (p61). To defend the home, it is necessary to defend the father. He is the principal socialiser and educator of these values and consequently the prime target of the feminist detractors of the family. Morgan dismisses the statistics which reveal the paucity of men's involvement in household chores: 'it becomes quite inappropriate to measure any parental contribution to child-rearing in terms of practical caretaking' (p54). What the father provides is his stabilising roles of breadwinner and the enactor of discipline. A society without fathers, she argues, would degenerate into a state of 'rootlessness – where there are no heritage or ties and people have no place or past, but

simply wander about the face of the earth ... a world
without responsibilities in which relationships are thin and
transitory' (p60). Her apocalyptic vision of society
destroyed by fatherless, mother-headed families had
already been heralded by the influential American
academic, Charles Murray.

Murray has argued that British and American society
have both developed a violent and amoral underclass
characterised by redundant males, unmarried mothers
and illegitimate children. His thesis – harking back to the
discredited Victorian pseudo-science of degeneracy – has
been a powerful influence on contemporary right-wing
politics.[14] Crime and social instability are viewed as the
consequence of the decline of marriage and the purge of
the father from the family. Blame for the criminal
behaviour of boys lies with the rise of lone-mother
households. In the 1990s, Conservative government
attempts to impose social discipline have demonised
female-led, one parent families as the cause of social
unrest and young male waywardness. The Conservative
politician John Redwood blamed the soaring welfare
budget on: 'Too many young women ... having babies and
'marrying' the state. Too many unmarried young men ...
walking away from their responsibilities as fathers' (*News of
the World* 17 September 1995). John Redwood and other
right-wing politicians like Peter Lilley promote a moral
authoritarianism in an attempt to secure a social order
damaged by their brand of deregulated market capitalism.
They are not concerned with domestic democracy –
encouraging fathers to share childcare and household
tasks – but in reasserting the male role of breadwinner in
order to police mothers in the upbringing of sons.

The fear of a declining male authority within the family
and in society, articulated by right-wing intellectuals,
politicians and social commentators since the 1980s, has
become, by 1996, a common theme in social democratic
political discourse. Amitai Etzioni, the founder of
communitarianism, has provided a link between liberalism
and this new politics of social discipline. In Britain, it has
met with the approval of Tony Blair and Shadow Home

Secretary Jack Straw. Etzioni argues that the contemporary family is failing in the task of transmitting self control and moral values to the young. Mothers, absent at work, are no longer ensuring the cohesiveness of family life and fathers continue to fail to take a fuller part in the practices of childcare. Etzioni claims his concern is with the role of both parents as agents of social discipline.[15] But Beatrix Campbell, in her critique of communitarianism, argues that his concern is primarily directed against mothers and not at men's reluctance to share domestic work and childcare. 'Etzioni's fire has been directed at mothers and not at the democratic deficit in domestic love and labour.'[16]

This convergence of social democracy and conservativism had already found a cultural home with the emergence in Britain, in 1992, of the 'Wild Men', an import from the US, inspired by Robert Bly's book, *Iron John* (Element, 1991). This 'mytho-poetic' men's movement was the first significant development in men's sexual politics since 'Men against Sexism' began in the 1970s. While the latter had taken its inspiration from the Women's Liberation Movement – men rejecting the masculinity of their fathers and embracing their more 'feminine' feelings – the 'Wild Men' were intent upon reclaiming their fathers and their own male potency. The caring and sharing New Man of the mid-1980s, a product of its consumer boom, had reflected the changing sensibilities of post 1960s, middle-class masculinities. But for Bly, the archetypal 'soft' man only proved that men had lost touch with their inner virility. Men's waged work outside the home had broken the bond between father and son. Boys raised exclusively by their mothers learnt to see their father through her eyes: 'If the son learns feeling primarily from the mother, then he will probably see his own masculinity from the feminine point of view as well' (p25). According to Bly, modern men are mother's boys. Unable to grow up and relate to women as adults, they become trapped in compliant relationships, leaving them feeling powerless and manipulated. The New Man of the 1980s is Bly's 'naive man'. He can be receptive, can feel the

other's pain, but he cannot say what he wants, he is too
frightened to say 'no'. The 'naive man' has no resolve. Bly
argues that beneath his nice exterior is a man full of
misogynistic anger.

Bly declares this unmanliness to be a crisis of men's
relationship with their fathers: 'Not seeing your father
when you are small, never being with him, having a remote
father, an absent father, a workaholic father, is an injury'
(p31). Abandoned to their mothers, boys do not acquire the
self-preservating aggression which sustains the boundaries
of selfhood. 'A grown man six feet tall will allow another
person to cross his boundaries, enter his psychic house,
verbally abuse him, carry away his treasures, and slam the
door behind; the invaded man will stand there with an
ingratiating, confused smile on his face' (p146). The
purpose of the Wild Men movement was to rediscover the
father within and tap his power. Groups of men attended
weekend gatherings in the countryside, using ritualised
dancing, drum banging and male bonding to make cathartic, primeval attempts to harness their 'masculine free
spirit'. Despite widespread but mostly sceptical British press
interest, Bly's simple assertion that men had a fundamental
problem being men found a ready constituency amongst a
middle class disoriented and demoralised by the new work
order and the erosion of traditional masculine certitudes.
The journalist Andrew Anthony attended one gathering.
The profile of the one hundred men attending was
remarkably homogeneous: 'Aged between late twenties
and early fifties, they are all – with only one exception –
white, heterosexual, overwhelmingly middle class, highly
educated, articulate and socially aware.'[17] Anthony
described the pro-feminist commitments many of the men
professed, but noted how little time was spent talking about
wives and girlfriends. However, men were not so reticent to
talk about their mothers. 'When one fortysomething man
confesses his anger at his mother's incessant demeaning of
his absent father and half-jokes: "You can't hit a 75-year-
old woman, even if she is your mother," the laughter and
palpable sense of endorsement is universal and just a little
disturbing.'[18]

Bly stressed that blame for men's failure to be manly did not lie with women. The problem lay with fathers not doing their job of parenting. But the mytho-poetic movement he spawned, focusing on men's feelings of humiliation and shame and seeing these as a consequence of a mother-dominated family, inevitably fed into the language of women blaming. In spite of his progressive intentions, Bly provided one impetus for a growing masculine language of complaint, directed at female power and authority in the home. Men's childhood experience of the domestic power of their mothers, refracted by a culture which disparaged male emotional dependency, readily fuelled the rhetoric of anti-feminism amongst otherwise liberal men. David Thomas argues that the male experience is determined by 'a deeply repressed psychic agony known as the Male Wound' (p36) which can leave men fatally flawed. This wound 'arises from the fact that at a very early age – approximately eighteen months – boys make a psychological transition away from the female norm, which echoes the genetic and physical transitions they made as fetuses in the womb' (p36). The result is a masculinity which is 'fragile' and 'delicately balanced' (p54). 'I do not think it is possible to exaggerate the degree to which male behaviour is motivated by the fear of other people's disapproval or contempt' (p55).

Thomas's grievance against feminism is most strongly felt in his discussion about the personal injuries done to divorced and separated fathers denied access to their children – 'Whichever way you roll the dice, the game of parenthood is more viciously loaded against men than the meanest crap shoot in Vegas' (p236). He likens the separation of a child from its father to the crime of rape. To prove this equivalence he posed a dilemma to various acquaintances: what would they do if a man they vaguely knew gave them a choice either to have sex with him or to have their children taken away. 'Naturally enough everyone to whom I have spoken whether male or female, says they would consent to the sex' (p234). On the basis of this rough straw poll he claims that 'coercive sex with an acquaintance ... is less traumatic than the loss of one's

children' (p234). But only one is a crime: 'Any man who
assaults a woman runs the risk of severe punishment
under the criminal law. Any woman who denies a man
access to his own children runs ... no risk' (p235). The
Thomas suggests this sounds paranoid but asks us to view his
statistical data which demonstrates that: 'an absolute
minimum of 20 per cent of all fathers ... will be
permanently separated from their own flesh and blood'
(p236). However, he doesn't explain why he chose such an
extraordinary and inappropriate analogy.

The most compelling cause of Thomas's lack of
reasoning is an element of paranoia. As Freud wrote: 'the
strikingly prominent features in the causation of paranoia,
especially among males, are social humiliations and
slights.'[19] Both Lyndon and Thomas are a part of the
revolt of the 'invaded', 'naive man': reacting against their
own niceness and ingratiating compliance toward women
with an aggressive defensiveness which polarises men as
victims and women as persecutors. Their argument
against feminism is sustained by portraying it in the most
simplistic of terms, conniving with a farcical parody of its
diverse intellectual and political tradition. In this distorted
world view the iniquities and the inequalities of the
domestic division of labour which have resulted in men's
alienation from family life are the fault of feminism. But a
reading of any A level sociology text book will demonstrate
that the privatised, feminised world of home and childcare
and the male dominated public world of power, work and
politics are the consequence of patriarchal relations and
the capitalist mode of production, not of feminism. These
are the historical forces and conditions which have shaped
men's relationship to women and created Bly's 'naive man'
and Thomas's 'male wound'. We have only been able to
understand the complex and difficult relationship
between mothers and sons because feminism opened up
the family to analysis and debate. It was a feminist, Nancy
Chodorow, who developed a psycho-sociological description of the mother-son relationship.[20] She argued that
structured into the father-absent, mother-involved family
is the son's experience of a premature separation from the

mother whose legacy leaves an enduring insecurity in masculine identities. Far from desiring an exclusive female control over childcare, Chodorow argues for shared parenting 'where love and relationship are not a scarce resource controlled and manipulated by one person only'(p217). But for anti-feminists Thomas and Lyndon, and others like the smirking champ of misogyny Tony Parsons, 'the shrill vixens of feminism' are simply the pure and hate-filled distillation of female revenge against men.

Avoiding 'the bends'

The Summer of Love in 1988, Acid House, and the subsequent early years of rave culture, witnessed a new generation of young men versed in the language of female equality and gay sensibilities, willing to sustain differing and more democratic expressions of masculinity. The 1960s was being revisited. But a reaction against this trend had soon emerged with Lad culture, its debunking of liberal sexual politics, its retreat into the chauvinism of male exclusivity and its parodies of sexism and male crassness. 1995 was the first anniversary of the Lad's house magazine *Loaded* (circulation 150,000 and top of the men's magazine range). Simon Hattenstone, writing in *The Guardian*, remarked on its 'get-your-tits-out-for-the-lads-but-not-while-the-football's-on' ethos and concluded that men were confused and 'not a little moronic' about sexuality. 'Confused, emotionally stunted men make for confused emotionally stunted magazines.'[21] Pete May, writing in *New Times*, the journal of Democratic Left, came to the defence of *Loaded*: 'Perhaps one of the reasons lads are revelling in childishness is because they're fed up being lectured at. There's a backlash amongst young men and young women ... against the old feminist orthodoxy that men are to blame for everything.'[22] May's claim for a feminist *orthodoxy* (as if the philosophies and practices of feminism have ever gained ideological hegemony in British society) colludes with the discourse of political correctness which has attempted to abrogate debates around fairness and equality between men and women.

His idea that women are to blame for men being blamed only repeats the old chauvinist story which points the finger at women in general and mothers in particular. But he also has another target, the New Man; 'let's be honest, when it comes down to sex appeal, New Men were wimps.' In fact, May's clarion call for men to reclaim and take pride in some naturalised, primordial form of maleness had already metamorphosed the New Man into the Wild Man, some years earlier.

Loaded's masthead, 'For men who know better', encapsulates the raison d' etre of laddism, the pleasure in debunking liberal propriety and revelling in an irresponsible and juvenile adolescence. Comedians like Rowan Atkinson, Rik Mayall, and Ade Edmundson, programmes like *The Young Ones, Bottom, Men Behaving Badly*, and Frank Skinner and David Baddiel in *The Fantasy Football League*, offer a masculinity which paints SEX in large simple brush strokes, disparages the complexities of emotions and relationships with rude innuendo and thrives on anal jokes, the fear of buggery and a fascination with death. A very English public school derived culture, it laughs at what men are anxious about; principally sexual relationships and their own masculinity. Davies Riley-Smith Maclay, an advertising research agency, reported the growing resentment amongst young professional men, aged 25–34, towards advertising which depicted men relinquishing control in areas of traditional power. Its report *The Best a Man Can Get?* argued that adverts promoting female authority 'confirmed the pressure [men] were feeling from other sources, both at work and socially.'[23] Lucy Bannister, its author, told *The Guardian*, 'Men feel that the beautiful and scantily clad muscle men that they have noticed more often in tv ads these days, offer them an ideal shape that they find impossible to achieve.'[24] Body insecurity, job insecurity, future uncertainty are the contemporaries of modern masculinities.

But whatever the hankerings of right-wing politicians and anti-feminists, younger men will not return to the chauvinistic certainties of male superiority. To turn the clock back would require a totalitarian assault on women's rights to education, equality of treatment under the law and access to cultural and political institutions. Equally however there will be no return to the rather po-faced moralism of 1970s anti-sexist politics. Many men have rejected chauvinism and want something different in their lives and relationships. In this period of transition, the most visible alternative – popularly dubbed the New Man – has been a masculinity which promotes self-effacement and 'niceness' as the proper way to respond to women. But it has not been an alternative in the real sense, only a cultivation of men's emotional deference towards women and men's fear of their own desire: a self-perception that male desire is inherently destructive to its object. Avoiding 'the bends' – the loss of desire, the loss of future – is about having desire, not denying it in an act of contrition and compliance. During a launch meeting for *Male Order* at the Institute of Contemporary Arts in London in 1988, a creative director from a leading advertising company declared that men would be frightened off by its anti-male tone. His remark prefigured those anti-feminists who construct men as victims: as if self reflection will cause men to collapse like punctured balloons. *Male Order* draws on feminism to deconstruct masculinity in order see what makes men tick. It is not anti-male, but a first step in defining new egalitarian and democratic languages of masculinity. And that's how I see *Male Order*: a first step in finding new ways to talk about men and masculinity. As the philosopher Wittgenstein wrote: 'to imagine a language means to imagine a new form of life.'

Notes

[1] From Will Hutton, 'High Risk Strategy', *The Guardian*, 30 October 1995.
[2] From Will Hutton, 'Why the poor remain silent', *The Guardian*, 13 February 1995.
[3] See Pamela Sammons, 'Gender, Ethnic and Socio-economic Differences in Attainment and Progress: a longitudinal analysis of student achievement over 9 years', *British Educational Research Journal*, Vol.21. No.4 1995.

[4] *The Guardian*, front page report and Editorial, 19 January 1995.

[5] From Alex Duval Smith, 'Giving up on Life', *The Guardian*, 3 December 1994.

[6] Radiohead, 'the bends', from the album, *the bends*, Parlophone, 1995.

[7] S. Freud (1900), 'The Interpretation of Dreams, *Pelican Freud Library*, Vol.4, p621.

[8] From Zoe Heller, 'Don't Look Back', the *Independent on Sunday*, 22 March 1992.

[9] Report in *The Guardian*, 31 August 1993.

[10] Report in *The Guardian*, 21 December 1993.

[11] *Ibid*.

[12] Neil Lyndon, 'Feminism's fundamental flaws', the *Independent on Sunday*, 29 March 1992.

[13] *Ibid*.

[14] Murray's most recent book *The Bell Curve: Intelligence and Class Structure in American Life* (1994) is another throwback to Victorian pseudo-science, this time social Darwinism inspired eugenics. He was invited to Britain by the *Sunday Times* in 1989 and again in 1993. On each visit he wrote for the *Sunday Times Magazine*. His ideas about the emergence of a British underclass have been published by the right wing Institute of Economic Affairs. See Murray (1990), *The Emerging British Underclass* and Murray (1994), *Underclass: The Crisis Deepens*.

[15] Amitai Etzioni's work has been published by the independent think tank, Demos. See 'Learning Right from Wrong' in *Demos Quarterly*, Issue 1, Winter, 1993; and *The Parenting Deficit*, Demos Publications, London 1994. See also Etzioni, *The Spirit of Community: Rights, Responsibilities and the Communitarian Agenda*, HarperCollins, 1995.

[16] Beatrix Campbell (1995), 'Old fogies and angry young men', *Soundings*, Issue 1. Lawrence and Wishart Ltd, London.

[17] Andrew Anthony (1992), 'Wild at Heart', *The Guardian*, 17 October 1995.

[18] *Ibid*.

[19] S. Freud (1911[1910]), 'An Autobiographical Account of a Case of Paranoia', *Pelican Freud Library*, No.9, p197.

[20] Nancy Chodorow, *The Reproduction of Mothering: Psychoanalysis and the Sociology of Gender*, University of California Press, 1978.

[21] Simon Hattenstone, 'Sex and the single man's mag', *The Guardian*, 10 April 1995.

[22] Pete May, 'The return of the British bloke', *New Times*, 25 November 1995.

[23] *The best a man can get? Current male stereotypes in advertising*, Davies Riley-Smith Maclay, November 1995.

[24] Quote from Stephen Armstrong, 'Bodies of Opinion', *The Guardian*, 6 November 1995.

Who's That Man?

JONATHAN RUTHERFORD

To imagine a language means to imagine a new form of life.

Wittgenstein

Men still have everything to say about their sexuality. You still have everything to say about your sexuality: that's a challenge.

Alice Jardine and Helene Cixous

A few months ago a middle aged man left a workshop on the politics of the family. He was upset. He said to me, 'A group of women were saying that they didn't trust men to look after their children. It was as though they were saying that all men are child molesters. Surely women want men to look after children more. I don't know what these feminists want'.

His affront and confusion reminded me of a meeting I attended on men's violence against women. It was about six years ago. Around two hundred men and women turned up to listen to women from WAVAW (Women Against Violence Against Women) and an American man called Tom Jones, who was involved in EMERGE, a Boston based project working with men who were battering their wives or lovers. It was a significant gathering around a political issue that had been defined by women. Three women from WAVAW spoke about the pain and humiliation inflicted by men on women. It was a

21

forceful and emotional account that left most men silent. A few spoke, but none of us could respond in a productive way to that depth of feeling. We seemed to be floundering for words. I left the meeting feeling that something important had happened, but that something was wrong. As men and women we seemed to be talking different languages. There had been little connection between us and I felt no wiser about how I should respond to a sexual politics that was extremely critical of me, but also offered me a sense of myself and something that I wanted.

This chapter is an attempt to make that sense. It's about myself, and about men who are white and heterosexual. About our relationships with women, with homosexuality and black men; how they are structured by heterosexual masculinity. In using this term, I don't want to imply that masculinity is a fixed, coherent and singular identity; rather it is determined in different ways in relation to, for example, race, class, and culture. In writing I have become aware how heterosexual men have inherited a language which can define the lives and sexualities of others, but fails us when we have to deal with our own heterosexuality and masculine identities. An incident happened when I was thirteen. Two boys approached me at school, they said they were going to ask me an important question. 'Was I', they enquired, 'a heterosexual?' 'No', I said. That was the reply they had expected. 'Then you must be a queer' was their response. I felt thrown into panic, because though I hadn't understood what the word meant, I assumed that sexual labels were for sexual deviance. I know that they spent several weeks practising their ploy on a host of confused but predictable schoolboys, who would all vehemently dismiss their allegation. It's an incident about naivety, but it also reflects the assumption that 'normal sexuality' is both beyond question and beyond description; women may be sexual beings, homosexuals are, but men are just chaps, the lads. Our language doesn't produce us as sexual subjects or a category in need of a label.

Heterosexual men have taken refuge in this idea that our sexual identities are absolute. The dominance of heterosexual masculinity, the ideologies that have supported it by silencing the experience of others, the power structures and privileges that it disguises, the active, daily subordination of women and gay men, the persecution of effeminate men, and the racism of men's colonial legacy – all these have been sustained by its capacity to remain beyond question, its contradictions out of sight. It is an identity that is in continual struggle to assert its centrality in cultural life, yet it attempts to ensure its absence, and to evade becoming the object of discourse. Heterosexual masculinity shifts its problems and anxieties, defining them as belonging to others. Our identity represents its own problems in the image of the compliant female, the black man as sexual savage, and the perverted homosexual. It organises its legitimacy by constructing the Other, that which is outside and questionable, what is different. In his book *Mythologies*, Roland Barthes writes that, 'Myth does not deny things, on the contrary, its function is to talk about them; simply, it purifies them, it makes them innocent, it gives them natural and eternal justification, it gives them clarity which is not that of explanation but that of a statement of fact.'[1] The myth of masculinity is its attempt to pass itself off as natural and universal, free of problems.

Today the masculine myth is being sufficiently questioned to drag it into view. Like the *Invisible Man* of H G Wells, whose death is signified by his return to visibility, the weakening of particular masculine identities has pushed them into the spotlight of greater public scrutiny. The reality of men's heterosexual identities is that their endurance is contingent upon an array of structures and institutions. When these shift or weaken, men's dominant positions are threatened. The past decade has seen such a crisis. The changing nature of work, and the disruption of work culture with the decline of manufacturing industries, the introduction of new technology and the subsequent deskilling of traditional male jobs are changes that have undermined traditional working-class masculinities. Similarly the high levels of male unemployment and the growing jobs sector employing part-time women have changed the face of the

labour market, and had a corresponding effect at home.
The past decade has seen the increasing exposure of child
sexual abuse and men's violence against their wives. The
changing position of women, in many different spheres is
undermining the certainties of the past. The divorce laws,
far from being the Casanova's charter predicted by the
popular press, have been predominantly used by women
leaving their husbands. These developments and other
structural changes have all contributed to the questioning
of taken-for-granted assumptions about men's role and
function in life.

To become an acceptable masculine man means
adopting the values of male superiority. Our sexual
identity is about shaping and defending them. We invest
part of ourselves in them, for they are reassuring mirrors
that reflect back an idealised image of masculinity and a
sense of belonging. Our sexual identities are a lifelong
project. We can attempt to carry through the ideology of
male superiority with all its consequences, and try to
emulate the archetypal image that embodies the idealised
man of our particular class and culture. Or we can accept a
more subordinate masculinity, enjoying the privileges
without having to take responsibility for the active
subordination that sustains our positions. That has been
our prerogative as men, to stand aside, shamefaced or
thrilled, while the sportsman, the sexual superstud, the
misogynist, the woman beater, and all the myths and icons
of male superiority, do the work for us. But these mirrors
are less reassuring than they used to be. There is
increasingly a note of hysteria about them. Life is not so
certain. It is at such times of disruption, as traditional
masculinities fall into crisis, that new images of masculinity
are produced. And, while the production of new images is
to redefine a dominant masculinity, the crisis creates the
opportunity for a wider questioning and sexual politics
amongst groups of heterosexual men.

Feminism and a radical sexual politics have grown up in
the fissures of a disintegrating ideology of masculine
authority; they have also encouraged this shifting of
attention onto men. Where the great enigma was once

female sexuality, Freud's famous enquiry, 'What does woman want?', can be turned around. Instead we can ask, 'What do men want?'. A growing number of books and magazine articles are asking this question; probing the male psyche, exploring the emotional male, and men's attitudes to everything from sex, divorce and quiche to our bodies and attitudes towards intimacy. It's a popular discourse with an erratic politics, but it is backed up by a much more rigorous theoretical feminism that has analysed issues of gender, male sexuality and the mechanism of male power. The women's movement has produced a language for what Alice Jardine calls the 'spaces of the ... Other'[2] – the blank pages of history, the margins of society where men have attempted to confine women. Similarly radical gay politics and black politics have produced new definitions of the world that are not attributable to the grand narrative of White Man. These are languages that have produced new meanings for their own constituencies, but they have also produced descriptions of the dominant masculinity, that contest its myth and force it into view. Yet despite this oppositional language and the assertiveness of the new political constituencies, heterosexual men have remained remarkably silent in the face of this unmasking and criticism. It's as if the growing demand from women for something more from men has pushed men into a defensive huddle shored up in their institutional power, without a language in which to answer. Exposed to a growing questioning men have used their silence as the best form of retaining the status quo, in the hope that the ideological formations that once sustained the myth of masculine infallibility will resurrect themselves from the fragments and produce a new mythology to hide us in.

About Men and Masculinity

The historical construction of our masculinity is closely bound up with Christianity's attitude to the human body: the separation of the superior spirit from the weak flesh. It's a tradition that has become the dominant mode of

West European thought. When Rene Descartes wrote his famous words, 'I think therefore I am', he was insisting on the primacy of reason. A history of masculinity is the struggle to tame and subdue the emotional and sexual self and to recognise the ascendant and superior nature of reason and thought. The dominant meanings of masculinity in our culture are about producing our bodies as instruments to our wills. Flesh, sexuality, emotionality, these become seen as uncontrollable forces and a source of anxiety. Male sexuality becomes not so much a concern of our relationships with other people, but with ourselves: a struggle between our intellects and libidos. We live within a culture that alienates men from their bodies and sexuality. We learn to repress them because they are the antithesis of what it means to be masculine. It's a repression that we project onto others. Our struggle for self control is acted out as mastery over others.

The dark illicit secrets and fantasies of heterosexual masculinity are projected as the property of others: our images of women, homosexuals and black people are created by the fleshy fears of heterosexual men. They are the Other which is our own denial: the huge penis of the black man, the devouring female and the plague-like seduction of the homosexual. Here are the images of men's own sexual anxieties and contradictions: a sexuality beyond reason and control, the flight from the maternal body, and our own homoerotic desires and fantasies. Men's struggle to produce order between our interior world and an acceptable masculine persona produces a regime that punishes others. And it is a sexual identity that divorces men from the consequences of their actions. The *Daily Mirror* ran a front page story last year.[3] A judge had recommended that a convicted rapist should receive a 'castrating' drug. The story concerned a man who was already receiving it. He is quoted as saying, 'I am glad I was castrated .... the drug has removed my physical performance and desire ... I am around young people all the time now and I feel completely safe'. This is the description of his sexuality as an alien force, some kind of disturbing visitation from which he needs protection.

Men accused of sexually abusing children frequently shift their responsibility away from themselves. Not only in the idea of the castrating wife and the seductive daughter, but also by blaming a sexuality that is beyond their control. In court men will cite alcoholism, drugs, unhappiness, a wife's refusal to have sex, social trauma or simply an isolated aberration as reasons for this loss of control. But this only serves to mask the reality, that they chose to do it. In their pursuit of a fractured ego, self-validation and pleasure, men are often immune to the destruction they are causing, as though it has nothing to do with them. It reminds me of a TV programme I watched a number of years ago. A group of women who had been raped sat in a studio with a group of men, all of whom were convicted rapists. As the women questioned the men about their motives, the men sank into passivity. As the women became more angry and upset, the men became mute; they seemed disassociated from what they had done. Within each lay a deep hatred and contempt for women, yet their language had no connection to it. Their only moment of connection was in the act of rape.

Psychoanalysis, by and large, has not been concerned to analyse the historical construction of masculinity. But two men who have made some attempts in this direction are Alfred Adler and Karl Jung. Adler had a clear view of the importance of power relations in social structure. He argued that the devaluing of femininity in European culture shaped the psychological patterns of childhood. The polarity of women's subordination and men's power becomes organised around the child's own submission and desire for independence, setting up a contradiction between masculine and feminine tendencies. He argued that these tendencies were usually led to some kind of compromise in adult life. But if men couldn't achieve this compromise, anxiety about weakness or appearing feminine led to an over-compensation of aggression and compulsiveness. Adler dubbed this behaviour the 'masculine protest ... the arch-evil of our culture, the excessive pre-eminence of manliness'. After Adler broke with Freud in 1911, his work disappeared into relative obscurity.

Karl Jung was another dissident from classical Freudianism. He wrote his ideas about sexual character in his essay 'Anima and Animus'. He argued that an unconscious personality (the anima for men and the animus for women) develops as a negative of the socially acceptable one. For men a strong authoritative masculine persona is based on the repression of vulnerability and dependency. The subsequent balancing act between these two facets of men's sexual identity, and their incompatible demands, creates tensions and contradictions, that threaten the myth of masculinity's seamless quality. Both Jung and Adler produced theories of masculinity that suggest that men repress emotion which cannot be expressed in social practice. And while neither theory can provide a definitive account of the construction of masculinity, they can be brought together as elements of the psychoanalysis of a historically constructed range of masculinities.

This repression exists in a state of tension. Cultural changes produce a sharpening or lessening of the repressed persona. Today the flux of meaning around masculinity has produced a 'debate' between them. The representation of different masculinities has produced two idealised images that correspond to the repressed and the public meanings of masculinity: what I'll call the New Man and the Retributive Man respectively. Retributive Man represents the struggle to reassert a traditional masculinity, a tough independent authority. The classic figure is Rambo. The film *First Blood* is still a feature of every high street video shop and the image of Stallone with his huge machine gun adorns the t-shirts, books and toys of tens of thousands of little boys. He advertises a destructive machismo as the solution to men's problems. He is John Wayne with his gloves off, wildly lashing out at everything that threatens and disappoints him. He confronts a world gone soft, pacified by traitors and cowards, dishonourable feminised men. It is a world that has disrupted his notions of manhood and honour. It threatens his comprehension of who he is. And his attempts to recreate order, and subdue the forces that threaten him, degenerate into a series of violent actions.

Violence is a common response when masculine identities are under threat. It is an attempt to destroy what Roland Barthes has called the 'scandal of the Other'.[4] It represents a retreat into physical force, whose fantasy is played out in toy shops across the country. Alongside the emergence of a host of beefcakes and hulks, copying the success of figures like Stallone and Schwarzenegger, there has been a similar spectacle of contrived violence for boys. Toys and tv programmes like Transformers, He Man, and Masters of the Universe, with their space age heroes, their space tanks bristling with weapons, are fantasies for little boys that suggest that their emerging masculinity is about control and mastery over others. They are the junior companions that sit with apparent ease alongside the violent retributive fantasies of adult cinema. They are fantasies that give full vent to the logic of male reason pursuing its power and subordination of others; a metaphor for men's own internal struggles. And nowhere are these struggles more acute than in the emerging sexuality of boys.

Stallone's hysterical assertions of maleness are a departure from the genre of war films. War is usually conceived of as a rite of passage, an opportunity for men to find themselves, to prove their masculinity and their capacity to tame their bodies and physical fear. But the emergence of the rogue male represents a distrust of the traditional class-bound gamesmanship, a belief that the rot has gone too far, and that the individual man has only himself to rely on for his own, and for national, salvation. It's a belief played out in the pursuit of survivalism, the obsessive concern with apocalypse and the search for self sufficiency, learning to kill and live in the wild. Both the filmic images and the reality represent a masculinity in crisis. A crisis that is closely allied to the perceived crisis in the Nation. The spate of Vietnam war films is also concerned with rehabilitating a masculine experience, albeit within more conventional boundaries. By depicting the catharsis of violence and men's endurance of it, the films can imbue masculinity (and America) with the idea of

Sylvester Stallone as Rambo in *First Blood Part II* (1985)

self sacrifice and a new moral strength. This was implicit
throughout the first Vietnam film *Coming Home*. It starred
Jon Voight as the disabled war hero living in a hospital and
Jane Fonda who becomes his lover. And while the film
centres around the futility of the war, and Voight's
opposition to it, his protest is only given legitimacy because
he has experienced the war. Because he has been there he
is invested with a morality not given to other male
protesters, who are depicted as hippy wimps. Despite his
mutilation the war has made him a bigger man than the
others. This narrative, linking masculine superiority to a
man's exposure and endurance of violence, undermined
the film's liberal pretensions.

The war film takes men's alienation and sells it back to
us as a source of power and pride. The byline in the advert
for the film *Hamburger Hill* is 'War at its worst. Fought by
men at their best'. The press outpourings at the time of the
Falklands war were obsessed with a nation's young
manhood proving itself. A number of dailies relished in a
retributive and violent masculinity that was reasserting
itself over a society that was mollycoddled and nannied. It
was synonymous with national pride. 'We are proud of our
fighting men. Sailors, airmen and now soldiers ... all have
been put to the test ... Britain still has the will to fight for
freedom. We have the men too. Lions led by lions' crowed
the *Daily Mail*. And Peter McKay, writing in the *Daily
Express*, brought it all back home: 'Men also like to fight
and are excited by the prospect of battle ... there has, in
the past few days, been a small outbreak of nostalgia for
men as brutes ... right now it must be quite hard being a
feminist'.

Asserting this kind of masculinity appeals to the latent
male violence that is endemic in our culture. It produces
the notion of traitors: cowardly men who have abrogated
their right to masculinity, and consequently to citizenship.
The problem with this virulent machismo is that its
connection to reality discredits it. The borderline between
legitimate violence employed by the state and male
violence that threatens social stability is quickly crossed.
The popular usage of Rambo as an archetypal Man was

abruptly shattered when Michael Ryan lived out the
fantasy in the carnage of Hungerford. The resulting
do-it-yourself psychology of the popular press uncovered
a lonely inadequate who employed a fantasy world to
shore up his fragile masculinity; not exactly the stuff lions
are made of. And the violence of football fans, despite
their virulent nationalism further undermines the
legitimacy of Retributive Man. The presence of British
fans sporting 'Keep the Falklands British' as they kicked
and punched their way across Heysal Stadium was a
hijacking of the patriotic rhetoric that surrounded the
Task Force in the name of a violent and aggressive
masculinity.

In contrast, New Man is an expression of the repressed
body of masculinity. It is a fraught and uneven attempt to
express masculine emotional and sexual life. It is a
response to the structural changes of the past decade and
specifically to the assertiveness and feminism of women.
This reassessment of masculinity is engaged in forms of
compromise that are clearly different from the image of
the Retributive Man and his flight from the insecurities
and instabilities of his identity into an idealised phallic
masculinity. But they are tentative moves that often
simultaneously invoke men's resistance to them. This
advert, part of a series titled 'Beware the Wolf in Sheep's
Clothing', plays on men's resistance to, and adoption of, a
more feminised image. For men to put our bodies on
display contradicts the codes of who looks and who is
looked at. It pacifies us. Men have held the power of the
look, the symbolic owning of women's bodies. Reversing
the gaze offers the symbol of men's bodies on offer to
women. The model in this advert snarls his unease and
disapproval, caught in a feminised image that strips him of
his masculine power. His snarl, and the title of the ad, both
warn the viewer (woman) that he still retains that animal
predatory sexuality that is proof of his manhood. It's an
image that confronts the insecurities of a masculine
identity in doubt. The model disavows his passivity
through his aggressive look, through demonstrating that
he still has control over definitions of who he is.

Beware a Wolf in Sheep's Clothing

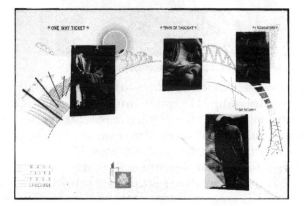

courtesy Davidson Pearce

'Beware a Wolf in Sheep's Clothing' came out about five years ago. We wanted to persuade men to wear fashionable clothes, when fashion was thought effeminate. So we developed the idea of the urban animal – a guy out on the prowl. Every once in a while you meet a man who exudes a threat, you accept that this guy is a little bit dangerous. We looked for models who were able to emit that threat, an image that other men would respect, and think, 'I wouldn't mind being him'. Yet he was wearing strong fashionable clothes. He was a loner who had no need of peer approval. It was a strategy to slowly persuade men into a new frame of mind regarding fashion.

Stage two of the campaign is 'Wool Talks Your Language'. It's quite different and reflects men's changing attitudes over the last five years. It's an image of men as fashionable, stylish and emotional. It's aimed at a man who no longer has to prove himself. It emphasises wool as an emotional fabric, that it's OK to cry. It's an image more men are willing to accept but we are treading carefully. It's OK in the South and metropolitan areas like Glasgow, but there is still a doggedness in industrial areas. Men are hanging on to older traditional things.

Bryan Ferry and fatherhood as fashionable accessory

Similarly the changing face of fatherhood is full of
inconsistencies and contradictions. The New Father is
fully entrenched in the Mothercare catalogue. In last
summer's edition he was on the front cover. On page 161
he is changing a nappy and on page 171 he is bathing
baby. He looks soft and gentle and, what's more, he's not
afraid to show it. He's late twenties early thirties, white and
classless in that conventional catalogue style. The idea of
putting men in the catalogue belonged to Mothercare's
chairman Kevyn Jones; it was a response to the increasing
number of men using the store, rather than to any detailed
market research. The new liberalised image of men
pushing buggies, attending births and cuddling babies in
public without fear of shame and ridicule, has been taken
up and encouraged in the media. A plethora of books have
been written in the past few years on fatherhood. Books
explaining the pitfalls, describing personal experiences,
reminiscing, being funny, giving advice, and generally
creating an instant folklore about dad. Fatherhood is
vogue. It looks nice and it's what women want. But while

the images outstrip the reality, men too want something different from fatherhood.

Fatherhood has also become a place where men can rehabilitate a tarnished image. Rockstars and personalities are eager to be photographed with their children. The picture of the boxer Barry McGuigan holding his baby, which appeared on the front cover of the *Observer* colour supplement in 1986 took the image to its ludicrous length. McGuigan in full boxing regalia is holding the baby in his gloved hand. It's obvious that he couldn't possibly have picked up the child, nor held it for much longer than the photo session. This is an example of the rhetoric that now surrounds fatherhood; what can lie below the surface is depicted in the two films *Kramer vs Kramer* and *The Good Father*. In the latter film Anthony Hopkins plays the role of a New Father who becomes embroiled in an attempt to win custody of his son; the film reveals the misogyny and power struggles that lurk below the surfaces of this image.

The struggle over paternity rights entered a new arena when an Oxford student, in early 1987, applied to the High Court for an injunction to prevent his girlfriend from having an abortion.[5] A subsequent article in the *Observer* in January 1988 reported that the student Robert Carver was now looking after the seven-month-old baby. An out-of-court settlement had entrusted the child to him. The article quotes Mr Chris Hegg, president of the Oxford University Society for the Protection of the Unborn Child: 'He has never asked for anything, not even for help with baby-sitting ... All he wanted was his baby to live and that is what he has achieved'. The growing interest amongst men in fatherhood has effected a new anti-abortion discourse shifting the emphasis from a woman's right to control her body to the rights of the foetus. David Alton, in promoting his Private Member's Bill commented to the *Observer*, 'Robert Carver has shown that abortion is not only an issue for women, and that men are prepared to shoulder the responsibility'. His comment is not however backed up by the facts.

There is little tangible evidence to show that men are now more involved in the care of their children. A recent

Family Policy Studies Centre Occasional Paper, *Inside the
Family*,[6] drew on evidence to argue that the division of
work within the family was broadly unchanged. Women
continue to be the houseworkers and carers. There have
been no significant studies of the changing relationship
between men and women; advertising agencies are loathe
to figure the New Man in food and shopping related
adverts, because they are areas where, they believe, women
are still predominant.[7] The new-look father of the
Mothercare catalogue is a rather two-dimensional figure,
in danger of becoming a fashionable accessory. But the
nature and extent of men's participation in childcare is not
exclusively determined by men's privilege, and to their
strategies to avoid the harder work of domesticity. The
lack of equal opportunities for women at work ensures
that few command salaries high enough to enable their
husbands to spend less time at work or to swap roles
completely. The gendered structure of work and the job
market impede rather than assist a more equitable division
of labour at home. Within these limits, changes have
occurred. Lorna McKee, writing in the *Guardian*, probably
sums up the present state of dad: 'Fathers have an open
script, ranging from a traditional distance stance through
to equal involvement, even role reversal'.[8] It's this
open-endedness in the contemporary meanings of
Fatherhood that offers the possibility of actual change.

The marketplace has produced a plurality of masculine
identities; different models of fatherhood, sexualised
images of men and new sensibilities. They are images that
reflect the underlying structural shifts; their connection to
actual practice and power relations is complex and
contradictory. There is no smooth linear movement that
can depict men's changing behaviour and attitudes. As the
'Beware a Wolf in Sheep's Clothing' adverts show, the
idealised images of Retributive Man and New Man co-exist
as competing meanings of the same masculinity. Different
institutions and experiences produce different syntheses
of one or the other. Similarly, the changing sensibilities in
men produce different responses to our power over
women.

It is difficult to gauge the changing trends of masculinity. One indicator is the magazines for men. The idea of a men's mass market periodical in the genre of women's magazines has been mooted in publishing circles for years. The belief has been that men are too conservative to buy such a product. But in 1986 the publishers of *The Face* produced the first self-conscious, non-pornographic magazine for men, *Arena*. It aimed to grab a corner of the fashion market. For a number of years *Cosmopolitan* has been producing *Cosmo Man*, which, unlike *Arena*, held a general rather than specifically fashion interest. This much smaller and more conservative version of its big sister comes out a couple of times a year, firmly bound to its sibling. The women's magazines *Options* and *Elle* have followed the trend with their own separate magazine or section for men. *Cosmopolitan* claims a readership of 500,000 men, but their interest is clandestine. Men won't buy it, but they regularly read their wives', lovers' or mothers' copies. Janice Winship, interviewing *Cosmopolitan* editor Linda Kelsey in *Marxism*

Today[9], asked her if she could characterise *Cosmo* man. 'I haven't really met him', she said. Her reply reflects the uncertainty about how much men are changing. There is a feeling that they have, but a lack of proof. This is why mainstream publishers continue to shy away from a fully-fledged mass market magazine for men.

The magazine *Arena* lives up to its name by being a gladiatoral stadium where two contending meanings of male heterosexuality battle it out. On one side are the images, reflecting the new, less rigid sensibilities. Pictures of young male models are portrayed in passive, 'feminised' poses, exposed to the camera. The heterosexual male reader is confronted with a challenge, the new object of his gaze is another man. We are invited to take pleasure from these male bodies and the clothes they wear. There is a sensuality about the images which until now has been completely absent from publications for heterosexual men. Yet on the other side, contesting these images, is the text of the magazine. The articles confirm a traditional male view of the world. The mirror is thrown away for the old objective authority, the interviews with wealthy fashion moguls, articles on money and sex. These are seen through the new consumer ethic, but are traditional all the same.

Steve Taylor, a member of *Arena*'s editorial group, acknowledges the contrast. 'Sexual politics doesn't appeal to any of us. For our generation – I'm thirty-five – that discussion was blown. It was no fun. We don't want to go back to it. I think it would be really yuck to have a *Cosmo* man style. Talking to men about their feelings would be a commercial death wish.' The current crop of magazine supplements for men is hooking into the new narcissism of men. 'Younger men aren't afraid to look at themselves any more', comments Marcus Van Ackerman, who edits *Elle*'s supplement for men, *Elle pour Homme*. And it's true. The idea of the 'Beware a Wolf' ad was to pursue men to take an interest in themselves and fashion. The lone predator image reflected a man who was both powerful and prepared to follow his own interests. It was a break with the gang. That was over five years ago. Since then the

Narcissism and the New Man

gang have caught up and fashion has become a status
symbol amongst men. This change is regional but it crosses
class. Designer clothes are not the concern solely of the
southern yuppy classes. They reflect a masculinity that has
partly detached itself from its formative links to traditional
class identities. It has become aspirational and more
narcissistic, affected by the consumer market and the
purchasing of style and appearance.

It's not that men aren't changing. The disruption to our
sexual identity has produced a new flexibility in
masculinity. But what hasn't happened is any attempt to
address this potential for change. Radical politics has
made little attempt to address men as a gender and to
offer alternatives. Nor is there a sexual politics that
engages heterosexual men, that can connect with the
market created identities, and argue for new, democratic
forms of heterosexuality and eroticism. While the women's
magazines regularly feature women's interrogation of
masculinity, magazines aimed at men studiously ignore
taking up such concerns. *Cosmopolitan* attempted such an

enterprise for their 15th birthday celebration, but they
kept it out of print. The magazine organised a day-long
event, 'Let's get together', which brought together 100
men and 100 women, and an array of speakers. The
theme was men and women's relationships, and it exuded
the kind of appeal that many sexual radicals and leftists
would have sneered at. Yet it represented a brand of
popular feminism that the Left has been unable to relate
to, or articulate. It created a forum for women to tell men
what they wanted and it allowed men to respond and to
talk about our own sexuality in an atmosphere that was
free of bar-room banter and wise-cracking.

The participants were a source of some embarrassment
to *Cosmopolitan*. Far from being the youthful beauties with
which the magazine associates itself, the people there
ranged in age from 16 to 60. All the men I spoke to had
been affected by women's demands for something more,
and different, from men. These demands could be
summarised as a desire for friendship, which they didn't
think men offered them, respect as their right, and equal
opportunities. A number of men sitting with me, into their
middle age, spoke about the changes to masculinity in
their own lifetime. It wasn't that they were suddenly
anti-sexist, but they were finding a language that could
engage with the demands of the women they knew, that
could begin to articulate their sexuality and identities in a
way that would have been impossible twenty years ago.
Finding that language is the beginning of a debate that
starts to uncover, in Foucault's words, 'the fine meshes of
the web of power'[10] that subordinate women and produce
male bodies and masculinities organised around self-
control and domination. The place where a radical sexual
politics can begin to engage with masculinity, is in the way
that individual men experience, live out and contest its
dominant meanings. How we negotiate our relationships
with other men and with women within the disjunction of
our lived experiences and the social structures and
expectations that shape our sexual identity.

Attempts to formulate such a sexual politics for men
emerged during the 70s in response to the rise of the

women's movement and, to a lesser extent, gay liberation. Its main form was the consciousness raising 'men's group', where men could explore areas of our lives, such as sexuality and relationships, that had previously been taboo subjects in male company. The appearance of the magazine *Achilles Heel* in 1978, produced by an independent collective of men, provided a broader theoretical overview, linking the new personal politics to a libertarian socialism. A series of national conferences attempted to create some kind of political coherence to the mass of fragmented activity. For a brief period the magazine and the conferences gave men's anti-sexist politics a national dimension. But the political coherence of these activities kept foundering on disagreements about what men should be doing: should men be developing a mirror image of the women's movement; or was such organising together only likely to perpetuate men's power.

Men's anti-sexist politics had one foot in the counterculture of the 70s and one in the libertarian left. As these began to wane, it lost its focus and radical edge. By 1982 *Achilles Heel* had ceased publishing. Men's anti-sexist politics was superseded by a more personalised, depoliticised concern with men's roles and emotions. Despite the radicalism of its rhetoric, its highly personalised account of the world disabled any possibility of political strategy, further reinforcing an image of men wrapped up in themselves and their personal lives. Pitted against this celebratory-style politics remained a strand of anti-sexist puritanism and 'mea culpa' politics. They both fed off each other creating entrenchment in simplistic vision. What neither recognised was that the whole 70s culture of sexual politics for men had increasingly little relevance as the 80s progressed. As in the relationship of young women to 70s feminism, young men's sexual politics was affected by quite different experiences. For example, while an older generation of men were arguing over the causes of men's emotional inarticulacy, younger men were playing around with style, blurring the gender dividing line. They were practising something different.

This form of sexual politics was specific to a generation;

it was also specific to a white urban radical middle class. Its concern with psychoanalysis and therapy ensured a language and politics that failed to take up the cultural construction of masculinity, and did not recognise the centrality of race and class in the shaping of different experiences and meanings of masculinity.

About Men and the Left

Despite recognising, in retrospect, its failings, men's anti-sexist politics did produce an important and radical critique, not only of men's heterosexuality and masculinity, but also the practice of the left. It had sat uncomfortably on the margins of a generally hostile and macho organised left. In terms of new priorities and practices it had little impact. But it ensured that a small constituency of men was created who supported feminism and gay politics. Within the unions and the Labour Party change has been slow. Traditional paternalism, and hostility to feminism, is still characteristic of the Labour hierarchy. Neil Kinnock probably spoke for a lot of other labour traditionalists when he responded to a question about parental attitudes to drug abuse.[11] He said, 'I am a father and no matter how much I try and convince myself toward the course of enlightenment, I know that, put to the test, I'm what people would call a reactionary'.

There has always been a left critique of class paternalism of Labourism and old-style Fabianism, but the style of the 'hard' or 'fundamentalist' left has invariably reinforced its strongly masculine tone. Its politics is dominated by male imagery: the clenched fist, the haranguing oration, the rhetoric of fighting and struggling. In the end, despite its intentions, it is a profoundly disabling politics and one that is far more likely to retreat into old certainties than develop new ideas. Both these traditions have been wary of sexual politics.

There is a left that is open to change. It is emerging in haphazard form; its development was apparent in some of the debates around the realignment of the left in the 80s. It is a new constituency that has no organisational form, but it is apparent in parts of the Labour Party, the Communist Party and, predominantly, outside the traditional institutions of the left. I would argue that it is informed by Feminism, a greater responsiveness to black and cultural politics, and to the ideas of radical democracy. But its emergence as a potential site for the organising and mutual interaction of these constituencies is hampered by its continuing legacy of some aspects of paternalism.

While it recognises sexual politics, it stops at the point of supporting 'women's issues' or the rights of the gay community. There is a concern with 'gender balance' and equal representation. And while there is nothing wrong with these, if they are not part of a wider understanding about how power operates, their success will be limited. Men's power is not simply a sovereign, repressive force. It can be that, but it is a more complex phenomenon, and also operates through the ways in which politics and problems are defined, and in determining what are the real issues and priorities. We end up occupying a series of discourses that can defeat the best intentions of positive discrimination and equal opportunities. The new emerging radical politics shares the predominant attitude of heterosexual men, that sexual politics is all about women and gay men and not ourselves. It reflects the culture of labourism, where politics is all about other people and their problems. Consequently, across the whole spectrum, the left has made a problem of feminism and gay politics and ignored the issue of heterosexual masculinity and the problem of men. It assumes that men don't have a sexuality, that we have nothing to do with sexual violence or childcare or the institutionalising of men's advantage.

In this left discourse heterosexual men remain unquestioned. Those parts of the left that acknowledge the validity and importance of autonomous social movements have never been able to develop much more than a rhetoric of alliances that constantly affirms a commitment to 'Women, Blacks and Gays'. This triumvirate is written and spoken about as though they were distant planets orbiting men's sun. The relationship between 'their' politics and 'us' is rarely considered, for to acknowledge them would throw white heterosexual men into the spotlight, and open 'us' up to scrutiny. To become the object of such a critical examination would mean relinquishing power and that, in all the rhetoric about alliances, is not something currently on the agenda.

Heterosexual men can avoid the demands of women in a style of politics where we don't talk about what we want and what we need. It reinforces the myth that men are neither a problem nor have problems. We perpetuate forms of organisation and practice that exclude people's needs and feelings. The physical space we occupy, our language and the organisational forms it produces, perpetuate a masculine presence. The subsequent hierarchies often exclude working-class and black men as well. Those who are angered and oppressed are marginalised by a politics that will not acknowledge that there is a problem, and that it belongs to the institutions that have been created in the image of a specific white masculinity – a specific sexuality that has narrowed the parameters of the socialist project and impaired its ability to grasp the way power operates to exclude women, and other groups. Today's socialist politics and organisations were founded at the beginning of the century and they still adhere to a masculine style long since out-of-date. The unwillingness of heterosexual men to take up a politics that engages with our sexual identities blocks the development of new more democratic cultural forms. This can only hasten the demise of socialism as a radical and emancipating force.

The Communist Party is an example of the disparity between rhetoric and practice. Looking through its literature a new political language has appeared. It talks about 'transformatory alliances', 'a marxist-feminist analysis' and 'new relations between men and women that will foreshadow a socialist society'. But this language conflicts with the rigidity and lack of pluralism in its organisation. Despite being the only left wing party to make a commitment to feminism, it remains an insistently male heterosexual organisation. In this respect it is similar to most other organisations in the labour movement.

This is the description by a man who used to be active in the Labour Party, recalling his branch meetings in South London: 'There was always a concern at the lack of black people, the minority of women and working-class people present. It was a question that was periodically discussed, with suggestions about how to make ourselves more accessible to 'them' ... What came across was that we should all make a bigger effort to accommodate the problems of more marginal groups. What never came across was that the speaker felt threatened, or put in question, or that anyone had anything at stake in these political issues. We colluded with this masculine facade of coping, because we'd feel ridiculous starting a discussion about what the subject meant to us. We wouldn't know what to say because left politics is all about other peoples' problems.'

The ambivalence of men to the new political constituencies has shown itself in our wariness about putting ourselves in the picture. What we need to produce is a sexual politics that articulates what our masculinity means to us and how it affects us, to contest the dominant images of masculinity. The rhetoric of alliances and the new emancipatory forms of socialism that are emerging out of the realignment of the left cannot succeed until men have shown we have a stake in changing and getting other men to change too. An increasing number of men have learnt the language of feminism, we often practise its rhetoric. But there is a tendency to set up hierarchies of awareness amongst ourselves. Sexist remarks from other men can be met by a wall of knowing silence that is intimidating and serves only to enforce a regime of masculine competitiveness. Perhaps it is a way for some of us to re-establish our 'belonging' to women, perhaps it is a strategy for disguising our uncertainty. Despite these rather flawed means of living out a feminist critique, many men have been profoundly influenced by feminism. It has provided an engagement with our lives that the detached politics of socialism has failed to do. Yet we are fearful of talking through its personal implications and what it means to us.

There is a defensiveness amongst many men that sexual

politics demands a spilling of our privacy; and that the
personal and moral dimension it involves mean establishing
a regime of gentle, loving men: a new moral order that
imbues guilt into those who fail to live up to the new
standards. But putting masculinity into the picture isn't
about insisting that all men should be nice, and fit into some
stereotyped image. Nor is it about creating a male confessional and a fetish of self-disclosure. It's about making
ourselves 'seen', making our sexuality and masculinities a
basis for discussion instead of assuming that men as gendered subjects don't exist. Power is not simply about limit-
ing the freedom of others. It's about who controls
definitions, who constructs the meanings of political
struggle. This power shapes human activity, it reinforces
and legitimises material power. Foucault writes, in his
History of Sexuality, that the success of power 'is proportional
to its ability to hide its own mechanisms .... For its secrecy is
not in the nature of an abuse; it is indispensable to its
operation'.[12] As men we operate within definitions of masculinity that hide the mechanisms of our power. While we
can write and talk sympathetically about feminism and
women, we evacuate questions of our own sexuality, our
own subjectivity and our relationship to feminism, we
don't disturb the actual power relations, that reproduce the
gender system.

Feminism has challenged the power of masculinity by
exposing its mechanisms. A sexual politics for men needs to
continue that process by redefining our identities and what
it means to be a man. Feminism has provided the rudiments
of a language and a way of seeing that we can use to make a
politics about emancipating ourselves. In the last part of
this chapter I want to write out something about our
relationships to those we have constructed as the Other –
women, gay men and black men. This is an attempt to make
some sense of the connections between our personal and
sexual lives and the broader structures that create violence
and oppression.

About Women

I was ten when I saw the film *Lawrence of Arabia*. I vividly remember the image of the lonely inhospitable desert, the soaring emotional music and the man alone. The man on his camel under a blistering sun, in a vast open space. He was the archetypal male hero, free of all human ties. An independent man driven by a mission, wracked by hardship, emotionally apart, linked to the world by loyalty, duty and an abstract sense of love for a cause. He reminds me of all those other boyhood heroes who had to be free of the ties that bound them down – women, children emotional relationships – before they could get on with doing what a man's got to do.

The appeal of the hero is his freedom from women: the snares and entrapments of dependency and vulnerability. 'Here I am', he says, 'free, self-sufficient, without anxiety, a man's man'. He presents us with a sexual identity free of doubt while he masters and controls his surroundings. Yet somewhere in the story there will be the nostalgic memory of a previous life of domestic happiness: a woman in his past. It's as though his masculinity can only function with an idealised version of a lost woman's love. Its reality in the here and now would end the image and reality of a self-contained independent man. The male hero is in flight from women.

Paul Theroux's book *Mosquito Coast* depicts a man in such flight. The central character, known throughout the book as Father, has an irrational and increasingly obsessive desire to escape a feminised and corrupted America on the brink of apocalypse and ecological catastrophe. He tells his son: 'No-one ever thinks of leaving this country. Charlie I think of it every day! ... And I'm the only one that does, because I'm the last man!' He can't name the amorphous threat to his existence, but he feels his life is in danger because 'They always get the smart ones first'. His search for an authentic existence leads to the jungles of Honduras, where he drags his family to lead a life of autarchy. His increasingly bizarre and desperate attempts to mould the world in his own image backfire on him and

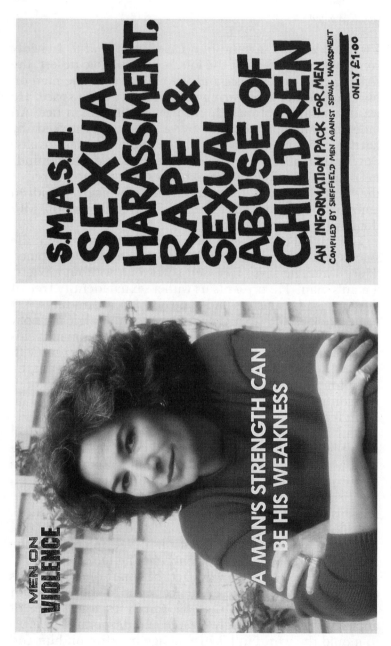

he is badly injured by a missionary, whose mission he burns down. Incapacitated he becomes wholly dependent on his sons and his wife, to whom he has referred throughout the story as Mother, a mere shadow who has obeyed all his whims. She decides to return down river to the town Le Ceiba, in contradiction to his order to continue upriver and deeper into the jungle. Father lies in the bottom of the boat like a baby, unable to move. He rails against his body and its weakness. Bodies are useless. He tells his son: 'Women, Charlie, they're in bad shape. They leak, they drip. It's terrible about women's bodies, how they leak. All that blood, all that useless fat'. When he discovers that he has been deceived and that they have reached the sea, he makes a last mad attempt to reach his goal, to be separate from the corporeal world. 'Listen to me, people. Grow wings and they'll never get you'. But his attempt to return to the jungle ends in his death and a cathartic howl: 'It was a child's shriek, thin and complaining and pathetic. 'Mother! Mother! Mother! Mother!'. Freudian interpretation of dreams represents flying as a symbol of the erect penis. The phallus of our sexual identity in ascendancy, freed from the ties that bind it to the ground, to women: 'I'll tell you who'll inherit the world – scavenging birds'. Yet despite Father's tireless pursuit of an authentic masculinity, to achieve a separateness, only death resolves his flight. The final irony is his plea for what he spent a lifetime running from, the maternal body.

Men have associated women with the earth, the flesh subordinate to men's reason. Mother Earth, green fields and lush pastures that men can bask in, that feed us. But she is also the mud and the dirt of women's bodies, the menstrual blood, the female sexual desire that instills panic. She is the landscape that we admire, yet tread warily across. She is to be feared and controlled. She is the vast mother with a cave between her legs. She embraced us when we were infants and ever since threatens to swamp us and swallow us up. She is the maternal body we must separate ourselves from. And woman is the temptress, the harlot who threatens our self control, the body we

MAN IN GREY

objectify, our pornographic defence against our mothers'
bodies. The mother and the whore, two images of
femininity that men's heterosexuality invents to reconcile
our contradictory desires for mother love and sexual love.
Freud summed up this aspect of our sexuality, which he
insisted was a 'universal affliction ... not confined to some
individuals', with the sentence 'Where they love they do
not desire and where they desire they do not love. They
seek objects they do not need to love in order to keep their
sensuality away from the objects they love'.

The moral archetypes that confront women – the
mother and the whore, the good and the bad – are a
projection of the contradictions within male heterosexuality. Men's subordination of women produces dominant
definitions of femininity fashioned for male desire. They
are meanings that belong to us. In this passage from
Barbara Cartland's *No Time for Love*, the male hero Wystan
Vanderfield, a man used to having his way with women, is
confronted by his Ideal Love Object asking for something
he cannot, this time, deliver.

> His arms tightened.
> 'Our spirits have found each other. You are everything my
> heart has been looking for and that is all that matters.'
> ... 'I love you! I love you!' he was saying ... and she heard
> her own voice tremulous,
> 'Oh Apollo ... I love ... you!'
> 'I love you' he said again.
> 'Will you not ... love me completely', she whispered, 'as a
> man loves a woman and makes her ... his ...'
> He seemed to stiffen and she knew in that moment that
> what she had said was wrong!

Perhaps the best contraception of all is the memory of
Mother.

Women's presence disturbs men. She mirrors what we
deny in ourselves, she is the Other that we fear; the
stickiness of our own repressed sexuality. We attempt to
control women through defining her, through producing
a pornographic female sexuality that will allay our fears,

images that we can control and conquer, that don't make demands that threaten to undo and expose us. Women are heterosexual men's achilles heel because we need her and at the same time that need challenges our masculine claim to rational superiority.

Feminism threatens the control men exert over women, it subverts the femininities that have brought men sexual stability and the ordering of our internal worlds. What happens when women no longer belong to men, when female identities and practice begin to refuse the patterns of male heterosexual desire? Men are bereft. We have fashioned her as the source of our solace, she fills an inner void, the wordless room that we occupy and neglect, she speaks that language, without her we are nothing. And yet, sometimes her presence threatens us with that same fate. There is a small scene from a television play that has always stayed with me. I cannot remember the play because it was years ago. A man in his late fifties is sat at a table. Opposite him sits a younger woman. He is deeply distressed. He is trying to explain something that he has done in the past, trying to make sense of it. I have this vivid recollection of him saying: 'I destroyed the only person I ever loved. It makes me heave'. The passion and intensity left the question why hanging in the air unanswered. It's a scene that reminds me of the conversation between Michael Ryan, hiding in his old school after his rampage through Hungerford, and a police officer. It was transcribed in one of the dailies. Again and again Ryan asks about his mother, 'Is she alright?'. She is who he needs most and she is the first that he kills. The logic of masculinity, its meanings and values that tangle us up, insist that men marginalise what has concrete value, what has been significant in the construction of our selves, in order to pursue the dominant meanings of masculinity, the mythologies of patriarchy.

About Other Men

The threat that women have posed to men, that they will expose our weakness and undermine the myths and illusions upon which our claims to superiority are founded,

He was a loner who found it hard to make friends or discover romance

MARKET DAY
MASSACRE

He was a marksman who took pot shots at neighbours in their gardens

Shy schoolboy who grew up to be Britain's biggest mass murderer of the 20th century

Doting mother's lavish gifts turned Ryan into a spoilt wimp

By NORMAN LUCK and ASHLEY WALTON

Hobby

Cut Rambo video imports, says MP

By PAUL WILKINS, Home Affairs Correspondent

Anger

A man in black shot my mummy, gran is told

Boasting

Ransom

Lonely in the crowd: Schoolboy Ryan (arrowed) is ill at ease and unsmiling amid his primary school classmates

'Mrs Rowland said the only person she remembered Ryan with was his mother. "I never saw him with a girlfriend," she said.'

'Denis Morley who worked with Ryan... described him as a "real mother's boy, a spoilt little wimp... He could have anything he wanted, she absolutely doted on him. But despite all her affection he would go home at night and beat her very badly."'

From the *Daily Mail*, 21 August 1987.

Sons must leave their mothers in order to become masculine subjects. Male culture constructs women as the Other, what men aren't. And if a man won't or can't leave her, if he remains that mummy's boy who hangs on to her apron strings, then he can never be a real 'man'. Ryan's rage and hatred of his mother was his dependency on her, a need that denied him access to a masculine subjectivity. In his own eyes, in the eyes of others, he remained a failure, 'a woman'. His first act on killing her was to find a woman to rape, to prove that he really could be a man. He failed, from then on 'the enemy' was everywhere.

has produced a male bonding, a collusion amongst men to resist the Other. This collective of heterosexual masculinity adorns itself with the trappings of male power and prestige but it is in fact a sign of men's trepidation, a place to which men can retreat in search of reassurance and validation. It is men's culture pitted against women's nature. The fantasies of those beer adverts celebrating a brotherly bonhomie miss the point. It's not just what is going on inside the pub that unites men, it's what the pub door is shutting out. Men have created cultures around drinking, sport and work that seek to shut out the troubling contradictions of male heterosexuality. They have produced a language that diminishes the central influence of women in our lives. Wives and sex become disassociated objects, in a language that originates in men's estrangement from their bodies and sexuality. The defensive nature of these male cultures is demonstrated when women attempt to break into them.

Men learn to invest the meanings of ourselves in the structures and images of male superiority. That is where the promise of patriarchy is supposed to lie, and why we maintain our collusion with the oppression of women. But in reality few of us ever connect with real power. Dreams of greatness and fame, of being Someone, rarely bare fruition. The reality of class and racial hierarchies ensure that the majority of men wait for a pay-off that rarely comes. Bruce Springsteen, while championing an American blue collar machismo, has articulated the bitterness and disappointments of men let down by the broken promises of patriarchy. In the song 'Adam raised a Cain', from the *Darkness on the Edge of Town*' LP he sings about masculinity as a pyrrhic victory:

> Daddy worked his whole life for nothing but the pain,
> Now he walks these empty rooms, looking for something to
>   blame,
> You inherit the sins, you inherit the flames
> Adam raised a Cain.

But while he sings about the illusory status symbols and the intangible goals of masculinity that never materialise, Springsteen is looking to feel at home in his sexual identity

A LETTER FROM MY FATHER

As long as I can remember, my father always said to me that one day he would write me a very special letter. But he never told me what the letter would be about. I used to try to guess what I would read in the letter, what mystery, what family secret could at

last be revealed. I know what I had hoped to read in the letter. I wanted him to tell me where he had hidden his affection. But then he died, and the letter never did arrive, and I never found that place where he had hidden his love.

Duane Michals

The broken promises of patriarchy

rather than change it. And in many of his songs the image of the father is like a beacon that will lead him to an authentic masculinity. On the LP *Nebraska*, the song 'My Father's House' senses the loneliness, but there is a strong compulsion to follow in the same footsteps as his father:

> My Father's House shines hard and bright it
> stands like a beacon calling me in the night
> calling and calling so cold and alone.

His preoccupation with his father is reflected amongst a much wider constituency of men for whom the generational gap between them and their fathers means also a difference in masculine values. We see in their traditional masculinities a source of our disappointment in being men.

Our fathers play a symbolic role in our transition to the masculine world, they become a focus for all the promises and status symbols we learn to expect will be ours. The mythology of his omnipotence is like a thick foliage that obscures his ordinariness. So many sons are soured and disappointed by their fathers. We invest meanings in them that they cannot fulfill. We are looking for a mythical figure, the perfect man we can aspire to, the good father who will love us. He begins in our lives as the phallus, a rival we must follow, and it is hard to shake off that image of an ideal man we should emulate. Even as adults they can continue to grip us in infant paralysis. Franz Kafka wrote *A Letter to His Father* in an attempt to exorcise his brutal father's hold over him. 'I was after all, weighed down by your mere physical presence. There was I skinny, weakly, slight: you strong, tall, broad. I felt a miserable specimen. And what's more, not only in your eyes but in the eyes of the whole world, for you were for me the measure of all things.' It is an identification that is usually a lifelong and unfulfilled quest for that intangible something that will make us whole. For in pursuing masculine meanings and our belonging in patriarchal culture, in our desire to be at home with our masculine personas, we reinforce the contradictions of our sexual identities.

Many of Springsteen's songs allude to a sense of loss, a time in men's lives, before adulthood, when we were authentic and complete. It is a masculine nostalgia that is the explicit concern of the film *Stand By Me*. The story is about four twelve-year-old boys who go off on a hike in search of the dead body of another boy, killed in a train accident. Their adventure is set against a backdrop of authoritarian fathers, problem adults and a predatory gang of older adolescent boys. The summer is finishing and the four boys are all due to begin new schools in the fall. There is a sense that a period of their lives is coming to an end, a time when 'We knew who we were'. Central to the film is the relationship between two of the boys, Gurdy (whose adult persona has written and relates the story) and a more worldly wise boy, Chris. The film reads like a requiem for the idea of a lost age of innocence, before the fall of male heterosexuality splits men from one another. This is the future that is depicted in the brutalised and cowardly bragging of the adolescent gang, whose threats of violence

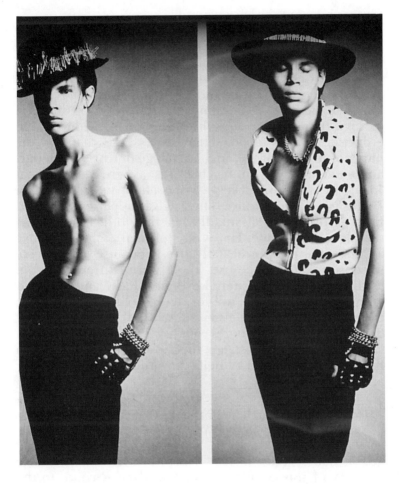

forever hover in the background.

The competitive aggression of the gang contrasts with the mutual aid practised by the younger boys. And while the film stays the right side of sentimentality, it is rooted in nostalgia. Central to this is the developing love and intimacy between Gurdy and Chris, which is not going to last. The message in the film is the transience of this kind of love between men, its hovering on the edge of an eroticism that is taboo. There is a sense that for the narrator his love of the mythical image of Chris is the only authentic moment in his life. It's a bereavement that Jonathan Garthorne Hardy writes about in his book *The Public School Phenomenon*. The English upper classes are a far cry from the 1950s middle America of the film, but the nostalgia is the same. Hardy says of men's schoolboy love affairs: 'these homosexual loves, because they were unconsummated, because they were different from anything that came later, were embalmed and secreted away ... England is full of these ex-lovers who are poignant, it is true, but also infinitely sad'. It is a repressed desire that literally oozes out of the poetry of John Betjeman, with his nostalgia for a lost middle England. In his poem 'Summoned by Bells', he writes of his passion for another boy:

> Here twixt the church tower and the chapel spire
> Rang sad and deep the bells of my desire.

It's a homoeroticism that runs through the heritage industry of this country: from *Brideshead Revisited* to the poet Rupert Brook. A mythical world of England at peace with itself coexists with an image of beautiful, intimate young men. It's an illusion born of a much harsher reality, as John Betjeman said of his schooldays. 'I never dared touch anyone. I thought I would have gone to gaol – and hell'.

Despite the marginalisation of homosexuality, it is ever present in our relationships with one another. Heterosexual men's common response is to render it invisible, to assume that it exists in crude, easily identifiable stereotypes. Yet men's language and behaviour is full of homoerotic content. In the City, a bastion of male power, markets are penetrated, good stocks are sexy, firms that are merging are getting into bed with each other, and their directors are referred to as likely bedfellows. Heterosexual male culture displaces repressed feelings and sexual interest in other men onto things, we let them speak for us. Workplace banter, men's horseplay, mocking references to effeminacy and the mimicking of 'queens' are practices that spell out men's own separateness from them, yet reveal their fascination. The historical regulation of homosexuality, the use of medical and psychiatric discourses to construct it as a sickness and deviance also constructs the limits of men's heterosexuality. He is the Other, a presence who simultaneously confirms the legitimacy of our own sexual identity, yet presents it with its own relativity, that it is only one identity amongst others, disturbing and disrupting our sense of normality.

The current eroticisation of men's bodies, the shifting of gay erotic images into mainstream popular culture, represents a blurring of sexual differences and a loosening of masculine rigidity. The original advert for Levi 501s, with Nick Kamen removing his clothes in the launderette owed much to this genre. But instead of frightening off heterosexual men from a product associated with such a sexualised image of masculinity, the advert paid off and the jeans became a big seller. It's an image that reflects a culture of sexual diversity, one that traditional masculinities have vehemently denied. But because heterosexual men repress our own homoerotic desires we fetishise gay men. The reality of sexual diversity, the plurality of sexual experiences in men's lives is subordinate to the dominant codes that define what is masculine legitimacy and what is different from that. Gay men have to continually contest their subordination and resist definitions of themselves that are often rooted in heterosexual men's fetishism.

And it is a fetishism that easily spills over into paranoia and violence. Freud contends that 'what lies at the core of the conflict in cases of paranoia among males is the wishful fantasy of loving another man'. AIDS has triggered off a wave of such paranoia where the gay man has become the persecutor, an object of vilification and pollution. Homosexuality as a plague is a metaphor that resonates loudly with heterosexual men's own anxieties about the enemy within, the fear that we may catch or be caught by it. The world men fashion for themselves produces its own problems of regulating homoeroticism. Our bodies and the minutiae of our behaviour become places of regulation and discipline. How we look at other men, how we touch them, the stance and rigidity of our bodies, the ways we speak to each other and the subjects we discuss, what feelings we show and the kinds of behaviour we exhibit – all these are codes that are used to police men, and that we employ to protect ourselves. Our relationships with each other are diminished by doubt and insecurity. I can remember all those times at school, the retribution and punishment we handed out to boys who were different, fat boys and effeminate boys. As we grew older we all learned to keep our heads down and follow the pack. We wouldn't have dared admit a longing for another boy, better to hit or humiliate him instead.

The White Man's Black Man

The black man shares a similar fate to the gay man in the heterosexual imaginary of the white man. Homoeroticism binds straight men to gay men with a mixture of fascination and loathing. We cannot be freed because homoeroticism is part of us, its denial structures our masculinity. Homosexuality and homophobia are historical constructed partners. Similarly the history of imperialism and the colonial experience has produced a meaning of blackness, of an Other, that constructs a sense of white supremacy and coherence in relation to this alien threat. The white man has embodied this meaning in the black man. He need not be present, but the idea of him, the knowledge of his existence, both disturbs and reinforces who we believe we are. Colonialism was never the simple material subjugation of military conquests and economic exploitation. It has been the destruction of black cultural identities, and the recreating of the black lived experience as the fantasies of whites. Whiteness became the order of things.

For the white man the black man is Other. He is the subject of a colonial discursive power that produces a myriad of images of him. It is a language of racist stereotypes and meanings, that have tied white men into a way of seeing the black man that subordinates, silences and often threatens to destroy him. Frantz Fanon, in *Black Skin, White Masks* describes the effect of this relationship on himself, a black man.

> I was responsible at the same time for my body, for my race, for my ancestors ... I discovered my blackness ... and I was battered down by tom-toms, cannibalism, intellectual deficiency, fetishism, racial defects, slave ships and above all else, above all: 'Sho' good eatin' '.
>
> On that day, completely dislocated I took myself far off from my own presence, far indeed, and made myself an object. What else could it be for me but an amputation, an excision, a haemorrhage that spattered my whole body with black blood?

But how would white men describe this relationship when what we have at our disposal is a history of vile language, deprecatory images and sexual fantasies. The words 'dark' and 'black' spill out from a deep contempt and fear, something of our own making. It is the black male body that has been fetishised as something primitive, containing a primordial sexuality that is the 'Other' to the white man's civilisation. White men have written their messages on the black male body, recording, photographing and constructing it as a spectacle for our dread and fascination. Medical photography has pathologised it and documentary photography has made it a problem or criminal. It has been eroticised and objectified in the name of fine art.

The white American photographer Robert Mapplethorpe has produced a book of photographs of the black body, predominantly male and naked (*The Black Book*). It features meticulously observed images that we are invited to admire and take pleasure in. But many of them, particularly of male genitals and parts of body dissasociated from the whole, beg the question of who these images are for. They seem to fit into contemporary erotic images of the male body, yet the narcissism is absent. They are the image of a white man's fantasy, on show for the consumption of white men (and women, although the images are homo-erotic rather than hetero-erotic.). The picture, 'Phillip on a pedestal' turns the body into an object of art, an ornament. What is it about my experience as a white man and my relationship to a history of racist and colonial imagery, that when I look at this picture I imagine chains around his legs, attaching him to the pedestal, not so much a slave, rather a domesticated and captive animal. It's a photograph that captures this particular black man and transforms him into an object of white men's desire. There is no democracy in this image, nothing reciprocal between the viewer and the object of his gaze.

The black man is rarely portrayed in relation to his family. If he's not an eroticised fantasy he is portrayed, particularly in the media, as a threat. The 'black rapist' who threatens 'our women', the violent young hood, the mugger; images that suggest a man incapable of fatherhood and familial responsibility. Not surprisingly black men are absent from the discourse of the New Father; for what exists above all in these representations is the body, a body that seems unconnected with emotions and family. So it is in the sports pages of newspapers that the majority of images of black men appear. Here he is valorised. The black man becomes 'our boy', 'black magic' tolerated and recruited into white society for his skills. The body of the black athlete is held in awe by white men. A white sprinter, quoted in Ernest Cashmere's book, *Black Sportsmen*, said;

> There isn't a chance of competing on level terms with black guys. Its depressing really. I trained hard all last winter and in one race I came up against a black who I knew hadn't prepared properly. He just blazed out and killed the rest of the field. It's got to be something natural.

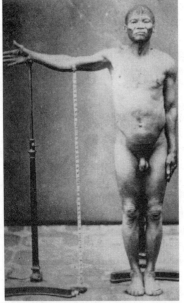

The Black Man as a body

It's a comment that reflects the idea that black physicality is more animal-like than white men's; the power of an uncivilised 'natural' force. In the same book Jim Smith, ex-manager of Birmingham City Football Club commented on the rise of a generation of young black footballers. 'They seem to use very little intelligence; they get by on sheer natural talent most of the time.'

The white man allows the black man one thing, his body. But it is a body filled with white fantasy and foreboding. For the white man the black man's physicality is what defines his presence. For the white man the black man is more violent, more of a rapist, more misogynist than himself. White men project their own misogyny and disgust with women on the black male. He becomes the constructed image of white men's repressed lust; imbued with an animal-like sexuality and a huge penis, a body closer to nature than the 'cultured white man'. These are images of what the white man denies in himself, his experience of a male heterosexuality as a dark and uncontrollable force. And a twist is added, for the white man really believes that the black man possesses these attributes. He comes to represent the idea of sexual insatiability, the illicit thrill of unbridled desire, and the fantasy of an orgiastic sexuality.

It is a fetishism that easily spills over into paranoia. The young black man can move in the white imagination from being a 'young colt' to a rampaging sexual menace. The lynchings of the deep south of America, the castrations that preceded them were like a ritual cleansing of white male misogyny and the guilt of homosexual desire. Black men were burnt alive, tortured, hung from trees, their genitals torn out in the name of often spurious accusations about sexual assault or rape of white women. The only sexual threat that existed was in the minds and deeds of the murderers. The Afro-American writer James Baldwin describes a lynching in *Going to Meet the Man*. The sexual desire and fear of the white man for the black body is acted out in all its sadism.

> The man with the knife took the nigger's privates in his hand,
> ... The white hand stretched them, cradled them, caressed
> them. Then the dying man looked straight into Jesse's eyes –
> it could have been as long as a second, but it seemed longer
> than a year. Then Jesse screamed, and the crowd screamed as
> the knife flashed first up then down, cutting the dreadful
> thing away, and the blood came roaring down.

The colonial imagination has constructed images of the black man as the 'dark villain' who will steal 'our women', the archetypal western nightmare of the 'black beast' running amok amongst the 'white virgins'. This is white masculinity as a fortress, protecting what it deems is its own from an alien threat. In actuality it is an imagery of our own making. The 'black beast' of our own sexual desires intersecting with and constructed by the history of colonialism. It is the source of that irrational fear of miscegenation. Of black men and white women being sexual together. It is the impetus behind that belligerent question that whites ask one another, 'Would you let your daughter marry one': the thought of their daughters being subjected to men's own fantasies of unbridled sexual intercourse, of a sexuality that obliterates women with its lust. 'Miscegenation' is when white men's projections onto the black body come home to roost. It disrupts the idea that white is a seamless subjectivity. Racism reinforces the idea of a superior, coherent white masculinity that is predicated on the notion of a black fragmented and disintegrated masculinity. When the white man looks at his image of black incoherence, he sees only his own completeness. Miscegenation, the black male body in our midst, shatters this relationship, threatening white supremacy.

The emergence of a black women's movement has prompted black men to begin a debate about black male sexuality, and the relationship of masculinity to race. It's a process to which liberal white men have an ambivalent relationship. The popularity of black women writers and the publicising of their struggles against misogyny and violence has ennobled them in the minds of white liberals. But in turn the black man has become the unspoken folk devil of white sexual political discourse. The struggles of black women can be appropriated by white men to confirm racist stereotypes and the idea that black masculinity is an inferior and defective copy of white masculinity.

This racism remains unspoken. Where it becomes evident is in the expectations of white men involved in sexual politics that black men should follow our lead. This universalising of a politics of specific experiences amounts to the old imperative of 'be white or disappear'. It's an issue that emerged in the final plenary session of the Breaking Out event (see acknowledgements in this book). An argument began about the language used to describe sexual politics and its concerns. There was a number of objections to the use of the word Eurocentric. In response an Afro-American man said, as I can recall, 'Understanding words like Eurocentric and what they describe has been crucial to our survival as black men'. It was significant that this growing argument ended the day, and was the main point of contention. A black presence disrupts the idea of how we as white men view the world. And what goes equally for how we have produced a response to feminism and sexual politics.

As we struggle to come to terms with feminism and gay politics we cannot ignore the way race has contributed to the construction of our sexualities and masculine identities. It is there along with sex and class and the struggle is for us to find ways of speaking about the complexities and contradictions that these forces create in our lives. For when those we have constructed as Other, as not belonging, whose presence has been marked by their silence and subjective absence, begin to define and speak for themselves, we are literally lost for words. These political constituencies organised around race and sexuality present us with a predicament. To either work out our relationship to their politics or remain part of the problem. The collective logic of white heterosexual masculinities is to project our sexual contradictions and repression onto others. Women, gay men and black men are constructed as a threat to the stability of our subjectivity, the potential subverters of our masculine order. The more the myth of masculinity is challenged the further the mechanism of men's power over others is exposed. We are then confronted with the choice of change or violence. The history of the colonial and patriarchal system has been one of terrible violence. For socialist men, changing our masculinity by developing a sexual politics is the only human alternative.

It means creating a politics that can speak out against the tyranny of present definitions of masculinity, yet one that doesn't simply construct men as the enemy – for then what are we to do? The unfolding dramas of the New Man as he plays off his new sensibilities with a system that privileges him, reflects that changing meanings of masculinity are not necessarily a threat to patriarchal relations. Rather they represent a potential for developing a sexual politics. One that can make tangible the contradictions, problems and desires of heterosexual men. That is a basis for dialogue with feminism and the creation of a politics around race and sexuality that can begin to go beyond the current fragments. The question what does a man want? is something we can ask of ourselves. What do we want? They are questions that speak for a desire to live a different kind of life in relation to others. To live our differences without resort to oppression. In short the way we want to be men.

Notes

1 Roland Barthes *Mythologies*, p.143. Paladin.
2 Alice Jardine, *Gynesis: Configurations of Woman and Modernity* p.72-73. Cornell University Press, 1985.
3 'I'm Glad I Was Castrated' *Daily Mirror* 12 September 1987.
4 *Mythologies*. Roland Barthes, p.151.
5 February 1987. The press took up the story of Oxford post-graduate Robert Carver who was attempting to stop his girlfriend from having an abortion. According to Tory MP for Basildon, David Amess, speaking in the House of Commons, Carver was not seeking a father's right but wanted to 'establish the right and legal protection of an unborn child capable of being born alive, under the ILPA' (Infant Life Preservation Act 1929). Carver took his case to appeal, but it was rejected in the House of Lords. Subsequently, it transpired, the woman did not proceed with the abortion.
6 *Inside the Family*, Melanie Henwood, Lesley Rimmer and Malcolm Wicks. Family Policy Studies Centre, 1987.
7 See Virginia Mathews, 'Merely Male in Admen's Markets', Guardian 30, November 1987.
8 See Lorna McKee, 'The dads who play at happy families' The *Guardian*, 19 January 1987.
9 *Marxism Today*, September 1987.
10 See Colin Gordon (ed) *Michel Foucault, Power/Knowledge*. Harvester Press, 1980, p.116.
11 *Everywoman*, 1986.
12 Michel Foucault, *History of Sexuality*, Allen Lane, 1978.

Look Back in Anger: Men in the Fifties

LYNNE SEGAL

'A new hero has risen among us' wrote Walter Allen in his influential review of Kingsley Amis' first novel *Lucky Jim* in January 1954.[1] The new hero is male, the 'intellectual tough' or 'tough intellectual'. He is rude, crude and clumsy, boasts his political apathy, his suspicion of all causes, and he is out to do nobody any good but himself. His heroism is that he is honestly self-serving, fiercely critical of all he sees as phoney, pretentious or conformist – a passion which expresses itself most easily in a rejection of all he sees as womanly, as domestic. He exudes a pervasive sneer or bullying contempt towards women.

Explaining the appeal of this young cynic tells us a good deal about the nature of men's lives in the 50s. Understanding men's lives in the 50s, it seems to me, is a good starting point for reassessing contemporary debate on the changing nature of men and masculinity in the 80s. Back in 1958 Kenneth Allsop was already wondering how a person in 1984 might look back on the 50s: 'I think that he will see a sensitive, emotional, intelligent but wretchedly neurotic society, obedient to protocol beneath the exhibitionist 'rebelling', and obsessively class-conscious'.[2] What he will not see are public forms of rebellion – exhibitionist or not – from women. Even though it was a woman writer, Storm Jameson (never of course placed in the ranks of Angry Young Men), who perhaps most clearly expressed what was best in 50s literary protest. 'What we need now may be just that insolent irresponsibility, the contempt for safety and comfort and riches, the passionate delight in freedom, the curiosity, the blind hunger for experience and new knowledge, of the mediaeval wandering scholar ...'[3]

What we also need now, and what was needed but largely absent then, for those who might wish to shed some light on the existential angst of the new man of mid-century Britain, was some greater understanding of the social and political reality surrounding the working and personal lives of men and women of the time. At a recent conference on the New Left of the 50s, 'Out of Apathy: 30 years of the New Left', Jean McCrindle, one of the handful of women who were part of that movement from its inception, expressed incredulity at the absence of women from the politics of the time: 'I just don't know, I don't know why women were so absent, so silent – there was a pathological absence of women, silencing of women, in those days'.[4] Exploring the reasons behind women's 'pathological silence' in those days can tell us something of the nature of men's lives at the time.

The most familiar images we have of the political climate following the defeat of the Labour Party in 1951 and the beginning of the Tory boom all conjure up its complacency, inertia, illusion: economic problems were solved, class conflicts dissolved, household harmony restored – so both Labour and Tory politicians declared. By the early 50s Keynesian economic policies had indeed eliminated mass unemployment and ensured a steady rise in the standard of living of the working class – further change, it was thought, was unnecessary. As central as a new myth of classlessness to this Butskellite consensus was the myth of sexual equality. 'The feminine sex is a social problem', Alva Myrdal had announced a decade earlier.[5] But now women's problems too were solved. Gone for good, it was thought, was the toil and misery of the pre-war working-class housewife, raising too many, unplanned, unwanted, underfed and unhealthy children, in desperate poverty and wretched housing. Child benefit, family planning, and other welfare provision for mothers and their children did cushion the post-war family from the kind of poverty it had often experienced in earlier times. Women may have returned to the home after the war, with the birth rate soaring and working women derided, but so too had men. There were many new demands placed upon women as wives and mothers, but, it was felt, women could hardly complain when unlike former times they were no longer alone in their interests and preoccupations.

Man About the House

The man's place was also in the home. Men too, in popular consciousness, were being domesticated; had returned from battlefield to bungalow with new expectations of the comforts and the pleasures of home. Both the popular and the academic writing of the 50s celebrates a new 'togetherness', harmony and equality between women and men in the home. The sociological writing of the 50s, for example, applauds the major and profound changes occurring in contemporary family life. In Britain the well known community studies of Young and Willmott on working-class families in the early 50s move quickly from describing the working-class husband of former times who was mean with money, callous in sex, harsh to his children and neither helpful nor affectionate towards his wife, to affirm the end of the absentee husband and a new partnership in marriage: 'In place of the old comes a new kind of companionship between man and woman, reflecting the rise in status of the young wife and children which is one of the great transformations of our time'.[6] The influential writing of John and Elizabeth Newson came to similar conclusions: 'At a time when he has more money in his pocket, and more leisure on which to spend it, than ever before, the head of the household chooses to sit at his own fireside, a baby on his knee and a feeding bottle in his hand'.[7] In some ways the domestication of men was real enough. Anthony Sampson in his *Anatomy of*

Britain (published in 1961) writes of the threat of domesticity to professional men's clubs. 'At lunch time they seem confident enough: but it is in the evenings, when the wife and family beckon, that the loyalty of the clubman is tested: and it is then that the crumbling of clubs is revealed. A few defiant masculine clubs, like White's, succeed in drinking and gambling till late in the night. But in most clubs, only a handful of bachelors, grass widowers and visitors inhabit the cavernous rooms. No doubt clubs will survive a long time, with their myths, their sites and the convenience: but the old misogynist zeal, which built the Empire and kept wives in their place – that has gone.'[8]

The box office hits of the day and the new Hollywood heroes (in a Britain increasingly Americanised) also seemed to reflect a post-war cult of domesticity so strong that it embraced men too: tough guys were on their way out. As Peter Biskind recalls, 'By the fifties, the tough, hard-boiled Hemingway male of the thirties and forties, the man who hid his feelings, if he had any ... who endured adversity alone with proud, stoical silence or wooden unconcern, had seen his best days'.[9] The new male stars of the 50s, tough but tender Rock Hudson, slight and sensitive Montgomery Clift and James Dean, were a different breed from Humphrey Bogart, James Cagney or Gary Cooper, then increasingly portrayed as neurotics or crazies. The new films generally put family ahead of career. And the female stars, whether Marilyn Monroe in *The Seven Year Itch*, Debby Reynolds in *The Tender Trap*, and *Tammy* or Elizabeth Taylor in *Giant*, were busy civilising men, and teaching them that their real desires were for matrimony and domesticity.

The new man of Hollywood, like sociological man of the 50s, may more often have been putting family first, but, as we shall see, his place within it remained decidedly limited. Re-assessing the 50s sociological and psychological writing on the family two decades later, Elizabeth Wilson suggests: 'To study this body of literature is above all to study how ideology operates by *excluding* whole areas of debate from the very consciousness of readers and authors alike ... The sexual division of labour, because it was taken for granted, was an *absence* in these works ... About this conflict [the conflict between women and men] there was also silence, for these books are about a myth – a myth of happiness'.[10]

But there are ways of seeing behind the myth to observe more of what men were actually doing in the home in the 50s, and the conflicts and tensions of family life at the time. 'Man about the house' is the chapter heading in an interesting handbook published in 1958 called *The Man's Book*. Aimed at middle-class men, the men deserting Sampson's clubland, it suggests what they might have been up to in the home: hammers, saws, smoothing tools, gripping tools, boring and drilling tools, scissors, nails, screws and glues are illustrated and explained. In another section, 'Outdoor Man', there is a chapter on gardening. The book contains not a single reference to children, housework, or any type of activity traditionally seen as 'women's work'.[11] It is noteworthy that the topic 'fathers' is rarely listed in the index of 50s books on the family, and when it does appear it is not in connection with issues of childcare.

In the research on English attitudes collected by Geoffrey Gorer in 1950 it is clear that the idea of quite separate roles for husband and wife was completely dominant. Gorer asked women which qualities they most desired in husbands, learning that the home was mentioned by less than 5%. What husbands most wanted from their wives was good housekeeping – sharing the husband's interests was mentioned by only 8%. Some wives did comment upon their husbands unwillingness to take part in any housework or childcare, like the 'typical 28-year-old working class wife' who complained of husbands being 'afraid of being thought a cissy; mine hates people to know he helps at all in the house; won't push pram ...'[12] Gorer reports that it is the younger married wives 'who are the loneliest members of English society, without even the faint friendliness of pub or cafe'.[13] Taking the sexual division of labour for granted, Gorer does not enquire into the nature or extent of men's involvement with housework or childcare, except to question whether father or mother is the most appropriate person to punish a very naughty child.

Richard Hoggart in his influential enquiry into working-class life published in 1957 also describes men sharing little of women's domestic life. A husband is not really expected to help in the home; ' "Oh, that's not a man's job" a woman will say, and would not want him to do too much of that kind of thing for fear he is thought womanish'.[14] Men pushing prams would still be thought 'soft' by most wives as well as husbands. What women want from men, Hoggart suggests, is not sharing in the home but a good and steady provider, and one who is not violent. The husband is always 'the boss' in the home and, even on the dole, 'he must still have his pocket-money'.[15] Fathers are not close to their children, at least up until the boy leaves school, when 'he is, probably for the first time, close to his father and finds his father ready to be close to him: they now share the real world of work and men's pleasures'.[16] The wife, in Hoggart's view, knows little of her husband's job, and will be working hard 'from getting up to going to bed'. A few younger husbands and wives may, however, be learning from middle-class husbands who, Hoggart feels, are more likely to help their wives if they can no longer afford paid help in the home. But we see few signs of the 'togetherness' being popularly celebrated.

It is in Young and Willmott's own study that we see some of the clearest examples of the separate worlds of women and men. Men are around the house more, they suggest: the home being less overcrowded is a nicer place to be, so 'men do not go to pubs so often as they used to'.[17] But what do they do in the home? As we learn from one woman informant, they go and fetch a bottle in 'so they can watch the tellie at the same time'. Young and Willmott use occasional washing up ('one or more times during the previous week') as the indication that most men do 'give some regular help to their wives'.[18] Or again in claiming that the sharing of responsibility 'is nowhere more obvious than over childcare', what we are told is that fathers are not so strict and punitive towards their children as they used to be. We can have no real idea what amount of shared housework or childcare did take place (as occasionally it might have) because the authors themselves, like those they interview, do not seriously expect it: the domestic partnership is one where the separate worlds of men and women are reconstituted inside the home itself:

> When they watch the television instead of drinking beer in the pub, and weed the garden instead of going to a football match, the husbands of Greenleigh have taken a stage further the partnership mentioned in an earlier chapter as one of the characteristics of modern Bethnal Green.[19]

Ironically Young and Willmot's stress on the importance of the mother-daughter tie in married life in Bethnal Green, alongside the terrible loneliness of the wives in Greenleigh ('it was all a misery ... I sat and cried my eyes out')[20], is perhaps the most compelling illustration we could find of the reality of the two worlds of women and men. Husbands, they suggest, are excluded from the world of mother and daughter: women are closer to their mothers than to their husbands. This, indeed, is precisely why in their conclusion they can proclaim 'the view which we have found and tested more or less daily for three years is that very few people wish to leave the East End'.[21] But it's only the women who are so lonely in Greenleigh ('It's like being in a box to die out here' reports Mrs Harper), the men, on the whole, like it: 'It's not bad here ... we've got a decent house with a garden, that's the main thing,' reports Mr Harper.[22]

The most impressive of these 'community studies' of the 50s is the description of Yorkshire miners and their families in *Coal is our Life*.[23] At odds with the cosy consensus of the time, Dennis, Henriques and Slaughter do perceive more of the ways in which women are oppressed by their dependence on their husband's wages and the organisation of their households around their husband's jobs. Significantly, this was one aspect of their analysis which was criticised at the time as merely a morbid preoccupation with problems of the past. Moreover these authors believe that the lives of women and men in the mining villages are but accentuations of typical working-class family lives whenever the wife has no prospect of professional or other social interests or activities outside the home. In this situation, they suggest, there can be little real sharing of anything between husband and wife.

Again unlike their contemporary colleagues, these observers stress the limitations of the new conditions enticing men from the clubs and pubs back into the home: 'Television seems to be making a slight difference in this respect, but it will be recognised that as a 'family activity' this is a passive and silent one, a relation between the television screen and each individual rather than between the family members'.[24] Even men's increased engagement in do-it-yourself household repairs and improvements, they notice, never seems to demand or encourage the growth of companionship between husband and wife. Men, in the mining villages at least, remain comparative strangers in the home, distanced from their children (particularly their daughters) and, if not engaged in the almost exclusively male social life outside the home, spend their non-working time in their garden or silently pottering about at home.

Husbands and wives in this study are seen as living separate almost secret lives, neither being able to enter properly into the other's world: the wife will know little or nothing of her husband's job and social life, the husband will take no responsibility for the housework or childcare. Few women said they found satisfaction in their sex lives, while husbands too in the 'almost business-like' arrangements of marriage experienced a suppression of affection and desire: 'As the years go by, and any original sexual attraction fades, this rigid division between the activities of husband and wife cannot but make for an empty and uninspiring relationship'.[25] For the husband to maintain his status and prestige in his social life with his peers, he must consciously distance himself from his wife and children, and be seen to do so. Behind this social distance between women and men, it is clear, as these authors stress, that women remain inferior and subordinate to men (unlike her husband, a woman spends no money on herself nor engages in any activities or amusements without his approval). The husband's greater freedom and power is accepted by both women and men, an apparent inevitability in a context where there is little employment for women, and where the jobs available for men are seen as peculiarly 'masculine': the miner's main source of pride in his work derives from its difficult, arduous, and dangerous nature. The passionate belief that only 'real men', and certainly not women, could descend down into the dark, dirty, dungeons of the minefields provides what status there is in a job which, for men, is poorly paid and hazardous.

Maternity Rules

The opposed social spheres of women and men described in *Coal is our Life* accords with other contemporary analysis, for example that of Elizabeth Bott, suggesting that the closer-knit the social network surrounding families, the more segregated the roles of husband and wife; the more isolated the family unit, the more symmetrical the roles.[26] This ties in with a belief some commentators expressed at the time that more traditional sexual divisions might persist in the older working-class areas, but were breaking down in the more isolated family units characteristic of the middle class and more geographically mobile urban working class. However, a closer look at the assumptions and practices of middle-class family life in the 50s suggests something rather different. Daughters of these middle-class men have written about fathers who were rarely at home, were ill at ease with their emotions, and attuned only to the mysterious demands of 'work', suggesting to Olivia Harris, for example, that English fathers seemed to be 'archetypally absent'.[27] Sheila Rowbotham has described how her lower middle-class father, though working from home, was so entirely removed from domestic life that he 'had to resort to creeping up on the kitchen in his carpet slippers to gain access to information ... To me he was simply a tyrant to be resisted'.[28] There were, of course, the exceptions. Sara Maitland's father 'bathed his babies, climbed trees, kicked footballs, hugged, kissed and played with his children. Above all he *taught us* ...'[29] But in general, it seems, that at

home, middle-class men, like their steady-earning
class equivalent, could expect 'a life well balanced
the TV set and the neatly-tended garden'.[30]

The wives of these men, meanwhile, were often f[...]
contented. Judith Hubback in her book *Wives Who Went To
College* published in 1957 described the dissatisfaction of
educated women tied to the home while their children
were young. But, like the women she interviews, she has
no solutions to the resentments and frustrations she
records: '... I get tired of having very few personal
contacts outside my family in which I am anything more
than my husband's shadow'.[31] 'Escape' to use their own
words, can come only perhaps when the children are no
longer young. The problem of combining family and
employment was publicly discussed in relation to
middle-class women, for example by Alva Myrdal and
Viola Klein in 1956 in *Women's Two Roles*, but they make it
clear that they are referring to married women who are
childless or have ceased to look after small children. In
discussing the positive aspects of women's engagement in
paid work, they suggest that what we need now is mainly 'a
change of attitudes among women themselves' as well as
better services; they do not contemplate change in the
services men provide in the home. Indeed, once again,
'fathers' do not even rate a mention in the index.[32]

It is not hard to explain the absence of any expectations
of men's direct participation in childcare or housework,
whether in the working-class or middle-class home. As
Denise Riley argues, the fixing and freezing of women as
mothers, and nothing other than mothers, was central to
the vision of the 50s.[33] Not even women could yet shift the
focus. Policing mothers at all times was the new wisdom,
popularised in John Bowlby's bestseller of 1953 *Child Care
And The Growth of Love* stressing 'the absolute need of
infants and toddlers for the continuous care of their
mothers'.[34] Bowlby's notion of 'maternal deprivation' was
used to explain every conceivable personal and social
problem, from educational failure and mental breakdown
to delinquency, divorce, promiscuity and general social
unrest.

Whatever may have been Bowlby's own intentions, which were primarily to assert and protect the interests of children, his ideas were an important part of the political campaign in the late 40s to return women to the home and increase the population of Britain. Not only feminists in the early 70s, but other writers on the 50s have commented on the use of 'maternal deprivation' as a justification for the housebound mother and neglect of the needs of 'working' mothers. Peter Lewis suggests 'it took the place in mid-twentieth century demonology that masturbation filled for the Victorians'.[35] The British psychoanalytic writing of the time also stressed the need for separate and distinct spheres for women and men as necessary for the mental health of the child: the father should remain the more distant and remote visitor from the outside world, in the words of D W Winnicot, 'the human being who stands for law and order which mother plants in the life of the child'.[36]

In line with expert opinion, the deluge of childcare manuals of the 50s either completely ignored the father's role in parenting, or treated paternal participation in childcare as a joke. *From Here to Maternity*, for example, warns husbands of the bizarre 'monkey business' they will have to put up with from their pregnant wives.[37] While *Happy Event*, another light and popular book for new mothers on 'the stark reality' of the first year with baby, has no tips for expectant fathers, it does open with a cautionary poem for mothers:

> When Baby's cries grew hard to bear
> I popped him in the Frigidaire.
> I never would have done so if
> I'd known that he'd be frozen stiff.
> My wife said: 'George, I'm so unhappy
> Our darling's now completely frappé![38]

Women, it seems, knew something about the limitations of men's new domesticity. As Betty Thorne, the wife of a Sheffield steel worker, wrote forcefully to the *Manchester*

Guardian in 1960 describing life on her street, 'The husband is an ornament or a nuisance alternately'.[39]

The general social concern with adequate mothering, and the assumed biological imperative dictating women's exclusive responsibility for it, had ambiguous effects on women. Mothering, at least ideologically, was given new value and importance. Housework or 'homemaking' was portrayed not as a drudgery but as a 'craft': the 'creative' work of efficient domestic consumption. Shopping was no longer to be seen as labour, but more as a type of leisure: a symbol of the 'good times' now accompanying and sustaining the golden years of economic growth in Britain. But women also faced new anxieties and accusations as incompetent carers and selfish slatterns, were they to complain too loudly of the secret isolation, boredom and strain accompanying their work in the home.

Complain, of course, some of them did. In a sudden public outburst of resentment in the *Guardian* Women's Page in 1959 we could have read: 'I love both my sons devotedly, but I suffer the most excruciating boredom in their company'. This was the confession of 'J.B.H.'; another woman writes, 'I have five children and I found those baby years, about which my child-loving friends wax lyrical, full of the most appalling boredom and weariness. It did not get better. It got worse with each one and it is just as bad with my grandchildren'.[40] But for these women, there was no alternative, not even one to ponder on, as the discontented were sharply reminded: 'Once a woman confesses boredom with any aspect of her God-given role of wife and mother it is a very short step to finding the whole thing intolerable, and to do so J.B.H. must have forgotten the millions of weary, bored women, in whom civilisation was built and depends for its continuance, and whom she has to thank for her position'.[41] (A short step, indeed, but one which it would take ten years to re-think!)

Meanwhile, the obvious backlash to the near obsessive focus on the importance of the mother child bond in the psychology of the day was the growth of a youthful rebellion against the oppressiveness of those dutiful

mothers attempting to act out the advice so freely heaped
upon them. An early warning had appeared in the US best
seller *Catcher in the Rye* in 1951, where parents, but mainly
mothers, exist to torment and warp the young.[42]
Unsurprisingly, 'domesticity' came to symbolise 'conformity' in the 50s: the extreme domestication of women,
with women represented as more 'feminine' (in both its
maternal and fashionable 'New Look' seductive forms)
paralleled the mild domestication of men, with men seen
as more home-based (if not more house-trained). Since,
through education and welfare provision, class differences
were now seen as surmountable, men who felt at odds with
their time, who, despite its greater affluence, felt bored
and dissatisfied, were to turn their anger against the ideals
of hearth and home. In particular, they turned against
women, against the powerful mother in the home
(powerful because she alone took real responsibility there),
with all the hatred and resentment they felt towards what
they called 'the establishment'.

Angry Young Men

Many young men of the late 50s identified strongly with
the tough, amoral, anarchic working-class heroes of Alan
Sillitoe in *Saturday Night and Sunday Morning* or *The
Loneliness of the Long Distance Runner*, men fighting for a
sense of freedom and fun against the dreary grey jobs and
marriages awaiting them. 'What I want is a good time. All
the rest is propaganda', the Sillitoe hero declares, in
rejection, as his author explains, 'of the double-faced
society that really takes no account of him'.[43] In these
best-selling books (soon to be made into films) women are
never to be trusted but treated as part of the system trying
to trap, tame and emasculate men. 'Women are all the
same', Arthur Seaton announces in *Saturday Night and
Sunday Morning*, 'whores, shrews, fools', enticing the
suckers into 'the hell that older men call marriage'.[44]
While these heroes see themselves as opposing all
authority 'fighting every day until I die … fighting with
mothers and wives, landlords and gaffers, coppers, army,

government'[45], in fact, the actual fighting is against the mothers and wives. There is no reflection on women's fate in life in Sillitoe's celebration of an aggressive, misogynistic masculinity: 'There was something about the whole situation which made him want to hurt her ... all you could do was end up by giving them a smack in the chop'.[46] Nigel Gray was later to point out in his study of post-war working-class fiction, 'Arthur is against all authority – except the authority of men over women. He fights the authorities with his mouth when they are out of earshot – that's cunning – and saves his muscle for women'.[47]

Sillitoe's individualistic angry young man shares the cynical, self-seeking character and quest of other contemporary heroes, whether created by John Wain, John Braine, John Osborne, Stan Barstow, David Storey or J P Donleavy. (The flippant and facetious Kingsley Amis hero – rather like the Waterhouse *Billy Liar* – is less physically aggressive, but no less contemptuous of all he sees as effeminate, sensitive or refined.) On the pop charts by the close of the 50s similar new working-class idols had appeared, Tommy Steele, Marty Wilde and Billy Fury, to drown out the sugary, suave sentimentality of Frank Sinatra: the yearning for 'Love and Marriage' with which the decade had opened had yielded to the new teenage dream 'Rock with the Caveman'. It is John Osborne's play *Look Back in Anger*, however, which has been hailed as most representative 'in every nuance' of the context of the mid-50s.[48] At the time leading theatre critic Kenneth Tynan welcomed its 'anarchy', 'instinctive leftishness' and 'automatic rejection of "official" attitudes'.[49] Writer and critic David Lodge wrote later of the impact Jimmy Porter, Osborne's young hero, had on his Royal Court audience in 1956: 'I ... remember well the delight and exhilaration its anti-establishment rhetoric afforded me, and the exactness with which it matched my own mood at that juncture in my life'.[50] (Lodge was then a military conscript on weekend leave, and conscription, as we'll see, played a not insignificant role in constructing the masculine mood of the moment.)

Osborne himself was always pathologically hostile to
women, as expressed in his great admiration for
Tennessee Williams: 'In Baby Doll, Williams has hit off the
American Girl-Woman of the last hundred years – spoilt,
ignorant, callous, resentful ... Make no mistake about it –
this Baby Doll kid is a killer. She would eat a couple of guys
and spit them out before breakfast ... The female must
come toppling down to where she should be – on her back.
The American male must get his revenge sometime'.[51] His
revenge, of course, is raping women. Jimmy Porter speaks
for his creator in expressing his fear of his middle-class
wife Allison, whom he systematically torments and abuses.
He compares her to a gorging python devouring and
draining men of all vitality: 'She'll go on sleeping and
devouring until there's nothing left of me ... Why do we
let these women bleed us to death? ... No, there's nothing
left for it, me boy, but to let yourself be butchered by the
women'.[52]

Life is dull, is what these rebels roar: life is unheroic,
there are no great causes left for men to fight in the
'Brave-New-nothing-very-much-thank-you' 50s world.[53] A
stifling domesticity has killed the spirit and guts of men,
and who is there to blame but women? Who indeed, if, like
Osborne and most of the other 'Angries', you believe that
class struggle is obsolete and Marx was a fraud? Even
Colin MacInnes had bought the 50s myth of classlessness.
Though less cynically apolitical than most of his literary
peers, in *Absolute Beginners* (1959) MacInnes created yet
another scornful, anti-social cult male hero who touched
the pulse of contemporary British youth: 'Do try to
understand that, clobbo! I'm just not interested in the
whole class crap that seems to needle you and all the
tax-payers – needle you all, whichever side of the tracks
you live on, or suppose you do'.[54] What was really
happening in so many of these novels was that class
hostility was suppressed and twisted into new forms of
sexual hostility.

In retrospect it is clear that the scorn which the Angry
Young Men hurled against 'the establishment' was a class
resentment, but one devoid of any collective class

consciousness. As many have since commented, these new writers were mostly university graduate ex-grammar school boys, from lower middle or working class backgrounds, moving fast, but not for them fast enough, up the class ladder. They faced a Britain as class-conscious as ever before, at least, that is, in its upper echelons, where power, authority and prestige still resided – and with it contempt and ridicule for the grant-aided student. ('They are scum', as Somerset Maugham blithely announced.[55]) Life was frustrating for the working-class grammar school boy, as Hoggart, from that background himself, had declared: 'He both wants to go back and yet thinks he has gone beyond his class, feels himself weighted with knowledge of his own and their situation, which hereafter forbids him the simpler pleasures of his father and mother. And this is only one of his temptations to self-dramatisation'.[56]

Another temptation was his desire for, yet fear of, middle and upper class women. Beware 'the perils of hypergamy' Geoffrey Gorer warned in 1957, referring to the process of men marrying upwards: 'Now I'm practically sure of it. *Lucky Jim*, *Look Back In Anger* and all that lot roused my suspicions; the clincher has come with John Braine's *Room at the Top*, which tells much the same story all over again, brilliantly and bitterly. The curse which is ruining, in fantasy if not their own lives, these brilliant young men of working-class origin and welfare-state opportunity is what anthropologists have dubbed hypergamy. It is a new pattern in English life, and apparently a very distressing one'.[57] Displaying the patronising and, inevitably, sexist perspective of the academic elite of his day, Gorer was nevertheless probably right to suggest that these educated sons of the working class felt in particular danger of losing their virility. Having abstained from the money and pleasures available earlier on to their less studious peers, and now perhaps attracted to women they felt less sure of being able to dominate, they liked to assert a particularly pugnacious manliness and heterosexual aggressiveness. One of the main sources of mockery that Amis, Wain or

Osborne use against their upper class antagonists is thus to deride their effeminacy, as in Amis' constant homophobic references, 'standing rigid with popping eyes ... they had a look of being Gide or Lytton Strachey'.[58]

Homophobia and the Fear of Unmanliness

But once again homophobia, coupled with new forms of sexual insecurity and fear of women, was not confined to those Angry Young Men who, like Amis, Braine and Osborne, were on their way through the political apathy and scepticism of the 50s to a true blue conservatism. These sentiments were overwhelmingly the spirit of the times. As others have noticed, there has always been a close link between misogyny and homophobia in our culture.[59] Though the persecution of homosexuals is usually by men against other men, it is also about the forced repression of the 'feminine' in men, and about keeping women in their place. Craig Owen, for example, has argued, 'homophobia is not primarily an instrument for oppressing a sexual minority; it is, rather, a powerful tool for regulating the entire spectrum of male relations'.[60] The 50s was not only a time when the symbol of the Happy Housewife embraced all women, when Hollywood could portray the career woman rather than the seductress as *femme fatale* (as in *All About Eve*). It was also a time of intense persecution of homosexual desire.

The social study conducted in 1951 by Seebohm Rowntree and Lavers, *English Life and Leisure*, and designed to influence and improve the cultural and spiritual state of the country, illustrates the anxieties of the time. Stating that everybody now agrees that there is a lot of homosexuality about, they add: 'It is only necessary to see a few of the unfortunate persons who have become addicted to it to realize how demoralizing and degenerating an influence it is'.[61] Moreover, they warn, 'sexual excesses are both a symptom of national weakness and a powerful secondary cause of it'.[62] This was a decade when, as Jonathan Dollimore points out, leading Law Lord Patrick Devlin explicitly associated 'immorality' with treason, demanding the 'suppression of vice' as inherently subversive.[63] This association was strengthened in 1951 with the defection of British diplomats Burgess and Maclean to the Soviet Union, and the concurrent McCarthy witch-hunt against communists and homosexuals in the US. There was a dramatic increase in police activity against male homosexuality in both Britain and the US, reaching its height here in the anti-homosexual drive instigated by the authorities in the early 1950s employing young detectives to act as *agents provocateurs*.[64] Persecution of homosexuals still continued at the close of the decade with, for example, homosexual MP Montgomery Hyde being forced by his constituency association to stand down.

Amidst this onslaught of persecution, imprisonment, and aversive therapy, homosexuals themselves came to view their own desire, in the words of Colin MacInnes, as 'a crippled state of being'[65] or like Quentin Crisp as 'a fatal flaw in masculinity'[66], or, like Mary Renault in her novels, as an affliction to be endured and overcome.[67] It is the black American writer, James Baldwin, who perhaps most movingly portrays the internalised self-hatred of the male homosexual, unable to conform to the masculine ideal of heterosexuality.[68] The plight of the male homosexual in the 50s, like the rage of the Angry Young Man, tells us much about the contemporary anxieties over manhood, especially in the area of sex. Colin MacInnes, for example, as his biographer Tony Gould illustrates, is as aware as any heterosexual stud of the importance of being manly, delivering this message in one of his unpublished novels: 'What you must do, son, is become a fucker, and not become a fucked. It's simple as that. Boys or girls, up the pussy or the arse, whichever you prefer, but you've got to remember there's a cock between your legs and you're a *man*'.[69]

The post-war contrast between wartime and civilian life, and the maintenance of universal military conscription marking men's entrance into adulthood ('a crash course in growing up', Johnson p.210), was an important aspect of the tension over 'manhood' in the 50s. Trevor Royle opens his book on military conscription 1945-1963, *The Best Years of Their Lives*, by observing that National Service cast a long shadow over boys in the 1950s, 'it was simply a part of the fabric of everyday life'.[70] The writings of David Lodge, Alan Sillitoe and others all testify to the uncaring brutality and crude insensitivity generated by the pointless monotony of conscript life. While B S Johnson in *All Bull* pronounces it 'tedious, belittling, coarsening, brutalising, unjust and possibly psychologically very harmful'[71]. The swearing, drinking and boasting bravado of male bonding were all the young recruit could hold on to as a way of getting through the daily tedium of army life. Intensified male friendship and comradeship were the only real but lasting pleasures of national service. Those like Colin MacInnes who remember military life with pleasure recall 'the unexpected egalitarianism, the unlikely friendships, the blissful irresponsibility'.[72] Army training relies upon strengthening the opposition between male and female, with 'women' used as a term of abuse for incompetent performance, thereby hardening and cementing the prevalent cultural links between virility, sexuality and aggressiveness. This serves not only to discipline men, but to raise 'masculine' morale against the threats of a more typically 'feminine' reality of enforced servility and conformity characterising army life. 'Effeminacy', as Royle observes, was 'the ultimate soldier's crime' and 'to some people, carrying a gun was like having a permanent hard-on'.[73]

The problem for the young male conscripts of the 50s, however, was that they never could climax their sexual fantasy. They were not actually killing anybody. At a time of heightened hostilities between east and west, with western chauvinism kept on the boil by US paranoia of the menace and danger of communist influence, and brand new fears of the Bomb and a war of total destruction, the men of the 50s had few prospects – as 'Jimmy Porter' regrets – of ever facing up to and defeating a concrete enemy. Trained for military action, fed on a Cold War diet of spying and betrayals, they were the first generation to live in a post-imperial Britain and observe the old Empire dismantled, the Empire 'given away'. One dramatic exception was the Suez crisis in 56, when Ray

Gosling, a railway signalman at the time, recalls: 'I can remember the feeling that ran down the line as they "stood behind Eden", the man who was to show them and the world that the Old Bulldog could bite as well as bark ... that they were still at the heart of "the greatest Empire of all time". They would send a gunboat and show the wogs how the lion still roared. There was not one man who at the time spoke against Eden, yet one could feel in the comments made their knowledge that the Empire was dead; pre-war Britain would never return, Eden would fail'.[74] And he did.

But the links between army life, masculinity and violence are also more ambiguous than they might appear. Actual violence and fighting did not necessarily accompany the near obligatory smoking, swearing, drinking, aggressively sexual boasting and phallic symbolism of military equipment permeating the all-male military culture of young conscripts. David Morgan, recalling his period of national service in the late 50s, for example, remembers little real violence. There were talks about fights, but the reality was more 'an overt disdain for anything that might appear soft or wet'.[75] It was more 'a taboo on tenderness' than a celebration of violence. In particular, at least in terms of public discussion, there was little room for tenderness in accounts of sexuality. The army did help create certain dominant patterns of masculinity, but Morgan is cautious in drawing the links: 'It was not that, simply, boys learnt to swear, drink, desire women, favour toughness, rely on their mates and so on ... It was more a matter of learning to identify masculinity and being a male with these traits and pieces of behaviour'.[76]

These same traits and pieces of behaviour were also dominant in the substance and style of the staple literary consumption of the 50s – consumed by boys and men – and significant numbers of women as well. As Ken Worpole suggests, the supremely popular books in Britain in the 1950s, selling in their millions, were about the experiences of male combatants in the Second World War.[77] I can remember, though unquestionably one of the most fainthearted and timorous girls at my all-girls school in 50s Australia, feeling obliged to read *The Wooden Horse* by Eric Williams. It typifies, like *Colditz Story* and others of the genre, the male adventure story linking masculinity and rugged individualism: men (usually RAF officers) fight for their freedom against the enormous odds of wartime imprisonment. These books were also a powerful influence promoting apparently 'apolitical' but actually intensely conservative politics and values. Strange as it might seem, Worpole points out, but in keeping with the elimination of any political analysis of recent history, not one of these wartime best-sellers ever mentions the word 'fascism': the enemy is 'German'[78]. The hero, moreover, is a man outside the everyday ties and responsibilities of sexual relationships and family.

There were, then, at least two opposed faces of masculinity in the 50s. There was the new family man, content with house and garden. And there was the old wartime hero, who put 'freedom' before family and loved ones. In the home, there were new responsibilities on men as husbands, though not yet as fathers: the marriage guidance literature of the day, for example, was now emphasising that men should be able to satisfy their wives fully sexually. Men were still seen in this literature as necessarily the sexual instigators and educators of women: one result was the growing visibility of impotence. A literature was appearing on the dilemmas of contemporary masculinity, originally stemming from social anxieties over male delinquency and educational failure, as well as rising divorce and family discord. In the US, for example, Helen Hacker published a paper in 1957 *The New Burdens of Masculinity* in which she outlined the conflicts in 'the masculine role'. Men were expected to be more patient, understanding and gentle in their dealings with others, yet 'with regard to women they must still be sturdy oaks.'[79] Hacker was also to describe the growing visibility of homosexuality as a flight from, and index of, the burdens of masculinity.

Whatever the burdens on men, evidence of new levels of antagonism in the old 'sex war' are evident in the ubiquitous anti-woman humour of men in the 50s. If the function of joking, as Freud has argued, is the reduction of anxiety, there were very deep levels of male anxiety at the time. *The Man's Book* of 1958 did not, as I have already indicated, refer to either women or children. 'What really useful advice could one give about women in a twenty-volume encyclopaedia?' they facetiously ask in their preface, and continue by explaining that their final section on humour '*Wits End*' is designed to give the last word to men: 'And that in itself makes, as they say, a nice change'.[80] If there was one thing men had in common at the time, as I remember well from my own father's humour, it was the jokey pleasures of insulting women. There are 46 jokes in 'Wit's Corner', every one of them insulting to women, many of them portraying the fantasy delight in destruction of, or violence towards, women: 'Here lies my wife/ Here let her lie/ Now she's at rest/ And so am I' ... 'No man regards his wife with pleasure, save twice: in her bridal bed, and in her grave' ... 'A gentleman is a man who never strikes a woman without provocation' ... 'But Eve from scenes of bliss/ Transported him for life/ The more I think of this/ The more I beat my wife'[81], and so on, and on.

We could suggest, as would some feminists, that this pervasive misogynist humour was simply a weapon used by men to discipline women, a type of propaganda for male dominance and a warning to women of the consequences of challenging it. The relationship between fantasy and actual behaviour is a difficult question. But however we make the connections I think we can conclude that there was considerable conflict and ambiguity about male identity in the 50s. In the late 50s the cartoons of Jules Feiffer began to appear in the radical paper *The Village Voice* in the US, and were soon to be syndicated worldwide. They portrayed baffled and tortured men confronted by neurotic women in a sad, sick world of non-communication. 'Men Really Don't Like Women' Feiffer confided in an article in *Look* magazine in which he is pessimistically perceptive about relations between men and women at the time: 'The American woman is a victim.

Her trouble is she is doing comparatively well as a victim.
Her problem is not taken seriously. Woman is a
second-class victim. And what is her problem? We all know
it is man ... Man has always seen woman as his enemy. But
he needs her'.[82]

Women and the Left in the 50s

Amidst this taunting and teasing of women by men in the
50s, few women were writing or speaking publicly and
prominently. But those who were presented a perception
of the world which complemented rather than contra-
dicted the perceptions of men at the time. Doris Lessing's
ambitious novel *The Golden Notebook* was published in 1962,
but is set in the atmosphere of the political despair and
disillusion of so many in the communist left of the late 50s:
'We have to admit that the great dream has faded and the
truth is something else'.[83] It documents its heroine Anna's
quest for authenticity and fulfilment, not through the
Angries anarchic anti-authoritarianism, but through the
earlier more romantic and serious D H Lawrence view of
sex as 'the quick of self'. Anna can express herself fully
and genuinely only through the love of a '*real* man'. Doris
Lessing shares the 50s anxieties over manhood, and an
England 'full of men who are little boys and homosexuals
and half-homosexuals ...'[84] She does, however, passion-
ately portray the sufferings of women as mothers and
lovers, trying to cope with the selfishness, dishonesty and
aggressive insecurity of men, as well as the anxieties,
embarrassment and self-disgust they had come to feel
towards their own bodies. She is aware of the boredom
and depression of women trapped in the home, 'the
disease of our time' she called it.[85]

But for Lessing, as for the wider world of the 50s, there
is no alternative. We cannot blame men. 'If I were a man
I'd be the same', she writes.[86] On the contrary, women
need to bolster men up 'for the truth is, women have this
deep instinctive need to build a man up as a man ... I
suppose this is because real men become fewer and fewer
and we are frightened, trying to create men.' Those

women who could articulate women's sufferings saw them as her inevitable destiny, as Margaret Drabble reflected in her first novel in 1963: 'What happens otherwise is worse than what happens normally, the embroidery and the children and the sagging mind. I felt all women were doomed ... born to defend and depend instead of to attack.'[87]

And ironically, though unsurprisingly, within a vision which as Dollimore argues 'fatally conflates the natural and the social, biology and gender', when the attack on the stifling nature of family life in the 50s finally did surface, in the writings of Laing and Cooper in the 60s, it took the form of an attack on women. An attack on the pathological possessiveness of those housebound mothers, mothers who had little option but to live life through the lives of their children. Mothers who could not leave their children alone were denying them autonomy and driving them mad: 'A young man has only to look a little cross with his manipulative, incestuously demanding mother to end up on a detention order as "dangerous to others" '[88], David Cooper thundered forth in 1964. R D Laing and his fellow anti-psychiatrists delivered the same verdict.

The left in the 50s was as silent as everybody else on relations between the sexes, accepting unquestioningly the belief that women's problems were solved. The same was true even of the younger, fresh thinking New Left which was born in 1956 out of the twin crises of Suez and Hungary. It grew rapidly with the rise of CND the following year, to make the first decisive break with both the politics of the Cold War and the politics of Stalinism. The New Left, unlike the church-like bureaucratic and economistic old left, had an exciting, enriching interest in contemporary culture. But as Stuart Hall, one of its founding members recalls: 'We were totally unconscious of questions of gender, totally entombed on that issue – even though we were beginning to think about personal life, even though we realized the boundaries of politics had to be ruptured to bring in those aspects of life seen as important to people.'[89] Another co-founder, Raphael Samuel has also spoken of the left's anti-feminism: 'we

were worse than the Labour Party (who did at least have
one third women members). Like Colin MacInnes we
romanticised the working-class male hero as the hope for
the future. There was some truth in this, but also a
blindness.'[90]

Jean McCrindle has written of searching for books 'that
would make sense to me as a woman ... There wasn't an
awful lot of encouragement from looking at women's
actual lives in the 1950s'.[91] Fear and confusion
accompanied women's sexual involvement with men
outside marriage, with no accessible contraception for
single women, no legal abortion, and a crushing stigma
and other penalties visited upon unmarried mothers or
'fallen women'. Inside or outside marriage, Jean McCrindle recalls, there was little open discussion of sexual
problems, and 'feminism' was utterly scorned as 'bourgeois': 'You were a comrade and wanted to be treated
exactly as men were ... *The Golden Notebook* describes very
brilliantly the kind of women who stayed active in the
party and they were often bitter, hard, and certainly didn't
identify with the quiet wives sitting in the corner making
tea while 'the comrades' discussed politics'.[92]

What we can learn from the silence about women on the
left, it seems to me, is not simply reducible to the
ineluctable sexism of the men (however obnoxious they
may or may not have been in their relations with women).
In what little they did write women were as silent as men
about any alternative solutions to the strains placed upon
women isolated in the home or, increasingly, going out to
work but expected to give complete priority to their
families. What was needed was a whole new way of looking
at the problem of marriage, childrearing, sexuality and
employment. But such thinking was not available to either
women or men at the time. The consequences, as Jean
McCrindle suggests 'were heavy with boredom and
frustration for women, and with guilt for many men'.[93]
The solutions, or attempts at them, were to inform the
sexual politics of the 60s and 70s, when both men and
women began in earnest to rebel against conventional
respectability, and to go searching for other routes

through 'the battle of the sexes' and the 'trap' of domesticity.

From this flashback to the 50s it seems clear to me that the relationship of men to home and family has undergone irreversible change over the last three decades. Though domesticity acquired a new salience for men as well as women in the 50s, questions of men's relationship to childcare, housework, violence in the home, were not yet on the conceptual, let alone the political, agenda. The point of much recent feminist writing on men and masculinity has been to suggest that nothing has changed. But what is more interesting and very much more useful is to explore how things do in fact change. Change, of course, is never a linear process: it always throws up new tensions and contradictions.

Note I am immensely grateful to Barbara Taylor and Peter Osborne for the generous encouragement they have given me and for their very many, invariably helpful, comments and criticisms.

Notes

[1] Walter Allen, p.286, reprinted in G Feldman and M Gartenberg (eds) *Protest*, Panther 1960.

[2] Kenneth Allsop, *The Angry Decade*, p.203, Peter Owen, 1964.

[3] Storm Jameson in Allsop, *op. cit.* p.201.

[4] Jean McCrindle 'The Left as Social Movement' talk given at *Out of Apathy Conference* on 30 years of the British New Left, organised by Oxford University Socialist Discussion Group 14 November 1987.

[5] Quoted in Denise Riley *War in the Nursery*, p.193, Virago 1983.

[6] Michael Young and Peter Willmott *Family and Kinship in East London*, p.30, Penguin, 1962.

[7] John and Elizabeth Newson *Patterns of Infant Care in an Urban Community*, p.145, Allen & Unwin, 1963.

[8] Anthony Sampson *Anatomy of Britain*, p.73, Hodder & Stoughton, 1962.

[9] Peter Biskind *Seeing is Believing*, p.252, Pantheon Books, 1983.

[10] Elizabeth Wilson *Only Halfway to Paradise: Women in Postwar Britain 1945-68*, p.69, Tavistock, 1980.

[11] Colin Willock *The Man's Book*, Edward Hulton, 1958.

[12] Geoffrey Gorer *Exploring English Character*, p.153, Nelson, 1955.
[13] *ibid*. p.66.
[14] Richard Hoggart, *The Uses of Literacy*, p.49, Penguin, 1957.
[15] *ibid*. p.50.
[16] *ibid*.
[17] Young & Willmott, *op cit*, p.24.
[18] *ibid*. p.27.
[19] *ibid*. p.145.
[20] *ibid*. p.150.
[21] *ibid*.
[22] *ibid*. p.132-133.
[23] N Dennis, F Henriques & C Slaughter *Coal is Our Life*, Tavistock, 1969.
[24] *ibid*. p.183.
[25] *ibid*.
[26] Elizabeth Bott *Family and Social Network*, Tavistock, 1957.
[27] Olivia Harris 'Heavenly Father' in Ursula Owen (ed) *Fathers* p.61, Virago, 1984.
[28] Sheila Rowbotham 'Our Lance' in Owen *op. cit.* p.209.
[29] Sara Maitland 'Two For the Price of One' in Owen p.35.
[30] Allsop *op. cit.* p.204.
[31] Judith Hubback *Wives Who Went to College*, p.75, Heinemann, 1957.
[32] Alva Myrdal and Viola Klein *Women's Two Roles*, Routledge & Kegan Paul, 1956.
[33] Denise Riley *War in the Nursery*, Virago, 1983.
[34] John Bowlby *Childcare and the Growth of Love*, Penguin, 1953.
[35] Peter Lewis *The Fifties* p.45, Heinemann, 1978.
[36] In Riley, *op. cit.*, p.88.
[37] Peter Rabe *From Here to Maternity*, Frederick Muller, 1955.
[38] Jane Hope *Happy Event*, Frederick Muller, 1957.
[39] Betty Thorne 'Life in Our Street', in Mary Stott (ed) *Women Talking – An Anthology from The Guardian's Women's Page* p.85, Pandora, 1987.
[40] 'J.B.H.', 'Bored Mum and "Talkback" in Stott *op. cit.*, p.240-241.
[41] *ibid*.
[42] J D Salinger *The Catcher in the Rye*, Penguin, 1951.
[43] Alan Sillitoe 'What Comes on Monday', p.59, *New Left Review* no.4 July/August 1961.
[44] Alan Sillitoe *Saturday Night and Sunday Morning* p.36, Pan, 1960.
[45] *ibid*. p.65.
[46] *ibid*. p.126.
[47] Nigel Gray *The Silent Majority – A Study of the Working Class in Post-War British Fiction* p.129, Vision Critical Studies, 1974.
[48] Alan Sinfield *Society and Literature 1945-1970* p.2, Methuen 1983.
[49] *ibid*. p.4.
[50] David Lodge, Afterword to *Ginger You're Barmy* p.215-216, Penguin, 1982.
[51] John Osborne 'Sex and Failure' in G Feldman and M Gartenberg (eds) *op. cit.*.
[52] Quoted in Sinfield *op. cit.*, p.27.

[53] *ibid.*

[54] Colin MacInnes *Absolute Beginners* MacGibbon & Kee, 1959.

[55] Quoted in Sinfield *op. cit.* p.177.

[56] Hoggart *op. cit.*, p.246.

[57] Geoffrey Gorer 'The Perils of Hypergamy' in *Protest*, p.315.

[58] p.26, Sinfield *op. cit.*.

[59] Eve Kosofsky Sedgwick *Between Men: English Literature and Male Homosexual Desire*, Columbia University Press, 1985.

[60] Craig Owen 'Outlaws: Gay Men in Feminism' in Jardine & Smith (eds) *Men in Feminism*, p.221, Methuen, 1987.

[61] Seebohm Rowntree and Lavers *English Life and Leisure*, p.212, Longmans, 1951.

[62] *ibid* p.215.

[63] Jonathan Dollimore 'The Challenge of Sexuality' in Sinfield *op. cit.*, p.52.

[64] See Tony Gould *Inside Outsider – The Life and Times of Colin MacInnes*, p.64, Chatto & Windus, 1983.

[65] *ibid*, p.99.

[66] Quentin Crisp *The Naked Civil Servant*, Jonathan Cape, 1968.

[67] Quoted in Dollimore *op. cit.*, p.74.

[68] James Baldwin *Another Country*, Michael Joseph, 1963 and *Giovanni's Room*, Michael Joseph, 1957.

[69] In Gould *op. cit.*, p.89.

[70] Trevor Royle *The Best Years of Their Lives*, Michael Joseph, 1986.

[71] B S Johnson *All Bull*, Quartet, 1973. See also Lodge *op. cit.* and Sillito, 1960, *op. cit.*.

[72] Colin MacInnes 'Pacific Warriors' in *New Society* 30 June, 1966.

[73] Royle *op. cit.*, p.116.

[74] Ray Gosling 'Dream Boy' *New Left Review* May/June no. 3, 1960.

[75] David Morgan 'It Will Make a Man of You: Notes on National Service, Masculinity and Autobiography' in *Studies in Sexual Politics* no.17. University of Manchester, 1987.

[76] *ibid.* p.82.

[77] Ken Worpole *Dockers and Detectives*, Verso, 1983.

[78] *ibid.* p.62.

[79] Helen Hacker 'The New Burdens of Masculinity' in *Marriage and Family Living*, no.19, 1957.

[80] Willock, *op. cit.*, p.viii.

[81] *ibid*, p.352-354.

[82] In Lewes *op. cit.*, p.63.

[83] Quoted in Jean McCrindle 'Reading *The Golden Notebook* in 1962' in J Taylor (ed) *Notebooks/memoirs/archives: Reading and Rereading Doris Lessing*, p.49, Routledge & Kegan Paul, 1982.

[84] Doris Lessing *The Golden Notebook*, p.395, Panther, 1972.

[85] Quoted in Jean McCrindle *op. cit.*, p.53.

[86] *ibid* p.51.

[87] Margaret Drabble *A Summer Bird-Cage* p.29, Penguin, 1987.

[88] David Cooper 'Sartre on Genet' *New Left Review* no.25, May/June,

1964, p.71.

[89] Stuart Hall, Introductory talk at *Out of Apathy Conference*, 1987.

[90] Raphael Samuel, 'Class and Classlessness' talk at *Out of Apathy Conference*, 1987.

[91] Jean McCrindle, 1982, *op. cit.*, p.55.

[92] *ibid.*

[93] *ibid.* p.53.

Race, Sexual Politics and Black Masculinity: A Dossier

KOBENA MERCER AND ISAAC JULIEN

Introduction

This chapter is essentially a collage of articles, images and arguments which document our activities and interventions around the cultural politics of sex and race. For both of us the context in which this work began was the Gay Black Group, a small nucleus of gay men of Asian, African and Caribbean descent which formed in London during 1981. That was the year Britain experienced unprecedented civil disobedience in its inner-cities as black people and their allies rose up to resist the increasingly coercive policing that has come to characterise the Thatcherite hegemony of the 80s. For us, 1981 was a profoundly empowering moment, mobilising energies and creating an optimistic mood about our capacities and abilities to challenge our conditions of existence. That feeling of empowerment came from the collective identity we constructed for ourselves as black gay men, enabling us to overcome both the marginality we experienced as black people and the individual isolation we felt as gay people.

Politics is about making connections – practically, with the forming of alliances between different social groups, and at a cognitive level with the recognition of diverse categories of race, class, gender, ethnicity and sexuality in the articulation of power relations. The Gay Black Group enabled us to start a conversation amongst ourselves, making connections between the patterns of our common experiences to recognise the structures responsible for the specificity of that oppression in the first place. An integral part of this process was the use of the word 'black' not as biological description but as an inclusive term of political identification and solidarity forged through common struggles against racism. This rearticulation of 'blackness' in the general resurgence of ethnic politics in the 80s is important as it signals the re-formation of the contemporary 'left' in Britain which is now made up of a diversity of oppositional social movements.

Recognising this diversity, and the fragmented character of the 'left', is one of the most urgent and most problematic political tasks facing oppositional struggles today. One of the many reasons why the Gay Black Group came into existence was that we found our specific concerns were excluded and invisible in the agendas of the white left and gay organisations and the black community organisations that many of us had also participated in. The white left didn't really address issues of race and there was no space for talking about gender or sexuality in black radical politics. The angry tone of the 'White Gay Racism' article reflects the frustration engendered by that double absence. As an initial formulation of our own agenda it also emphasises our frustration at the apparent reluctance of the white gay male community to join in a mutual dialogue on racial and sexual politics. Partly as a result of this, as Isaac explains in the 'Interview', many of us moved on into different directions to pursue the same goals – getting issues of sex and race on the left agenda in both white and black communities – through different personal, professional and institutional means. The growing strength and pride of the black gay and lesbian movement, which now supports numerous such groups across the country, and the burgeoning development of black feminisms, demonstrate the extent to which a critical conversation on sex and race has already started – and there's no turning back.

For ourselves, as a writer and as a film-maker, we've pursued this aim through cultural politics, necessarily engaging issues on a number of fronts. This has meant extending and deepening our critique of racial politics in the gay movement and the urban gay sub-culture to the broader underlying questions concerning the cultural construction of masculinity. 'Racism and the Politics of Masculinity' introduces ethnicity as a crucial factor in the social construction of manliness, suggesting that the racial dialectic of projection and internalisation through which white and black men have shaped their masks of masculinity is one of the key points at which race, gender and the politics of sexuality intersect. That article was addressed to white and black men alike, but here again we have encountered silence as the real barrier to any critical dialogue. At the 'Breaking Out' day conference – where the idea for this book originated – some white men said they couldn't understand big words like 'ethnocentrism'. There is a valid point here about the need for an accessible language for public political debate, but this complaint also conceals the fact that some people simply *don't want to talk* about the complexity that arises at the junction of sex and race. And as Isaac's poem 'Report-back' indicates, there is a symmetrical resistance to talking about sex in the black community – 'we don't want to talk about that kind of thing in public'. To break out of this impasse we need some critical overview of the concrete ways that race, gender and sexuality are talked about and 'put into discourse' in our society. What is required to start a critical conversation is an awareness of the political implications of the different frameworks in which connections between sex and race are already being made.

Metaphors, equivalences and analogies are commonplace; they may be illuminating, helping to extend one's political consciousness, but they may also be misleading. It is often said that racism and sexism are similar, as both involve the justification of inequality through ideologies which appeal to the 'naturalness' of bodily differences to rationalise the 'inferiorisation' of black peoples and the female of the human species. Yet to say that they are the same obscures and cancels out of the equation the specific forms of oppression experienced by black women – analogies can flatten out and reduce the complex play of differences in any social or political interaction.

The most pervasive type of equivalence is made by liberal centre-ground politics which regards blacks, women, lesbians and gays as 'minorities' who face the same problems of 'prejudice' and 'discrimination'. This equation leads to the same solution: equal opportunity policies or 'affirmative action'. Yet this compensatory approach assumes that we all want to be the same as the socially hegemonic white male who functions as the putative norm of 'equality'. In contrast to this fabian, welfarist model there is an extra-parliamentary discourse of the left which similarly argues that black people, women and any other marginal groups are all equally oppressed by the capitalist mode of production. It follows that we should all subordinate our differences to the revolutionary identity of the industrial working class who alone will lead us out of our misery and alienation. Since the decline of ultra-left parties and organisations in the 70s this type of argument is less prevalent, but when the 'new left' generation entered the official institutions of the local state, such as the Greater London Council during the early 80s, there was an odd reconciliation between these two versions of equivalence.

The GLC, under Ken Livingstone's administration, opened up a range of radical opportunities responsive to the demands of the new social movements; but what often resulted, in the scramble for the funding of different projects, was a bureaucratised form of calculation which forced blacks, women, gays and lesbians and other 'disadvantaged' social groups to 'compete' amongst each other to establish who was more oppressed than whom. If municipal socialism has shored up the welter of conflicts and contradictions between the fragments of the new social movements, then suffice to say that in the meantime the New Right has cheerfully played upon these fractures in their attacks on the progressive policies of the so-called 'loony left'. Ideologues of Thatcherism have had no problem making connections between sex and race and they do it – at the level of policy and legislation as much as in the popular press – in logics which reinforce the conservative sway of popular fears and prejudices. Through the all-too familiar rhetoric of the 'enemy within', the right orchestrates the spectre of blacks, women and gays along with any Other you care to mention, as constituting a *threat* to the status quo. In a climate of hatred, fear and loathing where the AIDS health crisis has brought numerous fears and prejudices out of the closet of social-democratic consensus, the need to understand *how* commonsense connections are made is today more urgent than ever.

These different paradigms of political articulation highlight two strands of thought worked through in the essays on representation reproduced here. What emerges is a recognition that politics always entails a struggle over representation. There is no one singular or absolute 'truth' about the connections between sex and race; rather, the same elements are subject to alternative systems of representation which have different degrees of power and influence over the ways we live through our social identities as gendered and racialised human beings. The recurring theme of identification in 'True Confessions' and 'Imaging the Black Man's Sex' describes our examination of the complicated and messy *ambivalence* we are implicated in vis-a-vis sexual representations such as pornography. Informed by the strategic politicisation of such questions by the women's and gay liberation movements, we have also registered a critique of the 'self'-centred way that 'the personal is political' has been interpreted. Seeking also to displace and reinflect essentialist versions of 'identity' in black politics which ignore the importance of gender, we suggest that to re-engage radical sexual politics in the sphere of everyday popular culture and to be open to the concerns of a *diverse national population*, we need to re-think how boundaries of race, class, gender and sexuality are constantly crossed and negotiated in the commonplace cultural construction of one's social identity. Can identity be re-constructed beyond a binary and hierarchical ordering of difference in which some of us, or maybe all of us, are burdened with the role of representing somebody else's Other? This is the question at the heart of the concern with *difference* that characterises the 'postmodern' political forms of the new social movements. What is at stake is the ability to politically intervene in this situation and assert that radical *equality* – at the basis of the vision of a socialist society – is the fundamental precondition of diversity and difference. Is it possible for a socialist discourse to articulate this concern for difference without reducing any one element of society to the privileged role of the singular agent of democratic revolution? We can only begin to talk about this when we recognise the everyday sites of antagonism and conflict – which include sports, the media, music and dancing – where actual men and women of diverse ethnic origins intermingle in the mutual construction of each other's racial and sexual identities.

This gives rise to another strand of thought: that perhaps in order to understand these everyday connections more effectively, we should return to unpack the 'unfinished business' of the 60s. Then, but not today, active dialogic connections were constructed between black people's, women's and gay people's struggles in markedly empowering and liberatory ways. The Afro-Americans' struggle for civil rights and then Black Power acted as symbolic leverage, a metaphorical catalyst for historical change, as its demands were taken up, translated and re-articulated in the emerging radical movements, from ecology to student revolts. In the collective political imagination of the left in Britain the signifier '1968' is still the mythical origin of a new phase of counter-hegemonic struggle. Indeed it probably was, which is all the more reason why we need to cut through the romantic, nostalgic, self-mythology of the 'new left' and recognise that in the history of Western modernity the democratic ideal of radical equality has often been shaped and charged by the symbolic resonance of ethnic struggles. In the modern democratic imagination '1789' signifies the simultaneous 'explosion' of the people onto the stage of history in Paris *and* Port-au-Prince.[1]

Feminist and suffragette movements in the nineteenth-century were crystallised around the iconic figure of the 'slave', and through participation in anti-slavery women reformed the 'democratic image' of the *people*.[2] In the 1960s, such democratic analogies and equivalences translated Black Pride into Gay Pride; the slogan 'the personal is political' was equivalent in its active interpretation to the statement 'black *is* beautiful'; expressive forms of collective solidarity signified in terms such as black brotherhood were re-coded with similar empowering connotations by the feminist emphasis on sisterhood. These links are always being made – in the late 70s the soul tune 'We are Family' by Sister Sledge was sung as an anthem on Gay Pride Week. What is at stake, and what is at issue, in such cognitive and organisational connections? Whatever happened to the dialogic intersections of the 60s? Was it all, like the idea of a 'rainbow coalition' today, merely illusory, or are there practical as well as ideological lessons to be learned from an excavation of our recent political past?

The answers are unclear because these issues are not discussed as much as they should be. We need to re-start the conversation. In the era of AIDS this is a public conversation that cannot be avoided or delayed – the intersections of racial and sexual politics are now on everybody's agenda. Any talk of alliances begins with the recognition of the need to re-start those old conversations. These are some of the questions that have preoccupied us over the last seven years or so, recurring across a number of sites of intellectual intervention and activity[3], and they recur here to bear upon the basic question: *can we talk?* As in any dialogue – over to you.

Issues in Search of an Agenda

White Gay Racism

Gay News, 1982[4]

'Black People Only'.

What does that statement mean to you? Does it threaten you? Does it confuse you? We have some questions to ask the white gay movement following our experience of racism at this year's Gay Pride Week, when our right to hold a meeting for black gays only was challenged by white gays.

Gay Pride has become a political act of affirming, accepting and exhibiting one's sexual identity to society, so to ask *whose pride?* one must automatically be a traitor, a renegade from the cause of 'gay liberation'. For Gay Pride is a political umbrella whereby such diverse tendencies as revolutionary gay men, gay SDP, Liberals, Tories, Labourites, humanists, etc are all 'united' (or contained) within the political category of gay. But what about gay blacks? What *about* gay blacks? Well, yes there are such persons but why should they want to be *autonomous?* They exclude other people – that's racism! We know that racism exists in the gay movement, some white people say, come to us, talk to us, above all *tell us how* we can stop being racist: we want to help you.

We are forced to question the idea of Gay Pride because of our experience of mainstream gay politics, and this is one reason for our formation as a group. This formation, as an autonomous group, has been met with an emotional hostility which was stated with vigour this year when many white gays expressed shock and confusion at the fact of their exclusion from our activities. *We* were the racists, who had unnecessarily raised the issue of race in a political context which is supposed to be free of such questions, as it is complacently assumed that 'Surely, if we are all gay, and therefore oppressed, we are up against the same thing: a homophobic society ...' But rather than dwell on the particular nastiness with which this was expressed when we held our workshop (and a white person who was asked to leave tore up our poster and threw it back into the room), we want to look into what may be at the roots of this angry and confused reaction, and confront the gay movement with this as a criticism of its political practice. What is it about black politics which makes it unworkable within the traditional organisation of gays? To answer this we need to look at a number of assumptions which surround both the category 'gay' and the politics which have become associated with it.

Mainstream gay politics tends to ignore the fact that the oppressive category 'homosexual' has been *constructed* through a whole complex of medical, legal, religious and political institutions and that the term 'gay' is trying to extricate itself from that. No, it's argued, the enemy is purely and simply a 'homophobic' society, the repressive spectre of heterosexuals at whom the confessional drama of 'coming out' is aimed. Coming out is about *telling* 'them', and once they've been told fear and prejudice will be broken down by the sheer force of all these confessions. Presumably, once this has happened on the streets, at work and in the home, gay people will be able to express their 'identity' free from homophobia and its enshrinement in the law. Yet this attitude conceals and obscures different experiences of being gay as it is argued that everybody has to 'come out' in the same way.

The popular exhortation to 'explode the nuclear family' is the clearest example of a gay ethnocentrism which assumes that every family is a white, patriarchal, nuclear family. Not only is there the assumption that merely confessing one's sexuality to this family will suffice to destroy its social, economic and cultural dominance, but that everybody's family is like it. We do not intend to explain here how our families differ but it must be said that, unlike the stereotypical nuclear family, the extended family system in black communities is a vital means of resistance, to white racism. Trying to subvert it by sexual confession is not, for us, the way to solve the contradictions we experience in being gay and remaining part of our families and communities.

But what do you do after you're 'out'? What are you coming out into? The drama of mainstream gay 'identity' will be acted out in a commercial entertainment called 'the scene'. A series of localised places where, for a price, your sexuality will be *allowed* or tolerated. And this identity will be played out through a tableau of roles, types and images – or are they merely commodities? And all this will be called a 'gay sensibility'.

And so in a curious manner post-60s 'permissiveness' comes full circle with 19th century medicine. If the Victorians' method of social control was to incorporate all those deviants whose behaviour deemed them unfit for bourgeois norms, then this modern politics of 'liberation' merely accepts the category of homosexual as pregiven truth and believes that this is the centre around which identity is made equivalent to sexuality.

One does not 'come out' as a socialist, a feminist or as a revolutionary (all of which are equally 'prohibited'), but gays do, it seems, because European culture has privileged sexuality as the essence of the self, the inner-most core of one's 'personality'. So it comes as no surprise to see the development of a particular stereotype of a gay man whose consciousness contains nothing else but sexuality, who is perpetually troubled by his sexual desires and who is always looking for the truth of his identity in his sex. If this is ever questioned one is seen as a 'moralist', guilty of a 'repressive prudishness', but it is necessary for us to question this consensus in gay politics because our experience tells us that being black is actually more important, more crucial, to the form of oppression that we face.

Indeed we question the idea of a 'gay desire', which sees this as a natural drive that must be satisfied at all costs, because there is something inherently oppressive about thinking of sexuality in this way. This 'essentialist' view of sexuality is in fact based on the prevailing Western concept of sexuality which *already contains racism*. Historically, the European construction of sexuality coincides with the epoch of imperialism and the two inter-connect. Imperialism justified itself by claiming that it had a civilising mission – to lead the base and ignoble savages and 'inferior races' into culture and godliness. The person of the savage was developed as the Other of civilisation and one of the first 'proofs' of this otherness was the nakedness of the savage, the visibility of its sex. This led Europeans to assume that the savage possessed an open, frank and uninhibited 'sexuality' – unlike the sexuality of the European which was considered to be fettered by the weight of civilisation.

The notion of a secret hidden truth of sexuality, which must be confessed, is clearly related to this, as it is based on the idea that sex is the most basic form of naturalness which is therefore related to being *un*civilised or *against* civilisation. The age old idea that sex is a dirty little secret that needs to be confessed always entails the binary tension of 'moral order' versus the 'chaos' of sexual abandon. And the gay movement has inherited this by claiming that the liberation of the homosexual lies in liberating sexuality.

We are not trying to deny the oppression of homosexuals, but we question whether it's possible to overcome this history of domination by focussing all our attention on sexuality. Rather, when we consider the way black gays are incorporated into the stereotyping and sexual objectification of the commercial 'scene', we realise that as black people we are implicated in the construction of sexuality in a doubly oppressive manner.

The 'gay scene' promotes a version of sexuality which says that what is needed to undo the history of homosexual repression is some kind of metropolitan gay savage whose sole purpose is to express his naturalness, his sexuality, for he is at his most natural when he is most sexual. Like the main character in the film *Taxi Zum Klo*, this gay savage promotes a sexualised political identity for gay men who will destroy bourgeois morality by fucking it to death, this is supposed to be the real liberation. No matter if this sexual campaign is conducted by reasserting 'macho' masculinity (viz the clone, the stud, heavy leather imagery, etc) since what makes this different from 'straights', makes it OK, is that gays are only 'playing' at being butch – so it doesn't really matter, it's just good fun.

In this *laissez-faire* attitude to sexuality, which the scene embodies because it's about making money, the black body will feature highly. Traditional notions of sexuality are deeply linked to race and racism because sex is regarded as that thing which *par excellence* is a threat to the moral order of Western civilisation. Hence, one is civilised at the expense of sexuality, and sexual at the expense of civilisation. If the black, the savage, the nigger, is the absolute Other of civility then it must follow that he is endowed with the most monstrous and terrifying sexual proclivity. If you are a white woman, you are in constant danger of being raped. And if you are a man then you can be fucked such that every vestige of morals and civilisation will be drained from you. But if this is too violent for you, there is always the Oriental. The Orient is anywhere east of Israel. The Oriental has no capacity for violence; he is mute, passive, charming, inscrutable. Imperialism involved a hierarchy of 'races' in the 19th century and the erotic fantasies about the oriental body were placed mid-way between Europe's state of enlightenment and the savage darkness and danger of Africa. This tradition has been continued by the international circuit of gay tourism which repeats this pattern of exploitation and objectification.

These are the images and stereotypes which govern the gaze of white people we encounter on the 'scene' and which we also challenge by our very existence as a political group. It is often said that these stereotypes, and the fantasies which support them, are quite harmless, that on the contrary, they are 'healthy' since they show that whites really 'like' black and Asian peoples. These are the assumptions that underlie the 'politics' of a group such as Black and White Men Together, which also recently formed in London. Groups like BWMT legitimate themselves by claiming that many black people appear to play along with these images and expectations. This has been said about women, that they 'really' enjoy rape and male violence, when what is really happening is that they are caught up in a structure designed to perpetuate male power, or in our case, white male power too.

But perhaps the most telling aspect of these sexual stereotypes is that they are not confined to gay society. They are at work in the policy discourses of the state, which employ similar sexualising interpretations of black people to legitimate certain forms of surveillance and social control. These themes – for example, that black men are not 'good' fathers because they are sexually promiscuous – are at work in the methods and interventions of social workers, housing officers and the police. And it is this intertwining of racism and sexuality that makes it necessary for us to concentrate on and prioritise black politics rather than a variant of gay liberation which has failed to tackle or even recognise its own racism.

If the white gay movement were more aware of its history it would not at all be shocked by the formation of the Gay Black Group, since the political form which both the gay and women's movement took were derived from Black Power and Black *Pride* in the 1960s. The example shown by Black Americans' struggles in the USA showed that a people with a specific history of oppression could organise themselves and their own politics without the need of a Party to oversee and co-ordinate it. We feel that the ignorance of these facts is born out by gay anti-fascist politics in Britain in the 70s.

In the anti-fascist mobilisations a recurrent rallying cry was this: if the Nazis and National Front were allowed to go unimpeded blacks would be repatriated but gays would be sent to the gas chambers since they had nowhere to go. Thus it was imperative that gays combat the fascists for their own good as well as that of black people. Now what is notable about the logic of this is that black people are assumed *not to belong here* – 'they have their own countries to go back to if things get too hot'. And a simple equation is made between racism and gay oppression without dealing with racism in the gay movement. In the end the problem of racism is cancelled out by the insistence that fascism is anti-gay as well as racist. So, after the demo, or whatever 'anti-racist' event it is, racism can be safely forgotten until the NF plan their next show of force.

The sort of fascism represented by the National Front is the most obvious political expression of racism and it is understandable that gays say they're 'against racism' by being anti-NF. But if there were a fascist state in this country it need not take the form that the NF, or its opponents, imagine. Over the last fifteen years the British state has dramatically increased its repressive measures, and these have been tried out first in Northern Ireland and on the mainland, on the black communities. The response of the white gay community to the 'riots' last year between police and black people was proof again that nothing has been learned. It was claimed in some quarters that there was a solidarity between blacks and gays in the area as the black youth involved had shown no hostility to the gays. (The possibility that the youth were completely uninterested was never considered.) And among some radical activists it was thought that this 'solidarity' arose because blacks and gays share a common enemy in the police, without an understanding of the *particular* reasons why black society is policed so repressively.

So our conclusion is that the slogan 'the personal is political' has not really been taken seriously by the gay movement when it comes to issues of racism. Since our group formed the only moves in this direction from members of the white gay community have been requests for us to tell them when white people are being racist, or to tell them how they can stop it. The gay movement needs to take its slogan to its limit and interrogate its own political practice, and to understand what autonomy really means, instead of habitually and unquestioningly repeating the liberal pluralist chant that, whatever 'colour' we are, we are oppressed in exactly the same way whether we are black, women or gay.

Racism and the Politics of Masculinity

Emergency, 1986[5]

Both *The Sexuality of Men* and *Black Masculinity*[6] address the same subject, which is the social construction of masculinity – an issue that has been radically re-politicised by the impact of feminism and womens' movements in Europe and America over the last decade. But any similarity between the two books ends there. Each offers a different perspective on why masculinity is considered to be a political problem and what is needed for its transformation. By reviewing the two texts together my aim is not to play one off against the other, but rather to create a space through the juxtaposition for a critical reflection on the way questions of race inflect these different analytic perspectives on the sexual politics of masculinity.

Broadly speaking, where Robert Staples' account of black male gender roles emphasises sociological and historical factors, the contributors to Martin Humphries' and Andy Metcalfe's book seem to stress the 'inner' psychological dimension of masculinity and its personal inscription on the 'self'. This contrast in viewpoints reveals the uneven development of sexual politics among white and black constituencies. I want to develop the argument that we need to understand these differences in order to begin a mutual dialogue that will enable strategic analyses and interventions in the myriad conflicts and contradictions between sex and race.

Robert Staples' central thesis is that black masculinity is a contradictory experience giving rise to a system of black male gender roles built upon conflicts which stem from the legacy of slavery. Thus Staples argues[7],

> I see the black male as being in conflict with the normative definition of masculinity. This is a status which few, if any, black males have been able to achieve. Masculinity, as defined in this (white, American) culture, has always implied a certain autonomy over and mastery of one's environment. It can be said that not many white American males have attained this either. Yet, white males did achieve dominance in the nuclear family. Even that semblance of control was to be largely denied to the black man.

Whereas prevailing definitions of masculinity imply power, control and authority, these attributes have been historically denied to black men since slavery. The centrally dominant role of the white male slave-master in the 18th and 19th century plantation society debarred black males from the patriarchal privileges ascribed to the masculine role. For example, a slave could not fully assume the role of 'father' as his children were the legal property of the slave-owner. In racial terms, black men and women alike were subordinated to the power of the white master in the hierarchical social relations of slavery and for black men, as *objects* of oppression, this also cancelled out their access to positions of power and prestige which are regarded as the essence of masculinity in a patriarchal culture. Shaped by this history, black masculinity is a highly contradictory formation as it is a *subordinated* masculinity.

There is a further contradiction, another turn of the screw of oppression, which occurs when black men subjectively internalise and incorporate aspects of the dominant definitions of masculinity in order to contest the conditions of dependency and powerlessness which racism and racial oppression enforce. Staples sees the legacy of the past writ large in the development of 'macho' attitudes and behaviour in contemporary society. 'Macho' is the product of these historical contradictions, as it subjectively incorporates attributes associated with dominant definitions of manhood – such as being tough, in control, independent – in order to recuperate some degree of power or active influence over objective conditions of powerlessness created by racism. 'Macho' may be regarded as a form of misdirected or 'negative' resistance, as it is shaped by the challenge to the hegemony of the socially dominant white male, yet it assumes a form which is in turn oppressive to black women, children and indeed, to black men themselves, as it can entail self-destructive acts and attitudes.

Describing this as the 'dual dilemma' of black masculinity, Robert Staples draws out its implications in concrete terms. More than any other socio-economic group in the United States, black male youth have the highest rates of unemployment. This is a consequence of the function of racism in the capitalist social order in which blacks are integrated at the bottom, as an 'underclass'. Yet, importantly, Staples shows how ideologies of gender cut across structures of race and class. The high rate of unemployment among black male youth is a product of institutional forms of racism in education – where low academic expectations become self-fulfilling prophecy – and the intense economic pressure on working-class black households which forces adolescents to 'drop out' of school in order to earn a wage and contribute to the family's income. But gender is an important and often overlooked factor here because in education and certain types of employment, such as service industries, black women fare relatively better than their male counterparts. Employers may regard black women as less of a 'risk', a perception informed by ideologies which represent the black woman as a reliable, obedient and faithful 'servant'[8]. Moreover, black males are more visible in unemployment statistics because their female counterparts are 'hidden' in the home, and unwaged domestic labour is not officially recognised as 'work'. Gender is also a decisive factor in the various 'solutions' which black male youth may adopt to escape the position of permanent wagelessness – joining the army or a life on the edges of illegality.

There is a close connection between the disproportionate representation of black male youth in unemployment data and their over-representation in crime statistics. At one level, the link lies in the fact that the criminal justice system is designed to protect and maintain the structure of white power, property and privilege created by the capitalist division of labour in the first place. However, although this explains why black citizens as a whole fail to enjoy equal protection from the law, against crime and violence, the mythical stereotype of 'black criminality' cannot be dismissed as mere ideology. The reality, in which this myth is partly grounded, is that black men become involved in illegality out of sheer economic necessity – crimes are committed 'in order to satisfy basic needs for food, clothing and shelter'. This does not 'excuse' black criminal acts but it does help us understand how the mythology intertwines with reality, and Staples shows that the 'macho' gender role underpins the survival strategies of the ghetto 'hustler'.

Gender is important because where black women, under the same circumstances of material privation, may turn to the extended family network for economic support, or negotiate the social security apparatus of the welfare state (with its own forms of oppressive surveillance), black males have developed various 'hustles' which involve illegality as a style of life. The figure of the 'hustler' is an institution in black urban underclass society[9] and while it is intelligible as a valid response to conditions of racism, poverty and exploitation, it does not challenge that system of oppression but rather accommodates itself to it: illegal means are used to attain the same normative ends or 'goals' of consumption associated with the patriarchal definition of the man's role as 'breadwinner', the counterpart to normative definitions of women's domestic role as 'housewife'. The figure of the 'hustler' is often romantically depicted as a social outsider, whereas in fact this life-style involves an essential investment in the idea that a 'real' man must be an active and independent economic agent, an idea which forms the cornerstone of patriarchal capitalism and its ethic of 'success'.

If the 'hustler' constitutes a kind of 'role-model' for

black men then it should be seen on a continuum with the problem of internalised oppression. Staples draws on Frantz Fanon's analysis of the dialectic of violence in the colonial situation[10] to examine the consequences of brutalisation apparent in the fact that certain crimes, from theft to crimes of violence which include the sexual violence of rape, are 'intra-racial' in character. Fanon argued that 'it is the coloniser who introduces violence into the home and the mind of the native', and Staples sees this insight as equally applicable to the 'internal colony' of black society in America where the racist violence of lynching forms the background against which the brutalisation of black men has taken place. Violence breeds violence and Fanon's view was that in the colonial context the native is forced to imitate and adopt violence as an instrument of the will. *But*, and this was the question Fanon sought to analyse with psychoanalytic concepts of 'internalisation', the colonised direct acts of aggression not onto the white male coloniser, the original agent of violence, but against fellow colonised men and women. Such intracommunal violence can be seen as an almost pathological misdirection of rage – as the outward expression of internalised oppression it is consonant with self-hatred.

Staples sees the phenomenon of black-on-black crime in a similar dialectic and shows that gender is absolutely central to its reproduction. This is most acute in the sexual violence of rape[11]:

> ... it is Fanon's contention that the African male is an envious man who covets all the European's possessions; to sit at his table, to sleep in his bed and to sleep with his wife. The rape of white women by Afro-American men often reflects this desire ... And it was due to this fear of the black male invading his domain, destroying his property, that the settler punished severely any black man who attempted to become familiar or intimate with the symbol of white privilege – the white female. Many of the lynchings in the South were brutal reminders to black men that intermingling with white women was regarded as an unmentionable crime.

However, Staples argues, the mythology of the black rapist, bequeathed by this violent history is now turned in on itself in contemporary American society as, 'most contemporary rape cases are intra-racial. Despite white fear of the omnipresent black rapist, only ten percent of all rape cases involve a black male and a white woman'. What is at issue here is the centrality of sex and gender to the complexity of internalised oppression.

Staples reminds us that the former black activist Eldridge Cleaver grimly described his rape of black women as practice for an 'insurrectionary act of revenge' against white America[12]. Rape symbolised a violent act of 'appropriating' the white man's 'property' for the patriarchal concept of woman as property lies at the root of rape. So, following Fanon's analysis, if inter-racial rape is a political act it is one of profound psychic *resentment*. It is this that also underlies intra-racial rape as the redirection of sexual aggression and violence onto the black woman allows the black man to escape the punishment of the white male. Above all, Staples makes clear, rape has nothing to do with human sexuality but concerns the complex dynamics of power as mediated by race and gender. Rape is 'an act of aggression (which) affords a moment of power' over others and in this sense constitutes a radically misdirected expression of the rage and frustration built up out of oppression and powerlessness. And if the 'majority of black rape victims are familiar with their attacker, who is a friend, relative or neighbour', then this merely demonstrates the extent to which black men have internalised patriarchal definitions of male power as brute force. As a response to powerlessness, the kind of 'power' acted out in the criminal violence of sexual abuse does nothing to challenge the underlying structure of oppression but only 'passes on' the violence of the dominant white male, via the psychic process of internalisation, into the black community and onto black women, hence triply reinforcing their oppression.

Is there a way out of this cruel and vicious circle? The value of Staples' analysis is that, alongside the documentation of such brutal experiences in the work of black women writers like Maya Angelou and Alice Walker,[13] he provides a useful framework for debating these issues on the contemporary political agenda. The question of race and crime has been on the British agenda since the moral panics around 'mugging' in the 1970s. Today however, when certain sections of the white left, led by deviant ex-hippy sociologists eager to influence Labour Party policies, have seized upon the stereotypes of black criminality to promote their so-called 'socialist strategies', Staples' analytic framework separates criminal *acts* from the essentialist and racist idea that blacks are prone to crime by their *nature*.[14]

The question of male violence has been placed high on the agenda by feminist organising. Women's collective resistance against the use of fear to control their lives has led to major long-term initiatives against the institutional sexism of the law and the state – women's refuges, rape crisis centres and legislation on women's rights in marriage, abortion and health care have all made inroads against the patriarchal legitimation of male violence. But, in white sexual politics, the issue of male violence has been conflated with other issues such as pornography.

The radical feminist argument that pornographic images 'cause' men to act violently towards women, advanced by the 'women against violence against women' mobilisation, and writers like Andrea Dworkin, conflates cause and effect. In my view this is a reductive argument which finds a convenient 'scapegoat' in pornography for complex structures of male behaviour. Inadvertently, this argument has aligned itself with the moral retrenchment against the 'permissive society' led by the Moral Majorities of the new right and people such as Mary Whitehouse. Yet although this has influenced recent legislation on obscenity, which makes pornography less visible in places like Soho, it is still pervasive on Page Three of *The Sun* and in the newsagents. One result of this line of argument is that, by making pornography synonymous with rape, certain feminist positions may reinforce the racist mythology of the black rapist, as Vron Ware has recently pointed out.[15] This stereotype is a mainstay of the ability of the right – National Front and 'respectable' Tory alike – to mobilise and manipulate the fears of the white working classes. Because of the absence of a mutual dialogue on the complex intersection of race, gender and power, this perspective on the politics of male violence has dire consequences analogous to the lack of sensitivity to questions of race and the Third World in certain feminist mobilisations against nuclear weapons which are thoroughly Eurocentric.[16]

Moreover, by framing 'the masculine way of violence' in the context of a dialectical relation to the state and its legal system, Staples' account contrasts with the way that the white anti-sexist men's movement has dealt with the issue of violence. Tony Eardley's contribution on this subject in *The Sexuality of Men* ignores the socio-economic context by locating the 'source' of the problem at a psychological level alone. After evaluating explanations which regard male violence either as an innate biological property or as an acquired response to environmental stress into which boys are socialised, Eardley concludes that

> ... if men's dependence and their emotional weakness is exposed they may well perceive it as a deep threat to their identity and their security. All men's worst fears about themselves and their ambivalent feelings towards women can emerge at these moments, and they (men) may react with defensive hostility or outright violence.[17]

While I would not deny the validity of this psychological account, the emphasis on inner feelings and the 'person-centred' stress on identity at the expense of environment is a limited way of addressing the issues. Eardley, and Jeff Hearn in his chapter on sexual harassment in the workplace, acknowledge that the capitalist ideology of competitive individualism plays a crucial role in determining the manifestation of male violence – but by treating this only as an aspect of male 'sexuality' they ignored other elements in the social construction of masculinity. Most indicatively, they ignore racial and ethnic differences and, in my view, this is a consequence of the way that the historical and sociological context is effectively made secondary, by the use of psychological concepts. By emphasising masculinity at the level of subjective interaction and individual identity, rather than men as a sociological group, the focus on sexuality is reductionist as well as being ethnocentric.

Similarly other chapters in *The Sexuality of Men* – on pornography, on 'macho' attitudes in the gay community, on men's ambivalent attitude to pregnancy – each reflect a perspective in which sexual politics is narrowed down first to 'sexuality', then to the 'self'. It seems to me that this 'self-centredness' is a key characteristic of white sexual politics, or rather, it is an interpretation of the radical slogan 'the personal is political' which is made in an individualistic manner which thus excludes questions of race and ethnicity because it is so preoccupied with the 'self', at the expense of the 'social'.

This is the site of an important and difficult contradiction. As Michel Foucault has argued,[18] the historical construction of sexuality in the West has made it the privileged point at which the 'truth' of one's self is to be discovered, and thus to deconstruct or reconstruct the politics of sexuality necessarily involves an examination of the self. The question is whether psychological or psychoanalytic concepts are adequate to this task? These questions are thrown into the foreground in the second section of *Black Masculinity* which looks at another legacy from the days of slavery: the myth of black male sexual 'superiority'.

The paradox here is that this myth, it is often said, is one that many black men do not want demystified![19] The notion that black men have a stronger capacity for sexual enjoyment or simply that black men 'do it' more and better – indeed the whole mystique around black sexuality per se – arises from the core beliefs of classical biologising racist ideology which held Africans to be 'inferior' in mind and morality also on account of their bodies. As the work of Fanon and other writers like Hoch and Jordan would show[20] images of the hypersexual 'savage' or the threatening, marauding 'buck', tell us more about the 'repressed' fears and fantasies of European civilisation than they do about black people's experience of sexual intimacy.

But, as was argued in the Gay Black Group article, we cannot extricate ourselves from these myths without recognising that we are already deeply implicated in their reproduction. As with the issue of criminality, Staples demonstrates that there is a kernel of 'truth' in this sexual mythology whereby it is grounded in reality. As a private experience, sex offers a 'haven from a heartless world', a zone of emotional expression and affirmation carved out against the daily oppression of racism. While this may give black male sexuality a certain expressive intensity, Staples shows that the micro-level of personal experience cannot be divorced from wider macro-forces which also entail political conflicts and contradictions. He suggests that by internalising the mythology of black super-sexuality, black men have developed a 'macho' role which trades off and perpetuates the stereotype and gives rise to exploitative uses of sexuality. Again, because black men are

> denied equal access to the prosaic symbols of manhood, they manifest their masculinity in the most extreme form of sexual domination. When they have been unable to achieve status in the workplace, they have exercised the privilege of their manliness and attempted to achieve it in the bedroom. Feeling a constant need to affirm their masculinity, tenderness and compassion are eschewed as signs of weakness which leave them vulnerable to the ever-feared possibility of female domination.[21]

From this perspective Staples identifies a range of issues – such as jealousy, infidelity, divorce and promiscuity – seen as symptoms of the underlying emotional conflicts in heterosexual relationships engendered by the ascription of sexual 'superiority'. In seeking to live up to expectations shaped by received images of black male sexuality black men may experience inter-personal and intra-personal conflicts and Staples regards such conflict as the 'dominant motif' of black male-female interaction.

However, it is at this point that various limitations in his sociological approach become apparent. First, as he is concerned with young 'singles' and their 'dating games',

Staples does not clearly relate these conflicts to the family. This is a major oversight as certain assumptions about black sexuality lie at the heart of the prevalent view that black households constitute deviant, disorganised and even pathological units which fail to socialise their offspring into the correct societal norms.[22] Second, although there is an acknowledgement of the diversity of sexual relationships within black communites, Staples underplays the political character of this heterogeneity. His discussion of mixed-race relationships is superficial and although it highlights the isolation which inter-racial couples or families may experience from both white and black communities, it does not examine why. Similarly, in his discussion of gay sexuality among black men he sympathetically emphasises the racial segregation of the gay 'scene' and the isolation which often undermines black gay relationships, yet there is no discussion of homophobia in the black community, which is another source of problems which black gay men have to contend with.

Above all Staples speaks in the neutral voice of an objective 'third-person' and unlike Fanon's existential approach which incorporates an autobiographical dimension, the use of positivist and functionalist methods evades the complexity of personal experience. By contrast, one of the strengths of *The Sexuality of Men* is the self-reflexive way in which the writers include the 'I' of actual experience in their reflections on masculinity. Here I have to qualify my earlier criticisms because clearly this 'first-person' approach opens the way to insights which it would be foolish to ignore. Nevertheless the problem remains that while an honest examination of actual experience anchors the radical slogan 'the personal is political', what happens to the political if it goes no further than the purely personal? Various contributors to *The Sexuality of Men* acknowledge the importance of small consciousness-raising groups in providing a means whereby men can actively interpret this slogan by connecting 'private' experience to the public domain of politics. In this way, as an organisational form, the C-R group may lead to a 'liberation' for many men and women, in much the same way as the exhortation to 'come out' in the gay liberation movement sought to transform self-oppression through public acts of affirmation. Yet it cannot be taken for granted that the C-R model has a universal appeal or usefulness.

The problem is that this model 'works' mainly in a culture that prioritises individual, rather than collectivist, strategies and solutions. The consciousness-raising group was in fact based on the idea of a 'therapeutic community' which developed in new forms of psychotherapy in the 50s and which subsequently influenced the idea of the 'encounter group' popularised in the hippy counter-culture of the 60s and 70s. It seems to me that as an organisational form for sexual politics it is limited because its style, language and mode of operation is accessible and useful mainly to people who have been educated to the point where the discourses of psychotherapy and psychology have become second nature. In our society this means white people from a middle class background. At the centre of this dilemma is the language of psychoanalysis. Tom Ryan's contribution adopts this vocabulary and ends up approaching normative modes of masculinity as clinical phenomena, bordering on the edges of psycho-pathology. Ryan is concerned with what appears to be men's emotional illiteracy, their seeming inability to articulate or even understand their feelings which thus manifest themselves in violent or aggressive ways.

All this is crucially important but the point is, by abstracting the psyche from its specific cultural, social and historical formation, Ryan's psychoanalytic discourse assumes that it has universal relevance and applicability. This conceals a dangerously Eurocentric assumption which demonstrates gross insensitivity to the different ways in which emotions are expressed in different cultures. How could you say that black men like Miles Davis or Michael Jackson, James Brown or John Coltrane are 'emotionally illiterate'? It is often said that black people are more emotionally expressive. Whether or not this has any validity as a generalisation, there is a grain of truth here as the expressive qualities of black music, from blues and jazz in the past to reggae and soul today, bear witness to a culture in which the open expression of deep structures of feeling is valued as an end in itself. When we also consider the popularity and consistent appeal of black musics in Western society we are forced to concede that there are other ways, apart from the academic language of the disciplines which begin with 'psy', in which men and women attempt to come to terms with the pains and pleasures of sexuality. The point I am making is that because of the narrow range of reference, the discourse of white sexual politics has been impoverished in its obsession with 'self'. This has led not only to the erasure of 'race' from its political agenda (quite literally in the case of *The Sexuality of Men* which stubbornly refuses to acknowledge that not all the men in the world are white or even that white male sexuality is informed by the ethnicity of whiteness) but also to an inability to engage in popular culture and to reach ordinary men whose masculinity is constructed as much by sport, music, the media and other cultural practices as it is by the Oedipus complex.

Despite its limitations, Staples' invocation of Fanon serves to remind us that there are other ways of making use of the intellectual and analytic resources which psychoanalysis makes available. In *Black Skin, White Mask* Fanon's project was to uncover the unconscious roots of what was then called the 'inferiority complex' of the 'negro'. Since then the term for this problem has changed; today it's called 'negative self image', and within the various strategies of the state and social policy for the policing of 'ethnic minorities' (backed up by sociological research on ethnicity), black subjectivity and black sexuality are already targetted as key points of intervention in education, social work, health care, psychiatry and housing. At each of these points connections between race, gender and the family have been brought into the view of officialdom and the state.

Moreover, in a context where black women's autonomous organising has raised similar issues for black political agendas, Staples' book is an important contribution to the development of black sexual politics. Where black feminists have argued that, 'we struggle together with black men against racism, while we also struggle with black men about sexism'[23] this book provides a viable framework for a mutual dialogue on sexual and gender-based antagonisms within black communities. But what I think is most important is that, through sexuality, Staples renews the fundamental issue of internalised oppression, an issue which does not fit neatly into the existing agendas of black radicals and anti-racists. In *Color*, a film by Warrington Hudlin[24], two black women address this sphere of our political existence. Reluctant to disclose 'the personal', one character says, 'I wish there was a way to show this film to black people only, then I'd talk about my feelings'. Similar responses, that we shouldn't 'wash our dirty linen in public', may meet this book, but we urgently need to come out of this way of thinking as it only perpetuates the cycles of oppression that cross the personal and the political.

If, by contrast, the book also reveals some of the absences, omissions and silences of the prevailing forms in which sexual politics is practised then it also addresses the concerns of white men and women, as the questions raised by race, ethnicity and cultural differences cut across the complacencies of a personalised politics that remains in the prison-house of sexuality and the culture of narcissism. How white feminists and anti-sexist men take on these issues is up to them; the point is that race can no longer be ignored or erased from their political agendas.

In the present political predicament of the left, in which traditional sources of allegiance and identity (such as class) are becoming increasingly fragmented, perhaps we should contemplate the idea that *there is nothing* 'beyond the fragments'. That is, rather than simply assume that the diversity of political interests and identities which make up the left today can be synthesised or brought together under a common programme, we should start to give more attention to the micro-capillaries of power and domination at work between relations of sex and race. In this way, by examining the tensions between the fragments, we might be in a better position to transform the larger structures of oppression that continue to exploit our differences and diversity as sources of division and despondency.

Interview

Square Peg 1987[25]

Ever since the 1970s Gay Liberation Movement, there has been an underground black gay community that was located outside of mainstream gay communities and outside of white gay liberationist and feminist movements, although there were always black people in the gay movement, such as myself.

In 1981 the Gay Black Group was formed which I joined a couple of years later. It was a space where you met other black gays and lesbians, and then people went off into different directions to work within the black communities or within different cultural activities to do different things. It was very important, because it could have been fixated around the issue of gay identity, but because of being black or coming from working class or middle class backgrounds you wanted to do different things, and being gay wasn't the only important thing in the construction of your identity. The Group went on to become the Black Lesbian and Gay Group, as more women joined, and there's now a centre for black lesbians and gay men based in Tottenham.

The way that lesbian and gay identities are constructed in Caribbean society is very much along the lines of something to be trivialised, they're figures of fun and ridicule. So you'll hear lots of references, in dialogue, to 'batty man' or 'anti-man', which is important because it's an acknowledgement that we *do* exist. In terms of a continuity with the construction of gay and lesbian identities here, in this country, one could look to the family. In our film, *The Passion of Remembrance* that's what we have done, we have made that connection[26]. In a sense all the arguments are still around the question, 'Is homosexuality a white man's disease?'. Every parent knows they're lying when they say that and so does every black person who says it. And in this sense, because that question still gets asked, one can't *really* talk about coming out, in the same way that you do post-1970s, post-GLF, for the older generations of black lesbians and gays. They had to survive in ways that they could and they weren't always able to make themselves visible.

There were other kinds of pressures, other demands made on Afro-Caribbean communities around the 1940s, 50s and 60s, with subsequent generations of black people being born in this country creating different identities for themselves. If one looks back at black cultural activities – in writing, in the theatre and so on, as well as grassroots organising – there have always been black lesbians and gay men at the centre of those activities, always. And if one looks to the United States, from the perspective of a diaspora culture, one can look to Langston Hughes or James Baldwin – they're the most visible figures of our continuity in black history.

If one looks at the statement 'The Black Lesbian and Gay Group', that's saying that we know we're black people in society and so therefore discriminated against in a particular way which excludes or disavows our participation in various organisations, social and cultural activities, etc. So that statement, first of all to be gay but not to disclaim a black identity, was very important; yet within that there was always the split, the tension, between rejection from your own community and a rejection from mainstream white gays. That has always been the pivot around which a number of political actions and gestures are made. For example, we wanted to involve the white gay community to address certain issues, such as racism, and to participate in certain black political agendas as well, and at the same time we wanted to question the black communities' heterosexism but not to do it from the stance that white gay liberationists or white feminists would do it from. That's not to say *all* the white gay liberationists or *all* the white feminists would adopt that stance, but there seemed to be this whole thing about, 'Well, of course the black family is patriarchal' and so on. A lot of racist and stereotypical assumptions were made around the black family, around black people, black sexuality and what it's like in the black communities in terms of sexual politics.

If one looks at the gay and feminist movements one can see that there has been a gesture made by the white feminist movement to address race. For them it seemed to be something on their political agenda whereas there has been only a deafening silence that fell over the white gay movement around issues of race. If one talked about patronising attitudes, it circulated at a level in which the issues get personalised, or maybe if one was talking about cruising and the ways black men are perceived in those spaces, somehow the issues were made invisible. I don't think there was any recognition or acknowledgement of there being black lesbians and gays who were trying to construct an identity, which after all was what the gay liberation movement was doing in the 70s. Somehow the white gay community saw this as a threat and could not take on race as an acceptable or respectable category. I can't speak about the white feminist movement in any great detail but from the literature that I've read there seems to be some collaboratory work done; and whether or not it's succeeded or failed, it was a space where such issues were taken up, with some recognition of black women's identity and difference. Now in some of the things I've read this has been taken up in a kind of tokenistic or patronising way, but that's another story.

For me it was always important to work with other black people. That was always a priority. I have made alliances with white gay men, but for me to address their racism wasn't my preoccupation because it wasn't a problem for me. It was something that the white gay male community had to deal with. So the strategy was always to work within the black community and to somehow put the issues on the agenda.

Today, now, in 1987, there have to be alliances made. Maybe at one time an essentialist discourse – one that constructs a fixed or essential identity – was necessary. But some people, like me, are sick of explaining ourselves. They want to formalise their time and energy doing things that are more constructive for themselves. So in terms of talking about political alliances, essentialism is something that won't work any more. One can see that the idea that

GARY'S TALE [26]

From fables, learnt young, we were told that in
princes and princess snow white blessed was
true beauty held, in all its disguises.

Self-hate is what we've been taught to consume,
from our history class to our white friends' whispers,
and sometimes our best black friends' jokes.

Our mother and father told us that I had 'good' hair
and my brother had hard coarse hair, and because
we were lighter we drew closer too, true beauty disguised.

And, oh England, now that we grow older, have these tales
changed?
It's all too predictable. You have told me a lie, that we
have had to live by.

Do we love ourselves, when I look into your eyes?
Are we an image of our own making?

Kiss me, before someone sees us.

Those pretty, pretty blue eyes that made me invisible,
Those pretty, beautiful dark brown eyes that also made me
invisible, as I looked in the mirror.

And if it's boys who like boys the rules don't change
and so now I ask, do we love ourselves,
when I look into your eyes?

Because the last fight, the last battle, territory, will be
with one's self,
the most important terrain, the psyche.
The mind will be the last neo-colonialised space to be
decolonialised, this I know because I have been there,
backwards and forwards.

Helen Levitt

Those pretty, beautiful brown eyes that also made me invisible
as I looked in the mirror.
Do we love ourselves, when I look into your eyes?
Are we an image of our own making?

(Gary turns and looks at Tony
and says)

Kiss me, before someone sees us.

REPORT-BACK[27]

We filled the space. One hundred peoples with black, green and soft brown eyes. Skins varying from beige sandness to ivory chocolate wood. Faces that were as sensitive and vulnerable as mine. Smiles that were charged with a certain knowledge – 'Yes, we know what it feels like to be black in the heart of the black community and still not feel safe, because of that difference, in whom we dare to love'.

Black gay people and lesbian people who in the discussions, seated patiently, listened to a black mother's plea: how unfair to her that *we* had been. Even though she robbed us of talking out our silence that has been forced upon us, in our lives. A space we seldom had, even if it was learning to begin to look at each other's eyes and say: 'Yes, we are beautiful, even though we sometimes didn't believe so'... and indeed we were.

We could feel the air meant something more to our existence that afternoon. An existence that if some had their way would be eliminated. Even when the brother told us that he would kick our heads in, we smiled because you see on this occasion he was outnumbered. In the room this afternoon were many other gay brothers, far bigger than he, which must have made him think twice. It was amusing. The way he looked, that was the indian boy, his face as cool as buttermilk and his hair blue black, I felt his warmth, but also the warmth of others on that vulnerable brave afternoon.

we all inhabit our separate identities simply reproduces power. Sometimes it's strategically necessary to be a bit of an essentialist – to say this is who I am, I exist – but sometimes that strategy doesn't work at all. Today, there's no space for it.

Territories of the Body

True Confessions

Ten 8, 1986[29]

I went through a lot when I was a boy. They called me sissy, punk, freak and faggot. If I ever went out to friends' houses on my own, the guys would try to catch me, about eight or twenty of them together. They would run me. I never knew I could run so fast, but I was scared. They would jump on me, y'know, 'cos they didn't like my action ... Sometimes white men would pick me up in their car and take me to the woods and try to get me to suck them. A whole lot of black people have had to do that. It happened to me and my friend, Hester. I ran off into the woods. My friend, he did it ... I was scared.

Little Richard Penniman[30]

In recent years questions of pleasure and desire have been in the foreground of debates around photography and the politics of representation. In many ways this reflects the political priority given to the issue of pornography in debates led by the women's movement and the gay movement. From our point of view one of the most notable features of this political activity around sexual representation is the marked absence of race from the agenda of concerns – it is as if white people had 'colonised' this agenda in contemporary cultural politics for themselves alone. While some feminists have begun to take on issues of race and racism in the womens' movement, white gay men retain a deafening silence on race. Maybe this is not surprising, given the relative apathy and depoliticised culture of the mainstream gay 'scene'.

On the other hand there is a bitter irony in this absence of political awareness of race in the gay male community, especially when we consider recent trends in gay sub-cultural 'style'. After the clone look in which gay men adopted very 'straight' signifiers of masculinity – moustache, short cropped hair, work-clothes – in order to challenge stereotypes of limp-wristed 'poofs', there developed a stylistic flirtation with S&M imagery, leather-gear, quasi-military uniforms and skinhead styles. Politi-cally, these elements project highly ambivalent meanings and messages but it seemed that the racist and fascist connotations of these new 'macho' styles escaped gay con-sciousness as those who embraced the 'threatening' symbo-lism of the tough-guy look were really only interested in the eroticisation of masculinity.[31]

If the *frisson* of eroticism conveyed by these styles depends on their connotations of masculine power then this concerns the kind of power traditionally associated with *white* masculinity. It is therefore ironic that gay men have ignored this ethnic dimension when we also recall that the origins of the modern gay liberation movement were closely intertwined with the black liberation movements of the 60s. The documentary film *Before Stonewall*[32] shows how the American gay community learned new tactics of protest through their participation in the civil rights struggles for equality, dignity and autonomy, led by figures like Dr Martin Luther King Jr. As Audre Lorde points out in the film, the black struggle became the prototype for all the new social movements of the time – from women's and gay liberation, to the peace, anti-war and ecology movements as well. But although gays derived inspiration from the symbols of black liberation – Black Pride being translated into Gay Pride, for example – they failed to return the symbolic debt, as it were, as there was a lack of reciprocity and mutual exchange between racial and sexual politics in the 70s. The marginalisation of issues of race in the white gay movement in Britain has already been high-lighted by the Gay Black Group article which questions the ethnocentric assumptions behind the exhortation to 'come out', regardless of the fact that as black gays and lesbians our families provide a necessary source of support against racism. However such concerns with cultural differences have been passed by as the horizon of gay men's political consciousness has been dominated by the concern with sexuality in an individualistic sense. Here other aspects of ethnocentrism have surfaced most clearly in debates around the cultural politics of pornography.

During the 1970s feminist initiatives radically politicised the issue of sexual representation. The womens' movement made it clear that pornography was condemned for objectifying and exploiting women's bodies for the pleasure and profit of men. This cultural critique, closely linked to the radical feminist argument that 'porn is the theory, rape is the practice', has had important effects in society as it found an inadvertent alliance with the views on obscenity held by the New Right. Mary Whitehouse and others also helped to politicise sexual representation, arguing that certain types of imagery were responsible for causing actual violence or abuse.

These developments have also highlighted conflicts of interest between women and gay men. Gays have often defended porn with libertarian arguments which hold the desire of the individual to do what 'he' wants as paramount. Such sexual libertarianism is itself based on certain ethnic privileges as it is their whiteness that enables some gay men to act out this 'freedom of choice', which itself highlights the consumer-oriented character of the metropolitan gay subculture. In this context what interests us are the contradictory experiences that the porno-photo-text implicates us in, as pornography is one of the few spaces in which erotic images of other black men are made available.

Our starting point is *ambivalence* as *we want to look, but don't always find the images we want to see.* As black men we are implicated in the same landscape of stereotypes which is dominated and organised around the needs, demands and desires of white males. Blacks 'fit' into this terrain by being confined to a narrow repertoire of 'types' – the supersexual stud and the sexual 'savage' on the one hand or the delicate, fragile and exotic 'oriental' on the other. These are the lenses through which black men become visible in the urban gay subculture. The repetition of these stereotypes in gay pornography betrays the circulation of 'colonial fantasy', that is a rigid set of racial roles and identities which rehearse scenarios of desire in a way which traces the cultural legacies of slavery, empire and imperialism. This circuit for the structuring of fantasy in sexual representation is still in existence. The 'Spartacus' guidebook for gay tourists comments that boys can be bought for a packet of cigarettes in the Phillipines.

Against this backdrop, Robert Mapplethorpe's glossy images of *Black Males* are doubly interesting as the stereotypical conventions of racial representation in pornography are appropriated and abstracted into the discourse of 'art photography'. In pictures such as *Man in a Polyester Suit*, the dialectics of white fear and fascination underpinning colonial fantasy are reinscribed by the exaggerated centrality of the black man's 'monstrous' phallus. The black subject is objectified into Otherness as the size of the penis signifies a threat to the secure identity of the white male ego and the position of power which whiteness entails in colonial discourse. Yet, the threatening phobic object is 'contained', after all this is only a photograph on a two-dimensional plane; thus the white male viewer is returned to his safe place of identification and mastery but at the same time has been able to indulge in that commonplace white fixation with black male sexuality as something 'dangerous', something Other[33]. As Fanon argued in *Black Skin, White Mask* the myths about the violent, aggressive and 'animalistic' nature of black sexuality were fabricated and fictioned by the all-powerful white master to allay his fears and anxieties as well as providing a means to justify the brutalisation of the colonised and any vestiges of guilt. Mapplethorpe's carefully constructed images (discussed in more detail in the following section) are interesting, then, because, by reiterating the terms of colonial fantasy, the pictures service the expectations of white desire: but what do they say to our needs and wants?

Here we return to that feeling of ambivalence because while we can recognise the oppressive dimension of the fantasies staged in such sexual representation, we are fascinated, we still want to look, even if we cannot find the images we want to see. What is at issue is that the same signs can be read to produce different meanings. Although images of black men in gay porn generally reproduce the syntax of commonsense racism, the inscribed, intended or preferred meanings of those images are not fixed. They can at times be prised apart into alternative readings when different experiences are brought to bear on their interpretation. Colonial fantasy attempts to 'fix' the position of the black subject into a space that mirrors the object of white desires; but black readers may appropriate pleasures by reading against the grain, over-turning signs of 'otherness' into signifiers of identity. In seeing images of other black gay men there is an affirmation of our sexual identity.

This touches on some of the qualitative differences between gay and straight pornography: because 'homosexuality' is not the norm, when images of other men, coded as gay, are received from the public sphere there is something of a validation of gay identity. For isolated gays porn can be an important means of saying 'other gays exist'. Moreover, pornographic conventions sometimes slip, encouraging alternative readings. One major photographic code is to show single models in solo frames, enabling the imaginary construction of a one-to-one fantasy; but sometimes, when models pose in couples or groups, other connotations – friendships, solidarities, collective identity – can come to the surface. The ambivalent mixture of feelings in our response to porn is of a piece with the contradictions black gays live through on the 'scene'. While very few actually conform to the stereotypes, in the social networks of the gay subcultures and the circumscribed spaces of its erotic encounters, some black gay men appear to accept and even play up to the assumptions and expectations which govern the circulation of stereotypes. Some of the myths about black sexuality are maintained not by the unwanted imposition of force from 'above', but by the very people who are in a sense 'dominated' by them. Moreover, this subtle dialectic between representation and social interaction is at work in the broader heterosexual context as well – to explore this dimension, and its implications for cultural politics, we pursue Michel Foucault's idea that sexuality constitutes a privileged 'regime of truth' in our societies[34]. From this perspective we may uncover issues around the construction of black masculinities in and through different forms of representation.

Social definitions of what it is to be a man, about what constitutes 'manliness', are not 'natural' but are historically constructed and this construction is culturally variable. To understand how and why these constructions are 'naturalised' and accepted as the norm we cannot rely on notions of ideology as false consciousness. Patriarchal culture constantly redefines and adjusts the balance of male power and privilege and the prevailing system of gender roles by negotiating psychological and personal identity through a variety of material, economic, social and political structures such as class, the division of labour and the work/home nexus at the point of consumption. Race and ethnicity mediates this at all levels, so it's not as if we could strip away the 'negative images' of black masculinity created by western patriarchy and discover some 'natural' black male identity which is good, pure and wholesome. The point is that black male gender identities have been culturally constructed through complex dialectics of power.

The hegemonic repertoire of images of black masculinity, from docile 'Uncle Tom', the shuffling minstrel entertainer, the threatening native to 'Superspade' figures like *Shaft*, has been forged in and through the histories of slavery, colonialism and imperialism. As the discussion of Robert Staples' *Black Masculinity* in the previous section shows, a central strand in this history is the way black men have incorporated a code of 'macho' behaviour in order to recuperate some degree of power over the condition of powerlessness and dependency in relation to the white male slave-master. The contradiction that this dialectic gives rise to continues in contemporary Britain once we consider images of black males in political debates around 'law and order'. The prevailing stereotype projects an image of black male youth as a 'mugger' or 'rioter'; either way he constitutes a violent and dangerous threat to white society, he becomes the objectified form of inarticulate fears at the back of the minds of 'ordinary British people' made visible in the headlines of the popular tabloid press. But this regime of representation is reproduced and maintained in hegemony because black men have had to resort to 'toughness' as a defensive response to the prior aggression and violence that characterises the way black communities are policed (by white male police officers). This cycle between reality and representation makes·the ideological fictions of racism empirically 'true' – or rather, there is a struggle over the definition, understanding and construction of meanings around black masculinity within the dominant regime of truth.

This paradoxical situation is played out in other areas of popular culture such as sport. Classical racism involved a logic of dehumanisation in which African peoples were defined as having bodies but not minds; in this way the super-exploitation of the black body as a muscle-machine could be justified. Vestiges of this are active today in schools for instance, where teachers may encourage black kids to take up sport because they're seen as academic under-achievers. But on the other hand there are concrete advantages to be gained from appearing to play up to such general expectations. Without black athletes it is doubtful whether Britain would win any medals at the Olympics – sport is a circumscribed zone where blacks are allowed to excel. And we have also seen how black people have entered sports not just for their own individual gain; by using their public status, they have articulated a political stance – recall those newsreel images of the Black Power salute at the 1968 Olympic Games.

Although black men have been able to exploit the contradictions of the dominant ideological regimes of truth, the political limitations of remaining within its given structure of representation became acutely apparent in the context of the black liberation movements of the 1960s. Slogans such as 'Black is Beautiful', and new idioms of cultural and political expression like the Afro hairstyle[35], signified the rejection of second-class citizenship and 'negative self-image'. The movement sought to clear the ground for the cultural reconstruction of the black subject – but because of the *masculinist form* this took, it was done at the expense of black women, gays and lesbians. Figures such as Eldridge Cleaver promoted a heterosexist version of black militancy which not only authorised sexism – Stokely Carmichael said the only position of black women in the movement was 'prone' – but a hidden agenda of homophobia, something which came out in Cleaver's remorseless attack on James Baldwin[36]. Revolutionary nationalism implied a very macho-oriented notion of black struggle and this pertains to Britain also as the term 'black youth' really means black *male* youth (their sisters were invisible in debates on race and crime in the 70s) and this has been taken, rather romantically, by some black male activists and intellectuals to embody the 'heroic' essence of black people's resistance.

This emphasis on politics as 'frontline confrontation' not only ignores the more subtle and enduring forms of cultural resistance which have been forged in diaspora formations, it also depoliticises 'internal' conflicts and antagonisms – especially around gender and sexuality – within the black communities. It was precisely because this one-dimensional masculinist rhetoric colludes and compromises black struggle within existing regimes of representation, that black women organised autonomously as feminists in the 1970s. The issues raised by black feminists – and it has only been with their interventions and leadership that questions of pleasure, desire and sexual politics have entered the agenda of black political discourse – all point us towards the 'unfinished business' of the 60s. And as Cheryl Clarke demonstrates in her essay 'The Failure to Transform'[37], the issue of homophobia in the black communities cannot be avoided any longer. Contrary to the misinformed idea that homosexuality is a 'white man's disease', something into which we've been corrupted, she shows that lesbians and gay men have always been an integral part of black society – active in politics, the church and cultural activities like music, literature and art – even though our existence is publicly denied and disavowed by self-appointed 'community leaders'.

Although the organisational forms of black sexual politics are only recently emerging, questions of sexuality, pleasure and desire have always been on the black political agenda in so far as our aspirations – for freedom – have always found cultural forms of expression. Above all, it is in the arena of music that black people have endorsed and re-articulated the radical slogan that 'the personal is political'. While the music of the Afro-Christian church – hymns, spirituals, gospel – sang of the intense desire and yearning to transcend the misery of oppression, the blues or the Devil's music of the street sought worldly transcendence in the here and now through the sensual pleasures of the flesh. And as Paul Gilroy has argued[38] it is this emotional realism and the candid expressive voicing of sexual desire that also accounts for the immense popularity of black musics among whites in modern Western societies. It is in the medium of music – always associated with dance and the erotic potentialities of the dancefloor – that black men and women have articulated sexual politics. Male-female antagonisms are openly acknowledged in soul; sex is celebrated in the blues, but it is also problematised; some of Billie Holiday's songs offer succinct critiques of black men's manipulative attitudes, but they also address the ambivalent 'messiness' of longing for their intimate embrace.

While machismo was big box-office in the 'blaxploitation' movie genre of *Shaft* and *Superfly* in the early 70s, black male musicians like Sly Stone, Stevie Wonder and Marvin Gaye undercut the braggadoccio to make critiques of conventional models of black masculinity. In this period, classic Motown like 'I'll be There' by the Four Tops or 'Papa Was a Rolling Stone' by the Temptations spoke of a whole range of concerns with reliability and responsibility in personal relationships, critiquing some of the vagaries in certain models of black family life and fatherhood. Today, artists and stars like Luther Vandross and the much maligned Michael Jackson disclose the 'soft side' of black masculinity (and this is the side we like!). We feel it is important to tap into and recognise these resources in popular culture because they reveal that masculinity can be constructed in a diversity of ways. If we attune our ears we may also acknowledge that black male artists in music have been involved in a 'struggle' around the political meanings of masculinity – in contrast to the 'emotional illiteracy' which is regarded as one of the most malignant consequences of patriarchal role models, the sexual discourses of black popular music enables and invites men to find a means of making sense of their feelings. It will be crucial for the left to realise that far from being 'mindless entertainment', music is the key site in everyday life where men and women reflect on their gendered and sexual identities and make adjustments to the images they have of themselves.

Once we can reclaim the camp and crazy 'carnivalesque' qualities of Little Richard – the original Queen of Rock and Roll himself – we can appreciate the way in which some black men have been in the popular vanguard when it comes to sexual politics. Little Richard's outrageousness was a model for many who have deployed the subversive potential of irony and parody like George Clinton's Parliament and Funkadelic, Cameo and perhaps even Prince, as they 'play' with stereotypical codes and conventions to 'theatricalise' and send-up the whole masquerade of masculinity itself. By destabilising signs of race, gender and sexuality these artists draw critical attention to the cultural *constructedness*, the artifice, of the sexual roles and identities we inhabit. In this way they remind us that our pleasures are political and that our politics can be pleasurable.

Imaging the Black Man's Sex

Photography/Politics: Two, 1987[39]

I want to talk about Robert Mapplethorpe's pictures of *Black Males*[40] as a cultural artefact that says something about certain ways in which white people 'look' at black people, and how, in this way of 'looking', black male sexuality is perceived as something 'different', something 'other'. Certainly this particular work must be approached in the context of Mapplethorpe's overall photographic oeuvre. Mapplethorpe first made his name in the world of 'art photography' by taking portraits of patrons and protagonists in the post-Warholian subculture of celebrity. In turn he has become something of a 'star' himself as the discourses of journalists, critics, gallery curators and collectors have woven a 'mystique' around his persona – the artist as author of 'prints of darkness'.

As he has extended his repertoire the fundamental conservatism of Mapplethorpe's aesthetic has become all too apparent: a reworking of the old modernist tactic of 'shock the bourgeoisie' (and make them pay) given a new 'aura' by his characteristic trademark, the pursuit of perfection in photographic technique. The vaguely transgressive quality of his subject matter – S&M rituals, lady body builders, black men – is given a heightened allure by his self-evident mastery of the technological apparatus. However, once we consider the author of these images not as the origin of their meanings but as a 'projection, in terms more or less always psychological, of our way of handling texts'[41] then what is interesting about the images of black men is the way they facilitate the public projection of certain erotic fantasies about the black male body. Whatever his personal motivation or artistic pretentions, Mapplethorpe's camera opens an eye onto the fetishistic structure of stereotypical representations of black men which circulate across a range of surfaces, from pornography to sport, newspapers and advertising, cinema and television.

The first thing to notice about the photo-text *Black Males* – so obvious it goes without saying – is that all the men are *nude*. As a catalogue of vantage points and 'takes' on the black man's body, the camera's gaze is directed to a single, unitary, vanishing point – an aesthetic and erotic objectification which reduces black male bodies to a homogenous visual surface thoroughly saturated with sexual meanings. We look through a sequence of individualised, personally named, Afro-American men, but we 'see' only *sex* as the essence of the text's articulation of meanings around the signifiers 'black/male'. According to Mapplethorpe's line of sight: Black + Male = Aesthetic, Erotic Object. Regardless of the sexual preferences or orientation of either artist or spectator, the sense generated by this system of images is that the essential truth of black masculinity lies in the domain of sexuality. In pictures like 'Man in a Polyester Suit' it is the penis and (apart from the hands) the penis alone that identifies the subject in the photo as a black man. Whereas the pictures of gay S&M rituals portray erotic subjects whose sexuality consists of 'doing' something, black men are defined and confined to 'being' sexual, they just 'are' nothing more or less than sexual.

This ontological reduction is worked through the specifically visual codes brought to bear on the construction of the image – the black male body is processed through the artistic genre of the Nude which thus presents the viewer with a source of erotic pleasure in the act of looking itself. As a generic code established by numerous artistic traditions in the West, the conventional subject of the nude is the (white) woman. Substituting the socially 'inferior' black male subject, Mapplethorpe draws on the codes of the genre to frame his aesthetic reduction of black male bodies to 'beautiful things'. As all references to a social, political or cultural context are ruled out of the frame, this codification of the black body abstracts it and fixes its essence in the transcendental realm of an aesthetic ideal. In this sense, because the aesthetic and erotic idealisation is so total in effect, the images reveal more about what the eye/I behind the lens wants-to-see than they do about the relatively anonymous black male models whose beautiful bodies we see.

Within the tradition of the nude the power relations involved in the construction of the image are effaced by patriarchal associations between masculinity and the active subject of the gaze and femininity as the passive object to-be-looked-at. As Laura Mulvey has suggested with regard to the sexual representation of women in Hollywood cinema[42], the aesthetic reduction of woman's body to the abject status of 'thinghood' is not so much an expression of sexuality as an articulation of male power over the apparatus of representation. Thus objectification not only involves voyeurism – seeing without being seen – it is fundamentally predicated on a certain male narcissism – paintings in the nude tradition abound with self-serving scenarios of phallocentric power in which male artists paint themselves painting a naked woman, a classical mise-en-scene of sexual fantasy in which women are reduced to mirror-images of what men want-to-see. Mulvey argues that the fetishistic structure of mimetic representation is characterised by this fantasy of complete mastery and control of all 'objects' in the artists' field of vision.

In Mapplethorpe's case however, the fact that both subject and object of the look are male sets up a tension between 'active' and 'passive' and this *frisson* of (homo)sexual sameness transfers erotic investment in the power of the look, the desire to master the other, to the site of racial difference. As Richard Dyer has observed, the masculinity of male subjects might be undermined when they are the objects of the gaze, to-be-looked-at by others, therefore numerous supplementary codes and conventions feature in gay porn and the male pin up genre – such as the taut, rigid and straining body pose; clothing details; narrative plot – in order to stabilise the libidinal economy of the look.[43] Here, Mapplethorpe appropriates elements of commonplace racial stereotypes to prop-up, regulate, organise and *fix* the aesthetic reduction of the black man's flesh to a visual surface charged and burdened with the task of servicing a white male desire to look and, more importantly, assert mastery and power over the looked-at.

As Homi Bhabha has suggested, 'An important feature of colonial discourse is its dependence on the concept of 'fixity' in the ideological construction of otherness'[44]. The circulation of mass media stereotypes of black men bears witness to such 'colonial fantasy' in that there is only a rigid and limited set of guises in which black males become visible and many of these constantly repeat and reinscribe *idées fixes* – ideological fictions and psychic fixations – concerning the nature of black male sexuality. As a fantasy of power over black bodies, Mapplethorpe's work engineers artful authority over his subjects by appropriating the function of the stereotype to affirm his own identity as the 'I' of the look, the sovereign, omnipotent eye with mastery over the other – it is as if the photographs are saying, 'I/eye have the power to turn you, you base and worthless social subject, into a work of art'. Like Medusa's look, each camera 'shot' turns the black man's body to stone, frozen and fixed in space and time, enslaved to the white man's imaginary.

This emphasis on mastery is also evident in the imprint of a narcissistic, ego-centred staging of desire which imposes an isolation-effect whereby it is only ever *one* black man in the field of vision at any one time. This is a crucial component of the process of objectification, not only because it pre-empts the depiction of a collective black male body and instead homogenises the plurality of socialised black male bodies to an ideal-type (young, healthy, dark-complexioned) but also because this is the precondition for the fetishistic work of representation in which an absence is made present. Like the function of the solo-frame in pornography, this promotes the fantasy of an unmediated, unilateral, relation between seer and seen.

In the superimposition of two ways of seeing – the stereotype which fixes the flux of heterogeneity, and the nude which sexualises – we see the fundamental ambivalence of racial or colonial fantasy, oscillating between erotic idealisation and anxiety in defence of the imperial ego. Stuart Hall underlines this split in the white eye's perception. For every image of the black subject as a menacing threat, the savage or native, there is an image of the docile and faithful servant or the amusing entertainer and clown. Commenting on this bifurcation, Hall sees this as an expression of

> ... both a nostalgia for an innocence lost forever to the civilised, and the threat of civilisation being over-run or undermined by the recurrence of savagery, which is always lurking just below the surface; or by an untutored sexuality threatening to 'break out'.[45]

In Mapplethorpe's work we can discern three camera-codes through which this ambivalence is re-enacted.

Firstly, as it is most clearly and self-consciously marked, is what could be called the *sculptural* code, itself a sub-genre of the nude. As Phillip pretends to throw the shot-put, the idealised physique of a Greek statue is superimposed on that most commonplace of media stereotypes – the black man as athlete, mythologically endowed with a natural muscular physique and with a capacity for grace, strength and machine-like perfection: well hard. As the major public arena in which black bodies are displayed, sport is a key site of white male ambivalence. The spectacle of black men triumphant in the rituals of masculine competitiveness reinforces the idea that they are 'all brawn and no brains', yet because the white man is beaten at his own game (soccer, cricket, boxing, athletics, you name it) the racialised other is idolised and idealised to the point of envy. This schism is played out daily in the popular press; on the front page headlines black men become visible as muggers, rapists, terrorists and guerillas; uniformly they only appear when framed by negative predicates and connotations. Now turn to the back pages, the sports pages, and the black man's body is heroised, any threat of violence is contained by a paternalistic attitude;

Daley Thompson, Frank Bruno and John Barnes are assimilated to the status of national mascots and adopted pets, they are not Other, they're OK because they are 'our boys'. England's national 'shame' in defeat at the hands of the West Indies team in test cricket is accompanied by the slavish admiration of Viv Richard's 'awesome' physique – the high speed bowler is both a threat and a winner. The ambivalence cuts deep into the recesses of the hegemonic white male psyche – recalls those newsreel images of Hitler's reaction to Jesse Owens at the 1936 Olympics.

If Mapplethorpe's gaze is momentarily lost in admiration and wonder, it reasserts its control by 'feminising' the other into a passive, decorative *objet d'art*. When Phillip is placed on a pedestal his body is literally putty in the hands of the white male artist – raw material to be moulded, sculpted and cast into shape. His body, like many others in this code, becomes pure plastic matter remade into the ideality of abstract aesthetic Form – with the tilt of the pelvis the black man's bum becomes a Brancusi. Commenting on aesthetic differences between still photography and moving pictures, Christian Metz suggests that there is a deep link between photography and death, as a residual 'death-effect' is often invoked by immobility and silence such that, 'the person who has been photographed ... is dead: dead for having been seen'[46]. Here, under the chilling intensity of Mapplethorpe's perfectionism, each black model is made to 'die' if only to reincarnate their alienated essence as aesthetic objects – we do not glimpse a real person, we are not invited to imagine what they are thinking or feeling as they are being photographed, because each body is 'sacrificed' on the altar of some aesthetic ideal to affirm the sovereign mastery of the white man's gaze which has the power of light and death.

In counterpoint, there is a subsidiary code of *portraiture* which 'humanises' the hard, phallic lines. Embedded in a humanist ideology in which the face functions as the 'window onto the soul', this code introduces a realist element onto the scene. But any expressive connotation is withheld by the model's direct look which does not so much assert an autonomous self, but like the remote and aloof looks of fashion models in glossy magazines it emphasises maximum distance between the viewer and the unattainable object of desire. This 'direct-look' does not challenge, it mediates the 'active/passive' tension and is contained moreover by the sub-textual work of the stereotype.

Thus in one portrait the profile invokes the 'primitive' nature of the Negro, the black subject once more subsumed to sculpture as his face is an after-image of an 'African' tribal mask, the cheekbones and matted locks connoting wildness, danger, exotica. In another, the chiseled contours of a shaved head, honed by rivulets of sweat, simulates the criminal mug-shot from the forensic photography of police-records. It also inscribes the anthropometric use of photography, measuring the cranium of the colonised so as to show – via the evident truth of photography – the 'inferiority' of the Other[47]. This is overlaid with deeper ambivalence in the portrait of Terrel; his grotesque grimace immediately connotes the 'happy/sad' mask of the nigger minstrel. Humanised by racial pathos, the figure of Sambo ghosts the scene, reinscribing the black man's supposedly child-like dependency on massa, which in turn affirms the idea that he is socially 'emasculated'.

Finally, two codes together – *cropping* and *lighting* – interpenetrate the flesh and mortify it into a racial sex fetish: a ju-ju doll in the white man's imagination. The body-whole is fragmented into micro-details – chest, buttocks, arms, penis, torso – inviting a scopophilic dissection of the parts that make the whole. Like a talisman, each part is thereby invested with the imaginary power to summon up the whole 'mystique' of black sexuality in colonial fantasy. The camera cuts away like a knife, allowing the viewer's gaze to scrutinise 'the goods' with fetishistic attention to detail – tiny blemishes on the body only serve to highlight the technical perfection of the photograph. Such fragmentation is common in pornographic imagery and certain feminist arguments have proposed the view that this represents a form of male violence, quite literally, that the cutting-up of women's bodies into visual bits and pieces demonstrates the sadistic impulses in men's visual pleasure. Whether or not this argument is tenable[48], its effect here is to suggest a kind of aggression in the act of looking, but this is not 'racial violence' or racism-as-hate, on the contrary, aggressivity as the frustration of the ego who finds the object of his desires out of reach. In this sense the cropping is analogous to strip-tease where the exposure of successive parts distances the object, makes it untouchable, so as to tantalise and arouse the desire that finds its denouement in the unveiling of woman's sex. Except here the unveiling which reduces woman from angel to whore is substituted by the metonymic unconcealing of the black man's private parts, the forbidden totem of colonial fantasy.

As each fragment seduces the eye to ever more intense fascination we can glimpse the dilation of a libidinal way of looking that spreads itself across the surface of black *skin*. Harsh contrasts of shadow and light focus attention on the shining polished sheen of the skin. Unlike the sexual fetish whose meanings are secret or hidden, the racial fetish of skin colour and skin texture is 'the most visible of fetishes', according to Bhabha. Its glossy allure serves a number of functions: it suggests physical exertion – the bodies of black boxers always glisten like steel and bronze in the illuminated square of the boxing ring; or as in porn, sweat acts as a signifier to suggest intense sexual activity, as if it took place 'just before' the photo was taken. Here in Mapplethorpe's images, the spectacular brilliance of black skin is a fixing agent for the fetishism of colonial fantasy; there is a slippage between container and contents as the shiny texture of the black skin is overlaid with the glossy luxury of the high quality print. As Victor Burgin has pointed out, sexual fetishism dovetails with commodity fetishism to inflate the value of 'art photography' – the valorisation of print texture is also part of the allure of glossy fashion magazines[49]. Here the consubstantiality of black skin and print surface also underpins the fact that, as art objects, Mapplethorpe's pictures are also commodity fetishes, fetching exorbitant prices on the international market.

The term 'fetishism' probably connotes deviant or 'kinky' sexuality, calling up images of leather and rubber wear as signs of sexual perversity. This is not a fortuitous example as leather clothes have a sensual appeal as a kind of 'second skin'. When one considers the fascination with black leather it suggests a simulacrum of black skin, an outward extension of an intense curiosity and fascination with black skin among white people. Freud's clinical theory of fetishism as a symptom of perversion is problematic in a number of ways, but the key idea that the fetish is a metaphorical substitute for the absence of the phallus[50] is important and useful because it enables us to understand the splitting of levels of belief such that two logically contradictory thoughts can co-exist in the unconscious. For Freud, the little boy being 'shocked' to see that women do not have a penis like his involves conscious acknowledgement of the fact of sexual, genital, difference but unconscious disavowal, hence, '*I know* (the woman has no penis) *but* (she has, through this fetish)'.[51] Thus alongside 'negrophobia', the fear of blacks among whites, there is a sort of 'negrophilia' manifest in the commonplace white fascination with black skin.

Such a split is captured in 'Man in a Polyester Suit' as the singular central focus on the black phallus both affirms and denies that most fixed of racial myths in the white man's mind: that all black men have got bigger willies than he has. The use of scale in the photo foregrounds the size of the penis which thus signifies a threat; not the threat of ethnic or racial difference per se, but a sexual threat, a source of sexual anxiety that the black man is more 'sexual' and thus more potent than his master. The black man's prick then is a phobic object, a fixation in the paranoid fantasies of the negrophobic which Fanon found in the abnormal fears of his white psychiatric patients and in the normal cultural artefacts of his time; then as now, in front of this picture, 'one is no longer aware of the Negro, but only of a penis; the Negro is eclipsed. He is turned into a penis. He *is* a penis'[52]. His big black dick is a 'bad object', a threat to the purity of white womanhood, to which the white male responds in rituals of racist aggression – the lynching of black men in the United States routinely involved the literal castration of the Other's strange fruit. This myth of penis size amounts to a 'primal fantasy' in Western culture as it is shared and collective in nature, so much so that modern science has repeatedly embarked on the task of measuring empirical pricks to show that it is not 'true'. In post-Black Power America where any public endorsement of this myth would transgress liberal orthodoxy, Mapplethorpe enacts the disavowal of this 'truth': I know it's not true that all black men have huge penises, but in my photograph they do.

This presumably is the little 'joke' acted out in the picture. But more importantly, the racism presupposed by it is effaced and white-washed by the jokey irony of the contrast between the private part and the clothing which consists of a 'cheap', polyester three-piece suit: the opposition of hidden and exposed, denuded and clothed, works around the metaphorical opposition between Nature/Culture that underpins the binarisms of racial discourse. Sex is confirmed as the 'nature' of the black man as his cheap and tacky suit confirms his failure to accede to 'culture': even when the other aims for 'respectability' (the signified of the suit) his camouflage fails to conceal the fact that he originates essentially, like his dick, from somewhere anterior to Civilisation. Finally, the tip of the penis shines: like the patient of Freud's for whom a 'shine on the nose' functioned as a sexual fetish, the totemic object of colonial sex fantasy – skin – is made all the more visible by its shine. Wherever black bodies appear in colonial representation they are saturated with sweat, always wet with sex. Leni Riefenstahl's ethnographic text *The Last of the Nuba* demonstrates the roots of this fetishism – what is shown in her photographs has precious little to do with the Africans' beliefs implicated in their body adornment and display, but like a blank page black skin becomes a *tabula rasa* for the inscription that addresses itself to European sexuality. Riefenstahl admits that her fascination with the Nuba did not originate with an interest in their 'culture' but in a photograph of two male wrestlers by George Rodgers (reproduced, in homage, on the inside cover of the book). As with her other collection, *People of the Kau*[53], the anthropological rationale for her voyeurism is nothing more than a secondary elaboration of the primal wish to see, and re-create, this lost image of desire again and again.

That Riefenstahl made her name as the author of cinematic spectacle for the Nazis suggests that this sexualising and racialising form of 'looking' cuts across gender, as women are as implicated in its fetishism as men. There may be a continuity of sensibility with the aestheticisation of ethnic politics in Mapplethorpe, but to call him a fascist would be pointless, it would only enhance his reputation as a vaguely 'transgressive' and therefore avant-garde author of art photography. It is more useful perhaps to note that in the discourse of his colonial sex fantasy about black male bodies, Mapplethorpe silently reinscribes that form of disavowal found in the most commonplace of racist statements, 'I'm not a racist, but ...'

In looking at these pictures I have been talking about a particular way in which white people 'look' at black people. The fetishistic figuration of the black male subject in Mapplethorpe's photography underscores the cultural politics of *ambivalence* which concerns the strange, uncharted and unknown landscape of the 'political unconscious' of the West in which black bodies function as signs of radical otherness. In revising this essay I'm also more aware of how the ambivalence cuts both ways, that I am also equally implicated in the fascination these images arouse and the fantasies and pleasures they offer. One analyses presumably to achieve critical distance, to break free of ideological interpellations: some of the terms used, 'the white man' or 'the black man' are methodological fictions or common-sense abstractions, constantly returning to the ground from which the analysis seeks to extricate its reading. However important it is to be able to make generalisations in order to open a public discourse on these issues, it is also necessary to account for the inscription of my own desires. The point is – and this is where that feeling of ambivalence and undecidability is most intense – I continue to want to look, *but I still haven't found what I'm looking for.*

I want to 'know' those black men in Mapplethorpe's pictures, but I cannot look the Other in the eye because I'm an-other too: our looks are lost in mutual misrecognition because, as in real life interaction, the possibilities of exchange between black men are always mediated by *our* Other, that abstraction of psychic and social authority we call 'the white man' who is never somewhere 'outside' the self, but as Fanon showed always already 'inside' all of us. The concept of ambivalence is drawn from the theory of Freudian psychoanalysis and yet elsewhere I have criticised this theory for its residual ethnocentrism. How useful psychoanalytic ideas will be for black artists and intellectuals concerned, like myself, with disentangling the complex construction of our diverse sexual/racial identities, is something I haven't made up my mind about. If there are decisions to be made, then this will be the next frontier, a starting point for a new kind of discursive exchange on the reconstruction of the sexual politics of ethnicity.

AIDS, Racism and Homophobia

New Society, 1988[55]

As a new kind of disease AIDS has undermined traditional confidence in the authority of medical knowledge. In the absence of a known cure or a clear-cut 'scientific' explanation, the pre-rational search for someone to blame has taken precedence over rational debate on how best we can protect ourselves. Between 1981 and 1983 there was an awakening sense of anxiety directed mainly at the white gay male community and the response was to perceive the disease as a 'gay plague'. But around 1984/85 when its transmission within the heterosexual population was reluctantly acknowledged, black people were then scapegoated as its 'cause'. When media queer-bashing reached its peak, somewhere around the time of Rock Hudson's death, racism took its place – Haitian migrants were blamed for 'importing' AIDS to the United States; researchers claimed AIDS originated out of Africa; Tory MPs argued for the compulsory screening of immigrants

THIS IS NOT AN AIDS ADVERTISEMENT[54]

parting glances, buddie's friend, tell us of no 'other'
other's tales,
inbetween the gaps, between mirrors and turned away eyes,
the civilising-pleasure-seeking-mission-tourist,
black boys bought for a packet of cigarettes, that exotic other

might just translate

how a small disease in a third world domain
became a first world problem with a little name

this is not an aids advertisement – feel no guilt in your desire
this is not an aids advertisement – feel no guilt in your desire

it's the heart afraid of breaking, that never learns to dance
it's the dream afraid of waking, that never learns to chance

this is not an aids advertisement – feel no guilt in your desire
this is not an aids advertisement – feel no guilt in your desire

some say love it is a razor that leaves your soul to bleed
some say love it is a hunger, an endless aching need
i say love it is a flower and you its only seed

feel no guilt in your desire
feel no guilt in your desire
feel no guilt in your desire
feel no guilt in your desire

this is not an aids advertisement
this is not an aids advertisement
this is not an aids advertisement
this is not an aids advertisement

parting glances, buddie's friend, tell us of no other 'other's' tales
inbetween the gaps, between mirrors and turned away eyes.
being an endangered species may now make me equal with you
this is not an aids advertisement – feel no guilt in your desire
this is not an aids advertisement – feel no guilt in your desire

*dedicated to the memories of mark ashton and lino palmieri

travelling from the Third World. Medical, media and government responses have veered from hysterical moral panic to casual indifference, but rather than come to terms with living with this new disease in our collective eco-system, official responses have consistently amplified a message of fear whose only effective outcome is to reinforce racism and anti-gay prejudice as 'acceptable' outlets for mass anxieties.

Black people are not somehow immune from the media-led hysteria and panic around HIV infection. Indeed where some silently submit to fear or even internalise racist misinformation, our vulnerability is revealed. Such morbid fatalism is as life-threatening as the vitriolic homophobia that seems a more prevalent reaction in some quarters of the black communities. And it was this homophobic response, noisily voiced from the floor by belligerent activist Kuba Assagai, that erupted at the recent conference on 'Racism and AIDS' organised by Brent Council and the London Strategic Policy Unit, held recently at the Commonwealth Institute. In the afternoon I led a workshop on moral panics which was frequently disrupted by the moral panic going on next door! Some men in the 'Women and AIDS' workshop provoked outraged and angry protest as they simply refused to believe that lesbians or gay men exist in the black community – although we were there in front of their very eyes.

If the conference was disappointing and failed to meet its objectives because of this disruptive factor, it nevertheless served an important purpose by publicly highlighting the problem of homophobia in some black people's response to the AIDS crisis. As Ansel Wong, Principal Race Adviser to LSPU, has said, 'It is crucial to confront this issue in an open forum as we have tended to avoid dealing with it up till now'.

Ancient Greeks painted images of their god Phobos on battle-shields so as to frighten away their enemies. In the 'war' against this new disease, where blacks and gays have been labelled as a threat, racism and homophobia activate similar psychological defence-mechanisms whereby people avoid their inner fears by projecting them externally onto some Other. In their book *Aids, Africa and Racism*[56] Drs Richard and Roslind Chirimuuta show how Western media have exaggerated questionable 'scientific' evidence about the reality of AIDS epidemiology in Africa. Media stories of continent-wide pandemics correspond not to available and correlatable facts, but to the racist fictions of preconceived ideas that blacks are, by their nature, dirty, diseased and sexually unrestrained. For example, Robert C Gallo's claim to have discovered the 'ancestral origins' of the HTLV-III virus in the African green monkey was eagerly taken up in the press (despite being to date unproven) because of its neat 'fit' with pre-existing myths of Africa as the Dark Continent – source of every conceivable human misery. Like any fable or just-so story, the identification of an 'origin' or ultimate cause gives a narrative shape and structure to incoherent facts, thus helping to assuage unmanageable feelings of fear.

The rationalisation of the fear of germs through xenophobia – the fear of ethnic difference – dictates discriminatory politics in practice. Restrictive health criteria were first introduced into British immigration law in 1905 in the midst of a major medico-moral panic about the 'degeneration' of the eugenic stock of the English and its implications for Empire. Jewish people were scapegoated then as TB carriers. By the 60s, when the Empire had turned in on itself, a minor outbreak of smallpox among Pakistanis in Bradford in 1966 caused a micro-panic on the part of the British Medical Association who demanded the medical surveillance of black immigrants. This was put into practice in the 70s by the 'virginity-testing' of Asian women.

Clearly there are links between these repressive precepts conducted in the name of 'national health' and the various 'final solutions' for AIDS advocated by the rabid Right such as tatooing, quarantine and extermination. In 1987 *Sunday Sport* even managed to find a Ugandan doctor, one Dr Walton Sempata, who pleaded with their journalist, 'Let me kill my patients'. At the conference these links were spelt out by Dr Frances Welsing of the Atlanta Centre for Disease Control who argued, 'If you do not know what happened in Nazi Germany, you will not understand the AIDS holocaust today'.

Dr Welsing expounded her 'Cress-theory' of white supremacy which holds that, because they are a minority in the global gene-pool, whites have an in-built 'inferiority-complex' which is manifested in the periodical genocide of black and brown races to maintain the ecological balance of the ethnic status quo. Referring to arguments which regard AIDS as the result of bacteriological engineering or germ-warfare experiments, her theory was disturbing and alarming precisely because it sounded so plausible. But Dr Welsing had *no proof* and this didn't seem to bother her at all. The trouble is there are too many such conspiracy theories around and whatever their source they always have the same logic which is to merely reverse the roles of victim and victimiser in the demonology of AIDS. In this case, the racist view which sees blacks as a threatening source of infection is simply turned on its head by the view which sees the evil intentions of 'the white man' as responsible for AIDS. Moreover, all this conspiracy theory is dangerously disenabling; after all if AIDS is the result of a plot – maybe the CIA or KGB are behind it – then what can you or I possibly *do* about it?

The notion of racial genocide has a strong appeal because it appears to be able to account for the fact that black lives *are* being lost to AIDS and Aids Related Complex (ARC) the world over. In some cities in the US where its incidence in the white gay male community has declined, the disease claims more lives from Latino and black women, men and children. This may be due to routes of transmission via intravenous drug abuse or unacknowledged bisexuality or it may be because racism denies minorities equal access to affordable health care services like counselling. Dr Welsing did nothing to help clarify these issues. Rather, by suggesting that condoms sold in black neighbourhoods are deliberately punctured – with no evidence whatsoever – her contribution only exacerbated fears and amounted to a rhetorical abuse of her authoritative status as a medical expert.

The need to counteract racism – 'to clear our name', as one woman in the workshop expressed it – is vital; but it cannot be accomplished by such unsubstantiated speculation which provides an outlet for justified anger but only obscures the more complex issue of how black people have had to cope with myths about our sexuality. The real problem is an implicit 'conspiracy of silence' which inhibits open public discussion of the uncomfortable fact that some of the stereotypes have been internalised within the black communities. The myth of black hypersexuality is one, unfortunately, which many macho men do not want to give up. There is absolutely no reason to suppose that the fear of homosexuality is any more prevalent among blacks than it is in white society, but the limits of tolerance towards gays shown by many black pentecostal and fundamentalist church ministers demonstrates that sexual hypocrisy is not the monopoly of the white establishment either. But, in the current climate of moral panic fomented by the government, this problem is becoming more apparent. In 1986 Caribbean and other minority parents led the reaction against the 'positive images of lesbians and gays' in Haringey schools – and in their campaign against the 'loony left' (Bernie Grant MP is leader of Haringey Council), the popular Thatcherite consensus is all too pleased to recruit black and other minority constituencies into its strategies.

We have to deal with the self-destructive consequences of this sort of persecution politics of scapegoating. As Simon Watney argues in *Policing Desire*[57] one of the fundamental psychic defence mechanisms in the social construction of 'normal' heterosexuality is the *disavowal* of the diversity of human sexuality. There have been and always will be lesbians and gay men in the black communities, but our existence is denied by a conservative sexual morality and a set of overly rigid attitudes which have developed in some black people as an 'over-compensation' against myths of slackness and depravity. Similarly, although it is never talked about, many black people have an almost neurotic obsession with cleanliness, which is not a bad thing, but it has partly developed as a reaction against the racist perception that we are 'dirty'. Above all, there is a parallel defence mechanism operating in the black psyche which says that homosexuality is a 'white man's disease' – paradoxically this merely mirrors the homophobia of the majority society. Thankfully, the avoidance of reality inherent in these attitudes was exposed and challenged at the conference by the presence of the Rev Carl Bean of the Los Angeles based AIDS Minority Project. His quiet confidence emphasised that it is not necessary to know the 'cause' of human suffering to know that people with AIDS need care, compassion and dignified treatment.

Pioneering safe-sex education in plain language to overcome fear, ignorance and loathing in the black community, his assertion of the Christian message of love showed the confidence of the Afro-American civil rights tradition which is sadly lacking here. His optimism about 'self-help' strategies contrasted with the demoralising dependency on local authority funding which char-acterises black voluntary sector initiatives in Britain such as the Black Community AIDS Team (still awaiting funds) and the advice work of the London-based Black Lesbian and Gay Centre. In the context of the wicked assault on civil rights in Clause 28 of the new Tory Local Government Bill, such efforts are now even more vulnerable than ever. With the impending dissolution of London Strategic Policy Unit (one of the last vestiges of the GLC), it will be virtually impossible to implement anti-racist safe-sex education around AIDS and HIV infection because this will be seen as 'promoting' homosexuality.

Antagonisms are intensifying at all levels. When Keith Davidson, headmaster of the all-black private John Loughborough school says he will refuse to 'give gay-sex lessons to his pupils'[58], we have to realise that the struggle against AIDS hysteria is not a simple black and white issue. Where black people are recruited for conservative sexual politics and capitulate to the exploitation of fear and prejudice, we cannot avoid realising that the attempt to censor and silence sensible sex-education is the *real* threat in this struggle as it's only common-sense that information and education is our essential resource in overcoming the politics of fear induced by AIDS.

Notes

[1] See Paul Gilroy 'Cruciality and the Frog's perspective: critical notes on black cultural politics in Britain', in *Emergency*, Spring 1988 and CLR James *The Black Jacobins*, Allison and Busby, 1980.

[2] See Angela Davis, *Women Race and Class*, The Womens Press, 1983.

[3] From film-making – *Territories* (Directed by Isaac Julien, 1984) and *The Passion of Remembrance* (Co-directed by Isaac Julien and Maureen Blackwood), both from Sankofa Film and Video Collective – to readings of Michael Jackson's music video, Kobena Mercer 'Monster Metaphors: Notes on Michael Jackson's Thriller', *Screen* V27 no 1, Jan 1986.

[4] Gay Black Group, *Gay News* no 251, October 1982.

[5] Kobena Mercer, Review article *Emergency*, no 4, December 1986.

[6] Andy Metcalfe and Martin Humphries (eds) *The Sexuality of Men*, Pluto, 1985 and Robert Staples, *Black Masculinity: The Black Male's Role in American Society*, Black Scholar Press (USA) 1982, dist. New Beacon Books, London.

[7] Staples, *op. cit.*, p.2.

[8] See Pratibha Parmar, 'Gender, race and class: Asian women in resistance', in Centre for Contemporary Cultural Studies, *The Empire Strikes Back*, Hutchinson, 1982.

[9] The black male 'hustler' lifestyle is also a focal point for the ethnographic narratives of race-relations sociology, see Kenneth Pryce, *Endless Pressure*, Penguin 1979.

[10] See, 'Concerning Violence' in Frantz Fanon's *The Wretched of the Earth*, Penguin, 1967.

[11] Staples, *op. cit.*, p.62-63.

[12] See Eldridge Cleaver, *Soul on Ice*, Panther Books, 1970.

[13] See Maya Angelou *I Know Why the Caged Bird Sings*, Virago 1985 and Alice Walker, *The Colour Purple*, The Womens Press, 1982.

[14] On the development of the New Right's hegemony over 'law and order' issues see Stuart Hall and others, *Policing the Crisis*, Macmillan, 1978; Jock Young's views on race and crime would appear to demonstrate an ideological capitulation to this hegemony, see his article, 'Striking back against the empire', in *Critical Social Policy*, issue 9, Spring 1984. Alternatively, Paul Gilroy offers an archaeological analysis of the political discourse on 'black criminality' in Ch.2 and 3 of *There Ain't No Black in the Union Jack*, Hutchinson, 1987.

[15] See Andrea Dworkin *Pornography*, The Womens Press, 1981; for a

critical account of this version of the politics of representation see Lesley Sterm, 'The Body as Evidence', *Screen* Vol 25 no 3 Nov 1982; and on archeological connections of race, gender and colonial power, see Vron Ware 'Imperialism, Racism and Violence against Women', *Emergency* no 1, December 1983.

[16] See Pratibha Parmar and Val Amos, 'Challenging Imperial Feminism', *Feminist Review* no 17, 1984.

[17] 'Violence and Sexuality' in Metcalfe and Humphries (eds), op. cit., p. 105.

[18] Michel Foucault *The History of Sexuality, Volume 1*, Allen Lane, 1978.

[19] See special issue of *Ebony* magazine on 'The Crisis of the Black Male', July 1983.

[20] See Frantz Fanon, *Black Skin, White Masks*, Paladin, 1970; Paul Hoch, *White Hero, Black Beast*, Pluto 1979; and Winthrop Jordan *White Over Black*, Norton (USA), 1968.

[21] Staples *op. cit.*, p. 85.

[22] See Errol Lawrence, 'In the abundance of water the fool is thirsty: sociology and black pathology', in CCCS *The Empire Strikes Back*, op. cit..

[23] From 'Collective Statement', Combahee River Collective, in Barbara Smith (ed) *Home Girls: A Black Feminist Anthology*, Kitchen Table/Women of Color Press (USA) 1983.

[24] From Black Film-makers Foundation, New York, NYC; exhibited in Britain in the 'Third Eye' film programme of the Greater London Council, 1985.

[25] Isaac Julien, *Square Peg*, no 16 Summer 1987.

[26] See collective interview with Sankofa on *The Passion of Remembrance*, in *Framework*, no 32/33, 1986.

[27] Isaac Julien, from notes after the conference on 'Black Communities Living and Struggling Together', organised by Lesbian and Gay Black Group, Brixton Recreation Centre, February 1986.

[28] Isaac Julien, *Emergency*, no 4 December 1986.

[29] Isaac Julien and Kobena Mercer, *Ten 8*, no 22 (issue on 'Black Experiences') Summer 1986.

[30] Charles White, *The Life and Times of Little Richard*, Pan, 1984, p.24.

[31] For an examination of how these issues erupted around S&M dress styles at the London Lesbian and Gay Centre, see Sue Ardhill and Sue O'Sullivan, 'Upsetting the Applecart: Difference, Desire and Lesbian Sadomasochism', *Feminist Review* no 23, Summer 1986.

[32] *Before Stonewall: The Making of a Gay and Lesbian Community*, directed by Greta Schiller; dist. by The Other Cinema, Wardour Street, London.

[33] The concept of 'colonial fantasy' is developed by Homi Bhabha, 'The Other Question – The Stereotype and Colonial Discourse', *Screen* Vol 24 no 4, Nov 1983. See also Homi Bhabha's introduction, 'Remembering Fanon' in the reprint of *Black Skin, White Masks*, Pluto, 1986.

[34] See Michel Foucault, *op. cit.* and on 'regimes of truth' see Colin Gordon (ed) *Power/Knowledge: Selected Interviews and Other Writings, 1972-1977*, Harvester, 1980.

35 See Kobena Mercer, 'Black Hair/Style Politics', *New Formations* no 3, Methuen, 1988.

36 See 'Notes on a Native Son', Eldridge Cleaver, *op. cit.*.

37 Cheryl Clarke, 'The Failure to Transform: Homophobia in the Black Community', in Barbara Smith (ed), *op. cit.*.

38 In 'Diaspora, Utopia and the critique of capitalism', Ch 5 of *There Ain't No Black in the Union Jack*, *op. cit.*.

39 Kobena Mercer, in Pat Holland, Jo Spence and Simon Watney (eds) *Photography/Politics: Two,* Comedia/Methuen, 1987.

40 *Black Males* (with an introduction by Edmund White), Gallerie Jurka, Amsterdam, 1982; see also retrospective catalogue, *Robert Mapplethorpe 1970-1983*, ICA 1983 and Robert Mapplethorpe, *The Black Book* (with introduction by Ntozake Shange), Schirmer/Mosel, Munich 1986.

41 Michel Foucault, 'What is an Author?', in *Language, Counter-Memory and Practice*, Basil Blackwell, 1977, p 127.

42 Laura Mulvey, 'Visual Pleasure and Narrative Cinema', *Screen* Vol 16 no 3, Autumn 1973.

43 Richard Dyer, 'Don't Look Now – The Male Pin Up', *Screen* Vol 23, no 3-4, September 1982.

44 Bhabha, *op. cit.*, p 18.

45 'The Whites of their Eyes: Racist Ideologies and the Media', in George Bridges and Ros Brunt (eds) *Silver Linings*, Lawrence and Wishart, 1981, p 41.

46 'Photography and Fetish', *October* no 34 (USA) 1985, p 83-85.

47 Anthropometric photography is discussed by David Green in 'Classified Subjects', *Ten 8* no 14, 1984 and 'Veins of Resemblance: Eugenics and Photography' in Holland, Spence and Watney (eds), 1987, *op. cit.*. On photography as a means of surveillance see Frank Mort 'The Domain of the Sexual' and John Tagg 'Power and Photography' in *Screen Education*, no 36, Autumn 1980.

48 See Ros Coward, 'Sexual Violence and Sexuality', *Feminist Review* no 11, Summer 1982, p 17-22.

49 'Photography, Fantasy, Fiction', *Screen* Vol 21, no 1, Spring 1980 p 54.

50 'Fetishism', in Sigmund Freud, *On Sexuality* (Pelican Freud Library, no 7) Penguin 1977, p 352.

51 As formulated by John Ellis, 'On Pornography', *Screen*, Vol 21, no 1 Spring 1980.

52 Fanon, *op. cit.*, p 120.

53 *Last of the Nuba*, Collins, 1972 and *People of the Kau*, Collins 1976; for a critical appraisal of Riefenstahl see Susan Sontag, 'Fascinating Fascism' in *Against Interpretation*, Dell (USA) 1970.

54 Isaac Julien, 1987: Credits: Music by Larry Steinbacheck, 1987, Bronski Music Ltd, Williams A Buog Ltd, Larry Steinbacheck courtesy of London Records; Videotape distributed by Albany Video, Douglas Way, London SE8 and London Video Arts, Frith Street, London W1V 5TS.

55 Kobena Mercer, *New Society* 5 February 1988.

[56] *Aids, Africa and Racism* is privately published and available from: R Chirimuuta, Brentby House, Stanhope, Nr Burton-on-Trent, Derbyshire, DE15 OPT.

[57] *Policing Desire: AIDS, Pornography and the Media*, Comedia/Methuen 1987.

[58] See 'Lefties Lash School for Ban on Gay-Sex Lessons', *Sun* 16 January 1988.

Getting a Bit of the Other — the Pimps of Postmodernism

SUZANNE MOORE

*If I Was Your Girlfriend Would You Remember 2 Tell Me All
The Things U Forgot When I Was Your Man
If I Was Your Best Friend Would U Let Me Take Care Of U And
Do All The Things That Only A Best Friend Can
If I Was Your Girlfriend Would U Let Me Dress U
I Mean, Help U Pick Out Your Clothes Before We Go Out
Not That You're Helpless, But Sometimes Those Are The Things
That Bein' In Love's About
If I Was Your One And Only Friend Would U Run 2 Me If
Somebody Hurt U, Even If That Somebody Was Me
Sometimes I Trip On How Happy We Could Be
If I Was Your Girlfriend Would U Let Me Wash Your Hair
Could I Make U Breakfast Sometime Or Could We Just Hang
Out Go To The Movies And Cry Together
2 Me Baby That Would Be So Fine
Sugar Do You Know What I'm Saying 2 U This Evening?
Maybe U Think That I'm Being A Little Self-Centred
But I Want 2 Be All Of The Things U Are 2 Me
Surely U can See*[1]

If I was your girlfriend ... so sings Prince on the hit single
taken from his *Sign of the Times* LP. Prince, precocious and
perverse — the perfect Postmodern Man. Slithering

between hetero and homosexuality, blackness and whiteness, masculinity and femininity. Simultaneously embodying a desire that in its urgency becomes disembodied, this song gives voice to an overwhelming want that pays no heed to sexual difference. Until he reaches the place where man and women can really be best friends and more ...

To hell with New Man, here's a True Man – one that can be all things to all women. And just as I'm packing my bags and getting ready to leave for the Promised Land, to this other world, the song ends. And it is only a song and Prince is only a pop star. And anyway he isn't my girlfriend. He isn't actually anyone's girlfriend.

A sign of the times indeed. This strange love song is about a yearning far deeper than simply wanting another person. Like all the best love songs it is about loss, about the self-defeating nature of desire. He wants to assert himself, his desire, his identity at the same time as dissolving away the masculine identity that constricts him. To travel to another place, another country, another identity; to fuse with it, be it and take it over – that seems to be his goal. Far from being the centre of the world, masculinity appears to be just a place on the map.

The dark continent that he wants to visit is naturally the world of the feminine. There lies the key to the perfect union – with himself, with another. But in sensing the possibilities of this kind of gender travel Prince both recognises the limitations of masculinity whilst clinging to them.

These days of course its much easier for all of us to travel – through strange places and other cultures. We try to be polite to the 'natives' and then return with anecdotes about how well we got on with the people. No, we weren't like those other tourists, we really got the feel of the place. We buy a piece of 'otherness' and bring it home to put on the mantelpiece. We didn't steal it, we bargained for it in the market place ... in their language. We were kind and cautious. Colonisation is a cruel word for such harmless holidays.

Yet the whole point about going on holiday is that you

know you are coming back. You may *be* another person while you are away. You may feel different but that is because your identity is firmly established elsewhere.

What I want to look at here is the new kind of gender tourism, whereby male theorists are able to take package trips into the world of femininity. The glossy tourist brochures of contemporary theory offer cut price entry into these exotic places. The land of milk and honey is waiting for you. The price is right. Come on down!

Barthes' Bass Line

'*Myth and Utopia: the origins have belonged, the future will belong to the subject in whom there is something feminine.*'
Roland Barthes in *A Lovers Discourse*[2]

'*Being an incomplete female, the male spends his life attempting to complete himself, become female.*'
Valerie Solanas in *The SCUM Manifesto*[3]

Barthes, like Prince, certainly knows how to whisper sweet nothings in many a feminist ear. At times his work offers us a utopian vision of a world where sexual difference as we know it has disappeared. Bodies simply glide in and out of varying subject positions – sometimes male, sometimes female, sometimes neuter. No more fighting, no more politics, only the body and its pleasures. What a wonderful world it will be …

Barthes' position is by no means unique. Freedom from the 'binary prison' is what many of us interested in sexual politics have been fighting for. A whole feminist culture has been built upon exploring ways of escaping the rigidity of masculinity and femininity. Through novels, plays, films, paintings, this imaginary world of no-man's land has been conjured up. And central themes have been myth and utopia.

Myth and utopia, the past and the future. These are the times when things have been or will be different. What Nietzsche called 'A new way of thinking, a new way of feeling' is envisioned in Barthes' work through the metaphor of femininity. Yet this projection of the past into the future neatly sidesteps the present where there exists actual subjects in whom there is *already* 'something feminine' – women.

What makes Barthes' work so seductive is that he always stresses plurality, multiplicity, fluidity, above the values of linearity and hierarchy. These are the qualities traditionally defined as female. The pleasures he describes in his erotics of reading and writing are those of 'writing the body' – the physicality of human communication. The 'grain of the voice', the 'rustle of language'. His celebration of *jouissance* (bliss, coming),[4] a pleasure so intense that it disrupts cultural identity, where the subject literally loses itself, has come to be seen as a celebration of the ultimate female pleasure. For Barthes writing itself is an essentially Oedipal activity – making love to one's mother tongue. Instead of a phallic morality based on binary opposition, Barthes invokes a sexual pluralism. This emphasis on the pleasure of the body, the link between the mother's body and the mother tongue all resurface in the work of Irigary and Cixous who, unlike Barthes, are concerned with the specific relationship of women to culture.[5]

One consequence of Barthes' rejection of phallocentrism is an essentialising of all that is 'feminine'. As many critics have pointed out the whole problem with essentialism (biology as the source of behaviour, anatomy as destiny) is that it cannot recognise specificity. All women become subsumed into the category of Woman which then comes to stand for a mythical and other worldly space. Barthes seems to think that to enter this world is transgressive in itself but he does not do so unselfconsciously. 'Who knows if this insistence on the plural is not a way of denying sexual duality?' he asks.[6]

But what is at stake here is not his denial of sexual duality *per se* but the denial of women. For if we all share the goal of escaping from this binary prison then part of that escape must involve the acknowledgement of women and their desires. We need neither an idealisation or impersonation of them. The valorisation of feminine pleasure in Barthes' work which is common also to

Kristeva's, Irigaray's and Cixous' writing fails to recognise that female sexuality is experienced differently, at different times, in different cultures.

As Ann Rosalind Jones writes: 'I wonder again whether one libidinal voice, however nonphallocentrically defined, can speak to the economic and cultural problems of all women'.[7]

This recognition of difference, not just of sexual difference but of all the other kinds of difference, has been a continual problem for feminism. Women first realising just how different their lives were from men's experience, were claiming a separateness, demanding a voice, insisting on their own identity. This led to a politics based on identity, on the feeling of authenticity, of at last having found oneself and then of having found others the same as you. Then a new layer of difference disrupted any cosy feminist or gay identity – differences of race, class, age and experience. So difference becomes painful, difficult and unsurprisingly we want to do away with all of it. We dream instead of indifference. We fantasise or theorise a world like that of Barthes – where oppositions no longer exist, where every small difference is simply the starting point for our desire. Stephen Heath describes it thus:

> Difference as desire: no difference, only differences, no one and other, no his-her, man-woman, nor hetero-homo (another difference definition drawn up from the man-woman norm), a new sociality, deferring places, in that sense a utopia.
> But whose desire?[8]

For whether it's Barthes writing about desire or Prince singing about it, the desire in question is, in all its confusion, still *his* desire *their* desire, *male* desire. So what I want to know is this – if Prince wants to be his girlfriend's girlfriend, what does *she* want to be?

Lacan – the lead singer

The work on subjectivity to which Barthes has contributed, has become of increasing important to sexual politics. It is no longer so easy to talk of the individual or the self as an autonomous and coherent unity but instead we have come to understand that we are made up from, and live our lives as, a mass of contradictory fragments. It is paradoxical that a politics premised on identity, on self-assertion, should produce and appropriate theories that undermine the very notion of a secure identity. Yet this is a contradiction that is valuable in many ways as it stops politics becoming the 'other' of theory and vice versa. Feminists began to try to unravel the construction of gendered subjectivity – how we acquire the social characteristics associated with masculinity and femininity – not out of a desire to read lots of complicated books on psychoanalysis, but so that we might find out how we could construct ourselves differently. In other words, to unmake the processes which we feel are oppressive we first have to understand how they work and why they feel so powerful.

This kind of thinking is a direct challenge to the various ideologies which say that men and women are naturally different, that they are born with innate male and female qualities (men as aggressors, women as carers, etc). Instead it questions many fundamental assumptions about what is often regarded as natural or 'just the way things are', and puts social and cultural conditions above considerations of biology.

Some feminists, though, cling to what they see as distinctly female traits, and claim for them both mythical and mystical properties. Women are supposed to be more peace loving and closer to nature. One particularly nauseating example of this is Susan Griffin's book on *Women and Nature* in which she claims that women are akin to cows, goats and even shellfish! Mary Daly, another high priestess of radical feminism, makes similar arguments: every wrongdoing is a symbol of patriarchal power which is monolithic and ahistorical, so that footbinding in China becomes the same as a hysterectomy in Los Angeles which becomes the same as witch burning in the seventeenth century etc, etc.[9] An analysis based on such a scenario has difficulty in dealing with how we might live with men on a daily basis or indeed how anything might actually change. We are offered once more wonderfully utopian visions of a matriarchal future; but by collapsing all women, regardless of race or class, into the category of Woman, we find ourselves faced yet again with an essentialist and essentially patronising view of women.

Rather we need to understand how particular subjectivities are lived at particular times. The recognition that femininity is an ideological construction does not make it possible to simply cast it off as a worn out piece of clothing. It informs every aspect of our lives, our dreams and our fantasies in a way that runs much deeper. Sensing this has led to many theoretical excursions into psychoanalysis in order to provide us with a theory about the unconscious. If we talk about femininity as an ideology then we also have to explain how it actually gets into our heads (and hearts) so that we often seem to be colluding in our own subordination.

Talking about the unconscious has proved as difficult and unsettling as it has productive. Juliet Mitchell's resuscitation of Freud and the influential work of Lacan has problematised not just the question of gender but the whole nature of identity itself.[10] Crucial to these theories is language, language as absolutely central in the formation of gender, as the way that we not only represent ourselves to each other, but as the only way we have of representing our selves in the first place. These discussions about language are more complex than some of the debates about the sexist nature of words themselves, and the power of naming (eg think of the different connotations of master/mistress, or batchelor/spinster), for they question the actual structure – the form of language not just the content.

In Lacanian theory the baby's self creation as a human being involves the perceptions it makes about its body, which are primarily sexual. The baby experiences itself as a mass of drives unaware of the boundaries of its own body. It has to learn to differentiate between inside and outside and so, as Mitchell describes, it is around the openings or gaps in the body (mouth, anus, etc) that meanings cluster, and these become charged with erotic significance. The first difference the baby learns is the absence or presence of satisfaction (of the breast then later the mother) and this difference is the primary difference that is later recreated in language. When the child enters the symbolic realm through the Oedipus complex, it is into a world already structured through language. Language operates as a system of differences, but the chief signifier of difference in our culture, according to Lacan, is the phallus, and therefore the child has to position itself in relation to this. Absence/presence of the phallus/breast thus becomes transformed into feminine/masculine. The baby assumes a gender position, for the only way we can make sense in language is to adopt a subject position by learning to say 'I' – pulling all the fragments together under one name. Yet this nominal identity is always a misrecognition of ourselves as unified, coherent subjects – as the origin of meaning, the speaker of the sentence. Contained within such a misrecognition though is always the reminder of the original loss that caused us to enter the signifying chain (language) in the first place – the first splitting from the mother. It is through language then that the unconscious comes into being and it is in the gap between language and the unconscious (the unconscious comes about because of the repression of desire) that desire exists. In Lacanian theory then desire can never be satisfied as it always carries within its expression traces of the original loss.

From this brief outline I want to emphasise three points. The first is this notion of the decentred subject, the subject-in-process, the subject as a site of contradictions – the 'I' of a dream can be someone else. Unlike the driving ego of some American interpretations of Freud, the ego is 'necessarily not coherent'.

The second is that *if* the phallus is the key signifier of difference, and that's a big if – many feminists have argued cogently against this[11] – then masculinity becomes set up as the norm and femininity can only exist as absence, as what masculinity is not. Of course no one actually possesses the phallus but men are able to make identifications with this symbol in a way that women are not. Femininity thus becomes, as Kristeva argues, that which cannot be represented, that which always remains unsaid – how else can you represent pure absence? And so women become objectified in every sense of the word in order to shore up men's subject position.

Thirdly is this still nagging question of desire. Desire is always desire for the other, the unobtainable – surely not always reducible to desire for the mother? Desire as a concept then is genderless, asexual, neither one thing nor the other. Its expression and object, though, must be, for we have all been through the Oedipus complex and have all learnt the grammar of gender.

Yet obviously men and women enter the symbolic world of language from different positions and always somewhat precariously. To assume a masculine subject position, alongside the phallus as guarantor of authority – as integrated into the symbolic realm – or to take a feminine position, as that which is outside or marginal to it, is not simply a question of biology. For both Lacan and Kristeva show that this feminine terrain of lack, of marginality, is open to men as well as women. It is this mobility of subject positioning that allows access to *jouissance* that is beyond the phallus, beyond man, and that can therefore undermine and disrupt all representation. Feminine *jouissance* then is where the phallus is revealed as the completely arbitrary rather than transcendental signifier of difference – there exists no difference, only differences. But is the unconscious, from which *jouissance* comes, itself gendered? For Lacan the answer is yes. The unconscious is the space of the other, it is woman. 'Feminine *jouissance* is therefore posited by Lacan as an ultimate limit to any discourse articulated by Man'.[12]

Psychoanalysis was itself founded by Freud who listened to the voices of hysterics. Heath describes hysteria as the oscillation between female bodies and male subjects – women trying to find some way of speaking their desire. But Lacan, who Gallop calls, appropriately enough, the Ladies Man, declares himself to be 'a perfect hysteric'. He can speak from the place of a woman though he actually enjoys the power of a man. Like so many of these new hysterics he can claim a feminine subjectivity; so if it's no

longer necessary to be a woman to speak as a woman, how
do you speak as a feminist? Alice Jardine tackles such
questions in her brilliant book *Gynesis*. By Gynesis she
means the putting into discourse of 'woman' or 'the feminine' as a metaphor for all that Western thinking has not
been able to represent.

'In France, such thinking has involved, above all, a rein-
corporation and reconceptualisation of that which has been
the master narrative's own non-knowledge, what has
eluded them, what has engulfed them. This other-than-
themselves is always a space of some kind (over which the
narrative has lost control) and this space has been coded as
feminine, as woman.'[13]

Significantly for us however it is this new rhetorical space
of woman that is 'inseparable from the most radical
moments of most contemporary disciplines', that is perceived as politically revolutionary in its ability to disrupt the
very foundations of our existing order. But what has this
conception of woman got to do with actual women? And
how might it affect our ideas about sexual politics?

For although such radical claims have been made at
various times by feminists of all persuasions, many of the
so called thinkers of postmodernism remain unaware or
truly indifferent to the voices of real women. Indeed why
should they when they have neatly managed to step into the
space of the 'other' without ever having to talk to a single
woman? Why should they be interested in a sexual politics
based on the frightfully old-fashioned ideas of truth,
identity and history?

For if psychoanalysis has problematised identity from the
inside out, then theories of postmodernism have problematised it from the outside in, until it no longer makes any
sense to talk of inside/outside or the subject in society. If
marxism gave us the alienated subject and psychoanalysis
gave us the decentred subject, postmodernism proclaims
the death of the subject – though it seems to have been on its
last legs for a very long time now.

'You make me feel ... mighty real' (Sylvester)

It is both impossible and in a sense improper to try to pin down the term postmodernism to a single meaning or definition, but if anything it can be characterised by a sense of 'profound binary crisis'.[14] Every opposition that is central to Western thought has been blown apart – essence/appearance, truth/ideology, time/space, signifier/ signified, etc. Frederic Jameson describes this as the rejection of all depth models, a sense of the end of everything, while Baudrillard talks of the 'death of meaning' and the 'loss of the real'.

The term postmodernism originates in connection with new styles in art and architecture where the purity of modernism has given way to a plethora of quoted styles and historical fragments that are brought together into a facade that revels precisely in its artificiality. Yet the critic Frederic Jameson sees it as more than a style and refers to it as the cultural dominant of late capitalism. He links it explicitly with multinational capitalism. He describes the feeling of living in a post-industrial society in terms of schizophrenia, dislocation and depthlessness. This schizophrenic 'structure of feeling' is one in which what was once separated into distinct categories becomes blurred. The old boundaries between art and mass culture, reality and spectacle, self and other, have broken down until everything takes on an almost hallucinogenic quality. Our culture, he argues, has become the culture of the image. As the mass media and information technology have come to dominate our lives, image has replaced reality. Our experiences are always mediated by and through images. For instance, the news is now news of soap opera stars, an actor is now president of the United States and we all have the feeling at some time or another of playing a part in a movie scripted by someone else.

Another characteristic of the postmodern experience is the transformation of time into a 'series of perpetual presents'. History, which requires a sense of continuity, has instead fragmented into a vast repertoire of images of the past that can be cut and pasted at will. The tampering with, not of the distant past but of recent history, and the sudden creation of old 'traditions' is something that those of us in Thatcherite Britain or Reaganite America know only too well. The media, whose function it is to turn every thing into appearance, is instrumental in this process.

If political rhetoric is now formed from a cut-up, a collage of bits of the past, this is only possible because what Lyotard calls the 'Grand Narratives' of our culture have broken down. By this he means that the big stories we told ourselves (or were told to us) about progress, science, truth, socialism, no longer seem plausible any more. The idea that things would progress in a predictable and linear fashion has been shattered and been replaced instead by lots of smaller, more localised narratives. In other words these big stories have been revealed *as* stories rather than absolute truths and have become somehow meaningless or irrelevant. In the process through which their narrativity becomes visible they lose their power of legitimation.

Lyotard links this both to a general crisis in representation and to a crisis within scientific thought. He argues that through the commodification of knowledge via information technology, knowledge and power have become two sides of the same coin. Instead of science being self-legitimating it has had to face up to the question, 'Who decides the conditions of truth?'. The notion of objective truth is no longer viable – the observer always changes the outcome of the experiment. The 'value' of knowledge is thus always relative. Instead the exchange value of knowledge/information has taken over from its use value and it becomes the new commodity form. An obvious example is trading on the stock exchange, where actual goods are never exchanged but merely information about them.

This questioning of the status of knowledge and of the dissemination and legitimation of certain knowledges above others, are implicitly feminist concerns. For if it is true that the Grand Narratives are breaking down, the question we have to ask this time is not whose desire, but whose grand narratives? And what will replace them?

Grand narratives, narratives of mastery, master narratives (you take your pick according to both translation and position): Jardine reads Lyotard's crisis of legitimation as implicitly gendered, as 'the loss of the paternal fiction'.[15] For Baudrillard this crisis is not just the explosion of the master narratives into smaller particles, but the folding in of all meaning on itself. The sign system itself is in crisis. The fundamental distinction between the map (representation) and the territory (reality), between signs and what they refer to in the real world, has broken down. He cites four successive phases of the image:

> It is the reflection of a basic reality
> It masks and perverts a basic reality
> It marks the *absence* of a basic reality
> It bears no relation to any reality whatever: it is its own pure simulacrum.[16]

So signs are no longer tied to one-to-one relationships with their referents, but have become adulterous, producing illegitimate offspring wherever they go – pure simulacrum. Meaning is carried weightlessly around this circuit which is no longer involved in exchange with the real, instead, in this 'liquification of all referentials', signs refer only to each other and reality becomes redundant. The threat of illegitimacy has undermined the paternal fiction – for these bastard signs reproduce amongst themselves, not knowing or even caring who their father was. In a system that is based on exchange, as is our system of representation, a system which rests on the Law of the Father, two things undermine it more than any other – illegitimacy and incest. So if the postmodern condition is for Lyotard linked with a crisis in the authority of the father, it is also for Baudrillard about the loss of the transcendental signifier (the phallus, God, Man) as guarantor of meaning.

But does this withering away of the phallus and its power have different implications for men and for women? For if as Lacan argues women enter the signifying chain in a position of lack (of the phallus), then what can it mean to be told that this negative relation is in fact the

condition of humanity? Does it mean that desire
unrestrained by a binary morality (having or not having)
can be released? And is this untrammelled flow actually
liberating? For whom? Men, women or both? It seems to
me then, that we have to stop talking as though this crisis
was somehow universal and neutral, and ground it more
firmly in the terrain of sexual politics; otherwise it does
what so much philosophy does and simply ignores or
subsumes both questions of sexual difference and political
practice.

Here, though, I want to say a couple of things about this
whole concept of 'crisis' itself. Firstly whether there *is*
actually a crisis of/in representation is still debatable. What
is certain however is that there is much representation of
the crisis (including this essay!) In fact so much
contemporary theoretical work takes for granted this
notion of crisis, that it has become almost the new
transcendental signifier. Maybe this is because, as
Umberto Eco says, 'Crisis sells well'. He goes on to say:

> But even admitting the considerable age of the crisis, I still
> don't understand what the hell it means. I cross the street on a
> red light, the cop blows his whistle and fines *me* (not someone
> else). How can this happen if the idea of the subject is in a
> state of crisis, along with the sign and reciprocal?[17]

Secondly, if there is a crisis, is it symptomatic of the
breakdown of everything as we know it – including
capitalism and 'patriarchy'? Or is it in fact simply a
by-product of capitalism readjusting itself? This question
is important if we want to pursue any political possibilities
– for, in much of the so-called postmodern work, going
with the flow, so to speak, is seen as a more positive
strategy than trying to stop it.

For example, the letting loose of the primary impulses
of desire, the 'Becoming – woman' that Deleuze and
Guattari[18] describe in their work, may not necessarily be
detrimental to capitalism. This metaphor of becoming
woman – the necessity of entering a feminine subjectivity
in order to have access to the *jouissance* of the maternal

body – is a way of 'being' sexuality that escapes sexual difference (that does not pass through the Oedipus complex). So even women have to 'become woman' in order to express desire that is free of the constraints of gender. The becoming-woman of the male subject is an osmosis into the space of the minority of the other. Woman acts as the place and the boundary of this otherness, but in this process she will lose her identity as the boundary is permeated. As her terrain is taken over, all boundaries dissolve and so in turn she is able to 'reterritorialise' what was once 'Man'.

Yet it may be argued that this dissolution of all boundaries produces a kind of psychosis that is absolutely necessary for capitalism to reform itself. As Dick Hebdige comments,[19] the ideal consumer is now the 'psychotic consumer' – completely decentred, unanchored and irresponsible. The model of consumption that had at its core the sexually repressed worker has given way to a new consuming subject. Stuart Hall describes this historical process that started to take place after the Second World War as the 'libidinisation of consumption'.[20]

Hebdige writes: 'The Ideal Consumer as extrapolated from a barrage of contradictory interpellations from advertising billboards to magazine spreads to T.V. commercials, is a bundle of conflicting drives, desires, fantasies, appetites'.

In real terms we can see that consumption is being redefined as an activity that is suitable for men – rather than simply a passive and feminised activity – so that new markets can be penetrated. More products are being aimed at young men and shopping is no longer a means to an end but has acquired a meaning in itself.

So far then I have suggested that much postmodern theory seems to be about a shifting in the position of masculinity, an uncertainty about manhood, a loss of faith in patriarchal authority. It comes then as no surprise that the strategies for living in this brave new world are 'feminine' ones. Baudrillard's work is particularly interesting in this respect, so let's look at it more closely.

Baudrillard – A Different Drummer?

'I consider woman the absence of desire. It is of little import whether or not that corresponds to real women. It is my conception of femininity.'

Jean Baudrillard[21]

In Baudrillard's world, reality is mediated by the image, it has become replaced by a system of simulacra. At times this simulation of reality appears more real than real – hyper real. In this strange place truth melts into falsehood and the imaginary into the real until no one can tell the difference any more. In a parallel move to Lyotard, who discusses the commodification of information, Baudrillard describes the ultimate commodity fetishism of the image. The exchange value of signs, freed forever from fixed meanings, from their use-value, is what enables simulation. So for Baudrillard meaning is no longer produced or consumed but *simulated*. As Meaghan Morris points out, the work-ethic and the theory of value enshrined in the marxist concept of production gives way in Baudrillard's work to this model of simulation.

The word simulation comes from Plato and refers not to a replica of something that actually exists but to an identical copy for which there has never been an original. According to Baudrillard, for instance, Disneyland is a simulation, but its function in proclaiming its status as unreality is precisely to make the rest of America look real. So if everything has become for Baudrillard a 'precession of simulacra', simulation becomes a technique for getting by. No longer should we oppose this by looking for some underlying reality or fighting for truth – instead we should actively participate in the simulation – take it to the limits, as it were. We should push everything as far as it will go, into excess, into 'hyperlogic'. As in much of his work, the concept of reversibility comes to replace that of opposition.

Well, of course, simulation as a technique for living or even understanding is incredibly problematic in many ways, but I want to again discuss this question of sexual difference. For who are already experts in simulation if not women? Femininity itself has come to be understood as existing only in and through representation, as constructed discursively rather than as being a reflection of some inner state of being. Femininity is the perfect simulacrum – the exact copy of something that never really existed in the first place. There are strong correspondences here with the psychoanalytic concept of femininity as masquerade. There is a decidedly postmodern feel in the blurring of essence and appearance, in Joan Riviere's essay 'Womanliness as a Masquerade', written in 1929, in which she describes womanliness as a mask. Stephen Heath comments:

> In the masquerade the woman mimics an authentic – genuine – womanliness but the authentic womanliness is such a mimicry, *is* the masquerade ('they are the same thing'): to be a woman is to dissimulate a fundamental masculinity, femininity is that dissimulation. The masquerade shows what she does not have – a penis – by showing the adornment, the putting on of something else.[22]

This showing of what she does not have is what, for Irigaray, makes the masquerade a way of women participating in male desire at the expense of their own. For the question remains in these dizzying spirals of inauthenticity, where is female identity? Where is female desire? If femininity is the perfect simulacrum, what happens if women refuse to play this game? Heath describes the failed masquerade as in fact hysteria – the hysteric 'misses her identity as a woman'. Simulation (what Morris fittingly calls 'the ecstasy of making things worse') as a technique, then, has very different consequences for men and women. In a sense it is what women have always been doing, still do. Their refusal to play this game (or their decision to play it according to their own set of rules) has come about through the political impetus of feminism and has often led to them being denounced as hysterical.

But for Baudrillard the feminine is only ever lack, only ever appearance. That is the only truth. Feminism, which in many ways refutes this, which says women have identities, women have desires, is for Baudrillard fighting a losing battle, for the power of the feminine lies in this superficiality rather than in chasing after the falsehood of depth. Or to put it another way the postmodern condition has always been women's condition. Yet because he has no coherent theory of power relations, Baudrillard cannot conceive that this is far from the ideal position.

His hostility to feminism is made even more explicit in his theory of seduction. Seduction is always in reality an oscillation between activity and passivity – you let yourself be seduced, you actively play the passive role. For Baudrillard seduction is not just a leading away from truth, an adulteration of production, it is the only truth. This is of course contradictory, for if the value of seduction is that with its artifice and superficiality it always undermines truth – then how can it be the truth? In an essay called 'French Theory and the Seduction of Feminism' Jane Gallop dissects Baudrillard's position with a scalpel sharpened by feminist frustration. If seduction is a threat to the masculine world, which he defines as against appearance, then how come he is in a position to tell women the whole truth about it? As usual he places himself above sexual difference and from this lofty position advises women how best to combat masculine power:

> Now, woman is only appearance. And it's the feminine as appearance that defeats the profundity of the masculine. Women instead of rising up against this 'insulting' formula would do well to let themselves be seduced by this truth, because here is the secret of their power which they are in the process of losing by setting the profundity of the feminine up against that of the masculine.[23]

So women instead should listen to what he says, be seduced by him! As Gallop wryly comments, 'A line if ever I heard one'.

The whole principle of seduction is that of reversability – the ability to swing one way or the other. So the best way to be seduced is also to seduce. Reversibility again replaces the concept of opposition, but Baudrillard, though he wants to seduce feminism, will not let himself be seduced by it, so he ends up making the kind of irreversible and absolute statement that he wishes to undermine. When it comes right down to it, for all his talk, he doesn't want to go both ways.

In another piece he writes:

> Imagine a woman who faints: nothing is more beautiful, since it is always at one and the same time to be overwhelmed by pleasure and to escape pleasure, to seduce and to escape seduction.
> Please follow me.[24]

No thank you. This ridiculously Victorian idea of a woman who swoons with pleasure, who is corpse-like and beautiful, betrays Baudrillard's reputation as a thoroughly modern man. I have never met a woman who fainted with pleasure – these days if people pass out it's usually because they feel sick!

This conception of femininity as passivity occurs also in his book *In The Shadow of the Silent Majorities or the End of the Social*. The title itself is interesting, for although he describes the masses as the silent majority, historically there are in fact lots of different silent or silenced majorities/minorities. So while the 'end of the social' may be good news for him, what about all those fighting precisely to be accepted within it?

The masses, which he nonetheless refers to as an undifferentiated body, are, he says, no longer interested in socialism or liberation but know somehow instinctively that 'a system is abolished only by pushing it into hyperlogic ... You want us to consume – O.K. let's consume always more and anything whatsoever: for any useless and abysmal purpose'.[25]

Hyperconformity is for him 'an impenetrable simulacrum of passivity and obedience, and which annuls in return the law governing them'. This silent mutiny of the masses is a 'fantastic irony' which he says is 'akin to the eternal irony of femininity'.[26]

So again Baudrillard follows the path of least resistance and his ecstasy in this is obscene – obscene is another of his buzz words referring not to the obscenity of that which is not usually seen but instead to the 'obscenity of the visible, of the all-too-visible'.[27] It seems as if in his role of the disappearing theorist sitting and watching the demise of Western civilisation, he somehow believes himself to be outside the processes he describes. Otherwise how can he tell us about them or why would he want to? If the 'masses' are so wonderfully annulling that which governs them, why do they need a Baudrillard to chronicle their strategies or give away their secrets? Surely that old-fashioned and deeply romantic separation of the critic and society, the outsider and his/her culture, is one that he cannot sustain. This separation has been attacked from many directions – marxism, feminism, structuralism, post-structuralism, psychoanalysis, and within the physical sciences as well. Indeed opposition to such a notion is central to anything that we might call postmodern thought.

Still, I suspect that Baudrillard for all his talk, in his heart of hearts does not really want to disappear, though he subscribes to the art of the disappearing theorist. One can view his work as an example of what he is describing – it is a simulation of theory, that always self-implodes, that is always seductive. It is an elaborate game and he says he likes gambling. Gambling is a favoured metaphor because, he says, there is always a sense of forgetting oneself involved. In gambling, he says, money becomes detached from social reality – one becomes seduced into a game of pure appearance in which a sort of metamorphosis occurs. The transmutation that occurs is the goal of his methods of seduction and simulation – a coming through to the other side: 'Becoming-animal, becoming – woman. What Giles Deleuze says about it seemed to me to fit perfectly'.[28] Gambling, a perfectly masculine metaphor, always presumes that you have something to gamble with. Money as social reality, rather than appearance, a sense of worth, of value, these are luxuries for some people. You can only play Baudrillard's game if you have something to play with. Baudrillard prefers to sit, paralysed, hypnotised, but amazingly not struck dumb, by the spinning of the roulette wheel.

Something Wild

'What are you going to do now that you know how the other half lives? I mean the other half of you?'

Lulu in *Something Wild*

So far I have been trying to describe how the theoreticians of the postmodern subject seem also to be describing their own crises about heterosexual masculinity. Rosa Braidotti asks the crucial question about this:

'I wonder what it is that makes them want to embark on this sudden programme of de-phallicisation? What is being exorcised by male thinkers in the act of their becoming 'feminised'?'[29]

To this I would answer that what is left out, what is not spoken about, is the uncomfortably prickly notion of power. Male power. In deciphering the language of the 'other' and then claiming it for themselves, these theoretical drag queens don the trappings of femininity for a night on the town without so much as a glance back at the poor woman whose clothes they have stolen.

In these theories psychic space becomes the primary site of inquiry until it almost subsumes any social context. This is the true 'end of the social'. It then becomes almost impossible to talk about social relations (and of course politics) except in a kind of totally abstract but crude way. Power is always the power of the mother, the phallus, the signifier, the simulacrum and so on. And yet Foucault, who describes power in a far more complex way – as a fine network of relations rather than as a possession – is useful here, for he also insists on the materiality of discourse. In other words, ideas are always embodied in the particular discourses and institutions which produce them, in all our ways of writing and speaking. That these theories repress the actuality that men are in a position of power over women means that this power can go unchallenged and resurface elsewhere. The silence about such matters is deafening. This is not to say that feminists or the left should ignore such theories and hope they go away. On the contrary I think it is crucial that we engage with them, use them, exploit them completely for our own ends ...

One of the ways we can do this is to look at how the mechanisms that I have described operating at a theoretical level can also be seen within popular culture.

Much of our enjoyment of music and films often seems to be bound up with experiencing something other to our daily lives. This 'getting a bit of the other' seems also to depend on women as the gateway to the other world, but increasingly black people and black culture is used to signify something radically different. Some kinds of 'otherness' remain just too threatening to be colonised in this manner – homosexuality for example seems to be seen as far too disturbing and difficult to offer this kind of escapism.

Escaping from, or at least exploring the constraints of, masculinity is a common theme of what the press has dubbed the 'Yuppy Nightmare Movie'. This whole sub-genre of films offers men at least the kind of nomadic subjectivity that allows a masculine identity to be dissolved only so that it may be resumed and reassured by the end of the film. *After Hours*, *Blind Date*, *Blue Velvet* and *Something Wild* are all examples of this. Judith Williamson's excellent review of *Something Wild* in the *New Statesman* made explicit what such a film might tell us about the male psyche.[30]

The plot of *Something Wild* starts with the kidnapping of a nice middle executive (Charlie) by a 'wild' woman (Lulu) for an afternoon of exotic sex. So begins Charlie's voyage into a whole other world and the souring of a classic male fantasy. Throughout his voyage this other world is signalled largely through blackness – black cultures and black music. At various points in the film we see rappers, ghetto-blasters and gospel singing. But although Lulu has facilitated Charlie's entry into this world, by the middle of the film she has become a pawn between two men – Charlie and her psychopathic ex-husband Ray. In fact the central relationship of the film is really between Charlie and Ray or perhaps at a symbolic level between Charlie and the repressed aspects of himself. Though forced into a passive role by the outrageous Lulu (not simply sexually – he also finds himself caught up in her lies to her mother), as soon as another man appears on the scene Charlie has to prove once more that he is in control, that he is man enough to fight and more importantly to win. One of the twists of the film is that Lulu's appearance is only a masquerade. She reveals herself later as Audrey – a much more 'ordinary' woman.

This theme, that of masculinity having to face up to its darker side is one that is shared with *Blue Velvet*. Here too a similar plot structure is used – two men are brought together through their relationship with a woman. In both *Something Wild* and *Blue Velvet* this is made visually explicit in shots where the good man and the evil man are literally mirroring each other. As Charlie knifes Ray, they stand for seconds facing each other. Their similarities rather than their differences are apparent. There is a comparable shot in *Blue Velvet* where naive college student Jeff comes face to face with the terrifying Frank. This caricaturing of innocence and evil, which occurs in both films, is carried all the way through *Blue Velvet* which operates with a series of simplistic oppositions – pretty-pretty suburbia versus inner-city decay, night versus day, virginal romance versus sadistic sex, purity and horror, and so on. As Jeff makes his Oedipal journey into the underworld, in this cartoon psychoanalytic drama, it soon becomes clear that these two versions of masculinity, the dark and the light, are really two sides of the same coin.

The catalyst that brings these two halves together (Charlie with Ray, Jeff with Frank) is the female character. But both Lulu in *Something Wild* and Dorothy in *Blue Velvet* end up as pawns in the struggle between the two men. As Judith Williamson writes: 'the gateway to the other world/underworld/innerworld is women or more explicitly sex with women'.

As with the theories that I have been discussing, the world of the feminine becomes a way of men exploring, rejecting or reconstructing their masculinity, of 'getting a

bit of the other' at the expense of women. At one point in
Something Wild, Charlie has to buy new clothes in a gas
station. He ends up literally dressed as a tourist in shorts,
cap and a T-shirt which says 'Virginia is for Lovers'. As with
the gender tourists of post-structuralism and postmodernism, he returns back home to a familiar environment and
his own clothes, respectable once more. Wild woman Lulu
has also now been turned into prim Audrey – who now
knows her place and in a reversal of the beginning of the
film hands him the keys to her car, lets him drive and sits
demurely in the passenger seat.

Although the insecurity of identity that these films offer
is pleasurable, it can also be unsettling if security is not
restored by the end of the film. It is thus inevitable that
these wild women either have to be revealed as basically nice
girls or punished in some way or another – look at what
happened to Simone, the black prostitute in *Mona Lisa*.
Lulu can be something wild but ultimately not so wild as to
actually threaten the underlying order of things. Something really wild is the Glenn Close character in *Fatal
Attraction*, in which the whole horror of the feminine is
unleashed in the form of this monstrous witch woman who
challenges and destroys all that is secure.

I wanna be black

> *I wanna be black I wanna be a panther*
> *Have a girlfriend named Samantha*
> *Have a stable full of foxy little whores*
> *I don't want to be a fucked up middle class college student anymore*
> *I just wanna be black*
> *Wanna be like Martin Luther King*
> *Get myself shot in Spring*
> *And lead a generation too*
> *I wanna be black*
> *I wanna be black like Malcolm X*
> *And cast a hex*
> *Over John Kennedy's grave*
> *And have a big prick too*
> *I just wanna be black*

> Lou Reed[31]

Lou Reed's song, a parody not of blackness but of white people's perception of it, is apt when we come to looking at another way of getting a bit of the other. For if women's function then is to represent those parts of themselves that men cannot speak about, blackness also increasingly becomes a signifier of authenticity, of naturalness, for white men no longer so sure of their own identities. Black music is often seen simultaneously as both authentic and rebellious. Soul music, especially if it is at least twenty years old, has now been reinstated as some kind of truth in a world full of artificiality. Its sound is organic rather than machine made. The fatal irony is, though, that this expression of self-assertion, of pride, was a form of resistance against oppression; although these songs were part of an historical struggle to claim an identity, they are now being used as the soundtrack for an identity based on consumption of everything from jeans to lager. Removed from their historical context, their 'otherness' becomes more marketable.

Obviously black music is not a unified entity but is full of different musics, and at the other end of the spectrum from soul is hip hop – the music of the 80s. Unlike soul, hip hop can be read as being about the fragmentation of any identity whatsoever. Simon Reynolds, in his music criticism, maps postmodern theory onto popular music with interesting results. He argues that if soul is about the Grand Narratives of truth, progress and morality, hip hop and house have abandoned their narrative structure for a different beat that dispenses with storyline altogether. Time is chopped up into Jameson's 'a series of perpetual presents' rather than bound by linear narrative structures. Much of this music is literally machine made and does not have a wholesome, warm or reassuring sound to it. Instead it is made of shattered fragments and contradictory voices. On top of all this is often blatant, almost paranoid, aggression – the rappers message 'I can do everything better than you'. Frequently criticised for its glowering sexist lyrics, this music may tell us a lot about masculinity. If things seem to be breaking down, or feel insecure, it is the male ego that will fight its way to the forefront with its mean self-assertion at the expense of everyone else.

This is a music born originally of poverty, of desperation, so maybe it's wrong to read it in terms of the individual psyche, but what does it mean to the white youth who dance to it every weekend? How does a different social context alter its meaning?

Reynolds, who prefers hip hop to soul, writes:

> To the oppressed, the cry 'I am somebody', the struggle to become the subject of your own life, has resonance. As someone who's been brought up to be aspiring, motivated and in command of myself, I'm fascinated by failure; I get my fix from cultural representations of self-squandering, drift and dispersal. Strong voices don't reach me, broken voices do.[32]

Postmodernly ironic (which means never having to say you're sorry), Reynolds tells us here that his pleasure is in this 'otherness' which for him is somehow the Real Thing. Whether blackness, like femininity, represents authenticity or disintegration is not the question. It is the way that they are always defined in other people's terms that makes them an object rather than a subject.

Williamson asks at the end of her review of *Something Wild*; 'For if sexy women and laid back blacks can be made to stand for repressed facets of the middle-class psyche – what of their own social reality?'[33]

Exactly. Irigaray asked a similarly 'scandalous' question of Lacan – yes, but is woman the unconscious or does she have one? When confronted with postmodern theory we still have to keep asking these questions for the coming together of what Gallop calls 'theory and flesh' will only be possible when female desire is recognised. If the whole question of power cannot be tackled, it is because these new hysterics with their male bodies and optional feminine subjectivities cannot speak of a desiring subject who is actually a flesh and blood woman.

Flesh, blood, power – these have become the really dirty words. Mention them to your postmodern man and he will try to change the subject. But the subject never can be changed until these issues are addressed. It's not enough to lay back and think of Baudrillard and fake a good time – instead ask yourself, Who's fooling Who?

Special thanks to Lorraine Gamman, Janet Lee and Shelagh Young.

Notes

[1] Lyrics from 'If I was Your Girlfriend' by Prince, Warner Bros Music Ltd, 1987.

[2] Roland Barthes, *A Lovers Discourse*, Jonathan Cape, London, 1979, p 14.

[3] Valerie Solanas, *SCUM Manifesto*, Black Widow, p 6.

[4] The French word *jouissance* has no single corresponding word in English. It is sometimes translated as bliss, ecstasy or coming. In Barthes book *The Pleasure of the Text*, he describes the two parallel pleasures that make up our enjoyment of a text – *plaisir*, which is linked to cultural enjoyment and comfortably reinforces the identity of the ego, and *jouissance*, a much more violent pleasure that dissipates cultural identity to the point of discomfort and which unsettles the subject's relationship to language and representation. So our pleasures come from both experiencing the consistency of self-hood and its collapse.
Toril Moi in *Sexual/Textual Politics* (Methuen, 1985) notes the differences between Barthes' use of *jouissance* as loss, as where 'the subject fades to nothing' and Cixous, who uses it to mean plenitude, where contradictions will be resolved within the Imaginary.

[5] For a good introduction to the work of Luce Irigaray or Helene Cixous see Toril Moi's *Sexual/Textual Politics* (Methuen) or *New French Feminisms*, Marks and Courtivron (eds), Brighton, Harvester 1980.

[6] Roland Barthes, *Roland Barthes*, trans. Richard Howard, Hill and Wang, New York, 1977, p 69.

[7] Ann Rosalind Jones, 'Writing the Body: Toward an Understanding of L'ecriture feminine' in *The New Feminist Criticism*, Elaine Showalter (ed), Virago, 1986, p 371.

[8] Stephen Heath, 'Male Feminism' in *Men in Feminism*, Alice Jardine and Paul Smith (eds), Methuen, 1987, p 22.

[9] See Susan Griffin's *Woman and Nature, The Roaring Inside Her*. The Women's Press, 1984

[10] Juliet Mitchell, *Psychoanalysis and Feminism*, Penguin, 1984.

[11] See for instance the work of the Woman Take Issue group or Alice Jardine's *Gynesis*, where she questions why the phallus should be *the* signifier of difference. She asks why not the breast or something else? p. 139.

[12] Alice Jardine, *Gynesis, Configurations of Woman and Modernity*, Cornell University Press, 1985, p 167.

[13] *ibid*, p 25.

[14] *ibid*, p 39.

[15] *ibid*, p 67.

[16] Jean Baudrillard, *The Precession of Simulacra in Simulations*, Semiotexte, New York, 1983, p 11.

[17] Umberto Eco, 'On the Crisis of the Crisis of Reason' in *Travels in Hyper-Reality*, Picador 1986, p 127.

[18] See for instance Deleuze and Guattari, *On the Line*, especially 'Politics' by Giles Deleuze, Semiotexte (New York), 1983.

[19] Dick Hebdige, 'A Report on the Western Front: Postmodernism and the "Politics" of Style' in *Block*, Winter 1986/1987.

[20] Stuart Hall, 'Reformism and the Legislation of Consent', CCCS Working Paper, Birmingham.

[21] Jean Baudrillard, 'Forget Baudrillard. An Interview with Sylvere Lotringer', in *Forget Foucault*, Semiotexte, 1987, p 95.

[22] Stephen Heath, 'Joan Rivere and the Masquerade', in *Formations of Fantasy*, Methuen, 1986, p 49.

[23] Jean Baudrillard, *De la Seduction*, 1979, p 22, quoted and translated by Jane Gallop in 'French Theory and the Seduction of Feminism' in *Men in Feminism*.

[24] Jean Baudrillard, 'Please Follow Me' *Art & Text*, March-May 1987, 23/4.

[25] Jean Baudrillard, *In the Shadow of the Silent Majorities*, Semiotexte, 1983, p 46.

[26] *ibid*, p 33.

[27] Jean Baudrillard, 'The Ecstacy of Communication' in *Postmodern Culture*, Hal Foster (ed), Pluto Press, 1985, p 131.

[28] Baudrillard, 'Forget Baudrillard', p 75.

[29] Rosa Braidotti, 'Envy: Or With Your Brains and My Looks' in *Men in Feminism*, p 237.

[30] Judith Williamson, 'And the coloured girls go ...' *New Statesman*, 10 July, 1987.

[31] Lou Reed, 'I wanna be Black', Lyrics from Street Hassle, Arista, 1978.

[32] Simon Reynolds, 'Fear of Music', *National Student*, October 1987.

[33] Judith Williamson, *op. cit.*

Boy's Own?
Masculinity, Style and
Popular Culture

FRANK MORT

Imagine yourself on Tottenham High Road on a winter Saturday afternoon. The pavements are blocked, but not with Christmas shoppers. A continuous stream of male youth are making for the Spurs ground. Look once and it might be the rituals of the class played out unchanged since the 50s. Look again. It *is* 1987, not 1957. What has changed are the surfaces of the lads themselves, the way they carry their masculinity. Individuality is on offer, incited through commodities and consumer display. From jeans: red tabs, designer labels, distressed denim. To hair: wedges, spiked with gel, or pretty hard boys who wear it long, set off with a large earring. And the snatches of boy's talk I pick up are about 'looking wicked' as well as the game. Which is not to say the violence is designer label!

From Tottenham High Road to *The Face*. Fashion spreads of Doc Martens and cycle shorts. Dole-style clothes for hanging around street corners. City wide boys and black rappers. Soul boys, wallies and razor partings dancing late night. Soho clubs and metropolitan style. Something is happening to 'menswear'; something is happening to young men.

The rise and rise of advertising and marketing aimed at young men is part and parcel of the current enterprise boom in the service sector and media industries. But what is going on here is more subtle than advertising hype and the profit motive. Young men are being sold images which rupture traditional icons of masculinity. They are stimulated to look at themselves – and other men – as objects of consumer desire. They are getting pleasures previously branded taboo or feminine. A new bricollage of masculinity is the noise coming from the fashion house, the marketplace and the street.

Masculinity and Old Youth

But where do I stand in all this? Why have I suddenly got interested in young men and their commodities? I cannot claim exactly to be a young man. Yet over the last five years I have been drawn into all the paraphernalia of youth style. Haircuts and hair gels, clubbin', hip-hop, rap and of course the explosion of style manuals targeting young men and women; right across from *Just Seventeen* and *Smash Hits* to *The Face* and *i-D*. Friends and colleagues have made some pretty rude noises about my juvenilia, from 'it's only 'cos you fancy the young lads' to 'it's because you (mis)spent your early twenties reading marxist texts about capitalism and class struggle that you're making such a dash for youth culture now!'

It's certainly true that I, along with a fair number of people reading this, am from the tail-end of old youth. For those on the left it was the youth formed out of post-68 politics. The youth that in metropolitan centres like London now often wield considerable cultural as well as financial power. The youth that are at the heart of formal politics on the left and who have been very badly shaken by the collapse of the socialist project.

For women it is the generation who have forged present-day feminism. For men from that generation sexual politics has forced itself into their world view in a major way. Over the last fifteen years men have been asked some awkward questions about the power they hold, their identities, sexuality and desire. One of the biggest questions the women's movement has put to men is this:

how can we negotiate a new settlement around sexual relations, a settlement which problematises men's identities and lays the ground for a different version of masculinity?

Winning the argument about men's need to change means persuading them that they *can* change. In other words, that what we are as men and women is not natural or God-given but constructed socially, by practices and institutions which shape our experience. It also means breaking open masculinity's best-kept secret, forcing men to look at themselves self-consciously *as men*, rather than the norm which defines everything else. And to do this needs more than biting critique. In fact it raises the whole question of the languages on offer to debate masculinity.

Along with theories of patriarchy and a discourse of rights, moral languages have been crucial to the political vocabulary of the present-day women's movement. Especially around the issues of sexuality, pornography and male violence, languages of morality have given women a public voice to raise consciousness *and* make demands of men. But moral discourses can often turn out to be double-edged. While empowering they can degenerate into *moralism*, a politics of 'thou shalt not's' and 'do's and don't's' which preaches only to the converted. More to the point, when moralism has been tied to certain forms of revolutionary feminism the upshot has been a total pessimism on the question of men. Men are thus cast as the monolithic oppressors of women. This comes close to an innate but unexplained essentialism, implying that men are incapable of changing *because they are men.*

Against this we need a more sophisticated account of masculinity – but not one so sophisticated as to let men off the hook! Point one is that we are not dealing with masculinity, but with a series of *masculinities*. Differences of class, race and sexual orientation may be some of the big structures at work here, though we should also be aware of how specifically – and at times contradictorily – masculinity is represented in particular discourses or social practices: work as opposed to the media, education as against popular culture, and so on. This makes visible the

very uneven access specific groups of men have to the
structures of sexual power. But it should not be a recipe
for simple forms of constituency politics, where black men
are produced as a category distinct from gay men,
working-class men and so on. Neat distinctions like these
are blind to the cultural cross-overs, the smudging of
boundaries between identities.

The fact is that individuals do not live out their
masculinity in quite that neat way. As men (and as women)
we carry a bewildering range of different and often
contradictory identities around with us in our heads at the
same time. One of the biggest problems of constituency
politics is that it wants to nail them down to 'real',
quasi-biological entities. Blacks, gays and the rest are
partly symbolic categories, though with real effects on the
way people live out their lives. What is the upshot of all this
for a politics of masculinity? Anybody working on popular
culture knows how awkwardly notions of fixed identity sit
with the fluidity of sexual images represented in fashion,
music, nightlife. There is a continual smudging, as well as
policing, of personas and lifestyles. So point two is the need
for a different set of languages to speak about masculinity
– languages which grasp masculinity as process rather
than as static and unchanging. Such languages do not just
drop from the sky. They have to be worked at, forged out
of what is currently available, however unpromising.

So far, from the men of old youth, two languages are on
offer. Neither of them to my mind is very promising. The
track being scrambled for more and more by men on the
organised left is that men have now learnt the lessons of
the women's movement and that everything is fine and we
can all get back to normal. With the left stuck in the midst
of Thatcherism's third term, expect that sort of argument
to be put forcibly – along with a demand to end
'diversionary politics' and rally around basic 'socialist'
objectives. What it actually means in practice is purely
passive support for feminism. Gender and sexual politics
are cast as women's issues. Men give women the moral
authority to speak, while neatly side-stepping the
implications for themselves.

A second approach is better. It is the version of masculinity put forward in men's groups and sections of the gay movement over the last fifteen years. It does involve men addressing the ways they are written into the structures of sexual power and taking active responsibility for their behaviour. Positively (and this was the argument put forward in the collection *The Sexuality of Men*, 1985) we are told that men need to get back in touch with their own 'alienated' emotions. Consciousness-raising, psychotherapy and interpersonal dynamics can bring men 'closer' to themselves, to each other and to women, by being caring, soft, sensuous and gentle.[1]

While wholly endorsing the stress on responsibility, the 70s new man brand of masculinity leaves me cold. It's not just that I personally don't find these images appealing (and I don't!) I suspect they have nothing to say to men who haven't been through men's groups or the old new left politics. The humanist gloss on feeling, the yearning for coherent identities is narrowly class specific (ie, middle-class) and highly eurocentric. Men whose identities are shaped by Afro-Caribbean or Asian culture, for example, speak of never having been inside that map of coherent subjectivity.

And it is here that the noises coming from the spaces and places of popular culture become important – from the marketplace, the fashion house and the street. If we are looking for a different vocabulary of masculinity, which speaks of some potentially progressive renegotiations of maleness, then we should at least pay attention to the ways young men are representing themselves and being represented in the culture of popular consumerism.

Wolf in Sheep's Clothing? The Rise and Rise of the New Man

Summer holiday 1987. Wandering down the main street of a small town in Crete. Window shopping. Suddenly I caught Nick Kamen staring out at me from a cardboard cut out. Frozen images of the by now famous 'bath' and 'launderette' ads. And behind them, rows and rows of the real thing: stonewashed, blue originals and black denims.

It was a blisteringly hot day but the shop was full. International marketing had made red tabs as 'def' for Greek youth as they were for Soho fashion victims or the lads of Manchester's Arndale Centre.

Opening up young men's markets has been a real feature of consumer trends in the 80s. Whether it's products like 501s or Brylcream, outlets from Top Man to Next, or magazines like *The Face* and *Arena*, advertisers and marketers are hot on the trail of the 16-24 year old male. The so-called new man isn't simply a marketing creation, very few successful trends ever are. But he did become publicly visible through the recent bout of media campaigns for key product ranges. Looking at the images of masculinity on offer and listening to the marketing talk about young men gives us a shorthand way into the sexual politics of the marketplace.

Cladding Britain's bums in denim is big business. Turnover knotches up around £630 million annually, so it's small wonder that the jeans market is hard fought over by all the leading brand names. Levis first traded their red tab, button fly jeans (the 501 comes from the original bolt of the denim) to Britain's youth in the early 1960s. They quickly acquired a cult status and were later to feature in the Victoria and Albert Museum's Boilerhouse show of the hundred best designer products, alongside Swatch watches and Citroen 2CVs. Market challenges from Lee, Wrangler and smaller specialist producers in the 70s brought a marketing rethink from Levis. But their decision to diversify into fashion casuals was disastrous. Jeans manufacturers are notoriously coy about sales figures and turnover, but it was common knowledge that 1981 to 1984 saw a slump in Levis brand share of the UK market. 'Bath' and 'launderette' were to spearhead the company's recovery. Targeting the all-important 16-24 year old male with a four million package in Britain alone, the campaign was meticulously planned.[2] A major TV burst from January to March 1986 was screened between youth viewing slots like *Brookside* and *The Tube* and was backed by a year-long showing at the cinemas. At the same time there was a designer press drive, mingling 501s with clothes by fashion doyens Paul Smith and Jean-Paul Gaultier in *Tatler, Smash Hits* and *The Face.*

The undisputed success of these promos, both in terms of shifting the units (Levis sales rose massively in the year from March 1986) and in carving out a distinctive genre of youth ads has led to a rash of 'me-toos' or copies. Almost every product range has claimed cred with young men and women by mixing a familiar – and increasingly tired – brand of retro imagery, post-modern graphics and Americana. Budweiser beer, Brylcream, Mates condoms, Lee jeans, Ford Fiestas have all had the treatment. So often they score on authenticity with a youth market through precise and detailed use of 50s and early 60s icons: Monroe and James Dean lookalikes, sideboards and pony tails, double-breasted suits and polo shirts. Now suddenly it's the turn of the 70s 'The Decade That Taste Forgot' – reviving flares and platform shoes.[3] But this bricollage of Anglo-American post-war cultural history is no straight copy or nostalgia. And the choice of the 50s and 60s has been no accident (whether 70s revivalism is a passing fad or something more significant remains to be seen). Ironically it is there as the crucial signifier of youth and modernity. Nearer the ground, walk into style venues like Kensington Market in London, or the dole-style of Birmingham's rag market and see the fascination for the culture of thirty years ago. The ongoing success of the jazz revival has got its roots in the same source.

Janice Winship has shown how this retro mood gives today's youth an ironic language to feel their way through the hard times and tight structures of the late 80s.[4] Images of affluence, the first teenagers, rock 'n' roll, are handled with a distinctly 80s sensibility. The Levis ads were a tongue in cheek parody of 50s style. Young men in launderettes – not a common sight then in Britain or the US! Mean and moody looks on inner-city streetscapes reference, albeit in sanitized and glamourised form, unemployment, making one's way in a world in which the young – and now unusually young men – are short on the crucial element it takes to get by in a capitalist society – money. They have only their looks, their style, their bodies

Two images that started it all:
'Laundrette' and 'Bath'.
Naughty Nick Kamen, ex-
Freeman's mail order model;
James Mardle, *The Sun's*
'stud in the bath'.

to display and sell. These are cultural images framed both by recession and by the more fluid sexual scripts of the 80s, rather than 50s affluence and tight gender roles. It's the same message coming through from the (post)feminist mags and ads for young women especially EMAP's *Just Seventeen* and IPC's *Mizz*. A commonsense dolestyle chic for streetwise girls.

The modern cityscape was where our Levis hero was launched. The James Dean type loner; vulnerable and arrogant, soft yet muscular, tough but tender. Nick Kamen played out a real life success story through his role in 'launderette.' Here was the Essex lad, ex-Freeman's mail order model, who got a date with Madonna by selling his looks and his body. But the story lines were really much less interesting than the visual messages coming over about the male body. This is where new man advertising breaks the rules, fracturing traditional codes of masculinity. In other words, it's where marketing imagery enters the realm of sexual politics.

Two features are especially worth noting. First, the fracturing and sexualisation of the male body, condensed around the display of the commodity – the jeans. Cut close-up focus on bum, torso, crutch and thighs follows standard techniques of the sexual display of women in advertising over the last forty years. But now the target is men. More to the point, male sexuality is conjured up *through the commodity*, whether jeans, hair-gel, aftershave or whatever. Though Kamen stripped to his boxer shorts and white socks and 'bath' began with a naked torso, it was the display of the body *through the product* that was sexy. Belt, button-flies, jeaned thighs, bottoms sliding into baths was what made the ads erotic, less the flesh beneath. And so the sexual meanings in play are less to do with macho images of strength and virility (though these are certainly still present) than with the fetishised and narcissistic display – a visual erotica. These are bodies to be looked at (by oneself and other men?) through fashion codes and the culture of style.

Something uncomfortable, transgressive even, is going on in these images. A point the *Sun* picked up early on with its profile of James Mardle, their 'stud in the bath.' Always on the lookout both to incite sex – and police the perverse – its picture spread recouped the new man for normative, 'liberated' heterosexuality. Narcissistic self-pleasure and ambiguous visual erotica had become raunchy hunks with unbuttoned flies, there to turn on 'sexy' women. As one of the captions put it: 'Girls! Is Your Guy a Page 7 Fella'. *Sun* readers were reassured that 'Mr Levi' was very 'mucho macho', as part of its 'hunt for a hunk week'.[5]

Through the autumn of 86 the new man was getting an airing at the popular end of the market. But these media and street-style images had long been claimed for the cognoscenti by *The Face* and the other avant-garde manuals. Here they figured in the bricollage of art, fashion, clubbin' and metropolitan space which gave the lie to the doom pundits who said that nothing had happened since punk. This seemed to be the next big thing. The look was frozen in high fashion plates and in street glances of Soho and Paris' *Les Halles*; a mutant blend of *Face* stylist Ray Petrie's Buffalo look, retro-rockabilly, fashion casualty, US B-Boy. The mix was Levis, flight jackets, DMs, cycling shorts, baseball caps, straw hats, safety pins, car emblems and cartoon characters that changed week by week. Yet as upmarket punters were forced to admit, high street urchins not quite in their Ivy League were into the same game.[6] Tottenham High Road, Newcastle's Cloth Market, Manchester Piccadilly – these other centres of excellence were awash with George Michael lookalikes, a weird mixture of soft profiles with hard edges. They owed a lot to the Burton empire. Though Sir Ralph Halpern was proving himself very much a *man* in the old mould, he had transformed Burtons from a seedy gents outfitters into the Top Man chain. Rows and rows of stonewashed jeans, soft pinks, pale blues and Nike trainers. A young wallies' paradise! While high street boutiques stocked Timberlands, college sweaters and Stone Island tops in pursuit of Italy's Paninaro look.

So the new man is circulating up and down market, as much part of mainstream fashion as the avant-garde,

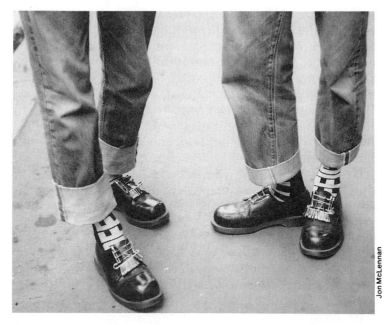

Jon McLennan

there in the dole queue and on the cat-walk. Current menswear is about blurring some of the divisions which have always dogged the fashion industry, perpetuating caste-like hierarchies between style and the mass market. Gaultier titillates haut couture by quoting from street style and gay subculture. Halpern's success story comes out of a similar sort of smudging. The store has picked up on both designer-led and subcultural trends, offering them to working-class youth. It may not quite be Boy George's idea of gender-bending, but the visual reassembly of masculinity through popular fashion has been a hallmark of the last few years. What is common to different ends of the market is the desire to play about with masculinity, to rearrange traditional icons of maleness. Mix 'n' match has got itself a new meaning. That young high street casuals are chancing their arm with their new *toilette* is clear. As one northern entrepreneur put it recently: 'it takes real bottle to wear some of my clothes, like silk boxer shorts at £15.99 a pair. You have to be prepared to put up with the hassle if you want to stand out from the crowd.'[7] Call it just another sort of boy's talk if you like, but in between the blag and the blather is a different language.

And as if this bricollage wasn't enough, circa 1986 in came Next, Woodhouse and the menswear magazines shouting about the return of the suit and classic styling. They were riding on the cultural spin-off of the City's Big Bang and the media-tech industries. But it didn't really matter if you deal in futures or in making the tea, the message was the same: loud pinstripes, wide braces, brogues and double-breasted jackets. Too many pundits have written off these yuppies and sloanes as icons of the new male conservatism – prissy gents or upper-class gangsters. Yet again there was as much a self-conscious playing around with the *idea* of a city gent, even when you really were in the City! We caught glimpses of them celebrating the Tory election victory in the summer of 87, or clutching at their computer terminals a few months later on the City's black Monday. Even here there was the same hyper-cultivation of the male body, a similar narcissism.[8]

So much of what is going on here is part of a visual culture, put together in fashion spreads and ads, street looks and glances. Haircuts, the cut of jeans, ways of walking and being are points of comparison between young men, not now just as aggressive competitors, but as stylists in the same club. They encourage men to look at themselves and other men, visually and as possible objects of consumer desire, and to experience pleasures around the body hitherto branded as taboo or only for women. The effect of all this is to open up a space for some new visual codes of masculinity. What's now cool is not the assertion of a fixed masculine identity, but a self-conscious assemblage of style. Pre-punk, the overriding concern of all youth subcultures was to offer coherent images to young men in opposition to the symbols coming from the dominant culture. In more theoretical language we could say that the epistemology of subcultures was about establishing fixed – and usually male – identities and chains of meaning. You were either a mod, skin, rasta, etc. Punk played about with all that. It upset realist commonsense which said that one thing equalled another: that Swastikas meant you were a Nazi or bondage gear meant you were a pervert. In the world of current youth style the aim continues to be about seeing identities as in flux and stressing a plurality of signification. There is no single, dominant message being pushed amid the bricollage, for: 'We're in the age of micro-narratives, the art of the fragment.' The result is some fairly scrambled messages about masculinity. 'Simply revel in the diversity. Revel in your diversity, say it loud and proud', proclaims *The Face*.[9]

The same noises, the same dissatisfactions with fixed identities are coming from younger gay men who are self-consciously taking up similar icons of style. For a young gay crowd their critique is of the early role model of assertive, out gayness – the now despised seventies clone. Certainly in London pubs and clubs like The Bell or Jungle, biker imagery, high camp and retro rub shoulders together. And there has been a spin off into straight venues. Just as in the late 70s Eurobeat and HiNRG (musical trademarks of the gay man) jumped across to a straight market, so now venues like Manchester's Hacienda club, or certain nights at The Wag in Soho, advertise themselves as mixed. Notice too at these sites how a sort of camp is back in fashion (and not just for a gay crowd). Exaggerated movements, extravagant gestures, hype, are all part of the repertoire.

By Christmas 1986 it had all got too much for the tabloids. Lumping these disparate male markets together, they came up with 'the toyboy'. Pics and tales of young, stylish lads snapped in their boxer shorts; the supposed playthings of older women. As usual the *Sun* led the field, treating 'lady' readers to its 'Good Toyboy Guide' – a list of haunts where these youngsters could be picked up. Clubs, wine bars, trendy clothes and record shops, we were told, all had potential. After all, if 48 year old 'rock granny' Tina Turner could 'boogie the night away' with her 'German hunk', so could any ordinary woman.[10] Toyboys were a distinctive popular response to the new man syndrome. Just as much as *The Face* and *i-D*, in their own inimicable style the tabloids caught hold of something of the cultural and sexual politics of the 80s, claiming them for Christmas fun and popular culture. And anyway, if Nick Kamen did pose in his underpants, Doc Martens and raincoat, with a headband round his right ankle, it was all in a good cause – his career! What enterprising lad wouldn't do the same in Mrs Thatcher's Britain.

Hand-tailored, eight button, double-breasted suit in gaberdine, £250; gaberdine ski-pants, £69.50; belts from £15. All at World Service, Neal Street, Covent Garden, London WC2

'Suddenly it's as if everybody wants a degree in creative shopping':[11]

Popular Capitalism and Young Men's Markets

Ever since the teenager first became visible in the sales-talk of marketers and advertisers in the 1950s, young men and women have rarely been out of sight of the consumer economy. At various points over the last thirty years young men have been high profile in the fashion industry.[12] Carnaby Street in the 60s and unisex slightly later led to the growth of male boutiques not just in 'swinging London' but across the country. As a teenager in Manchester in the late 60s I well remember how important these places were. They provided me with an alternative version of masculinity from the images on the football terraces and in pub culture. So I am not arguing that the 80s new man is totally new. But nor am I saying that nothing has changed. The current syndrome does throw up different *types* of male imagery which are the visual endpoint of rapid shifts in our patterns of buying and selling. For we are not just talking images here: images are underscored by the economics and cultures of consumption. Opening up new markets, more sophisticated design and marketing technologies, above all changing lifestyles – taken together, these have been branded the retail revolution.

Superstores and retail parks in out-of-town complexes. Next, Top Man and the rest on the high street. Sunday trading and arm-chair shopping. These are the forces changing the face of the shopping experience. We are often told that the retail revolution is consumer-led and that retailers are simply responding to new consumer preferences and higher disposable incomes. Certainly where young men are concerned Levis, Brylcream and the rest are part of the sectoral upturn in the fortunes of the British economy. Retail sales have been rising steadily since their trough in the worst recession years of 1981 and 1982 – when the clothing industry was especially hard hit. Record retail sales recorded in 1986 and early 1987 noted fashion and footwear as the fastest growth areas.[13]

Obviously all of this is regionally specific, much higher in the buoyant south and south-east. It is also driven by a quiet revolution going on in work patterns. Direct purchasing from the manufacturer, mechanisation of work routines, franchising – these are some of the technologies of Thatcherite restructuring. One result is the ever growing casualisation of the labour market. More and more part-time youth and female labour that is low-paid, non-unionized and without rights. Another spin-off is the massive boom in credit and loan facilities. Britons are addicted to charge cards and plastic money like no other EEC country. We boast of eleven million Visa and eight million Eurocard holders. Spending on the never-never has never been so acceptable (and so necessary!), rising three times faster than incomes since 1980 and producing its own growth industries – debt-collectors and re-possession merchants. Young men's clothing chains like Burton and Next offer easy instant credit. Students, the unemployed, as well as those of us in work are tempted to buy now and pay later – at high rates of interest.

Marketers may blank out these unspoken conditions of production and consumption, though they wax lyrical about some of the qualitative changes which have ushered in the consumer upturn. They are interested not just in charting rising sales figures or increased profits, the talk is all of shifting *patterns* of consumer spending linked to a rethink by the marketing profession. A designer-led, retail revolution, visually exciting, which responds rapidly to changing lifestyles and consumer demand – these are recurring themes. Rodney Fitch, of Fitch and Co, the consultants responsible for promoting Next, pinpoints the moves quite precisely:

> the consumer is changing. The consumer's ideas, expecta-
> tions and attitudes towards retailing, towards how they will
> buy, let alone what they will buy … are all in a state of flux.
> High street shopping simply mirrors changes in our society
> and demonstrates that you are responsive to them … design
> has become part of these competitive retail strategies. Design
> is a visual thing and therefore the end result is visual
> change.[14]

Two basic concepts ring the changes. One points up the move towards market segmentation and diverse lifestyle profiles. The other underlines the design input, and especially the emphasis on visuals, in the marketing brief. The argument runs like this. The cultural as well as economic splintering of what in the 60s and 70s were solid market blocs – the working class, youth, the housewife, etc – calls for a rethink. The market has filled up with segmented consumer profiles both up and down the scale: C1s, C2s, yuppies, sloanes, the working woman, gay men, the young elderly. A changed situation demands a different type of campaign. This is where the design input comes in. Lifestyle advertising, where the message is more 'emotional' than rational and informational, feeds off design and visual imagery. The idea is to create a mood where consumers experience their quintessential individuality in the product. *Campaign* makes the point that: 'Lifestyle advertising is about differentiating oneself from the Jones', not as in previous decades, keeping up with them.[15] Levis jeans, Dr White's, Saga holidays all work with this brief. Put that simply, it sounds as if the advertising profession had just discovered individualism as a way of selling commodities. Of course, the special, unique *you* has been the staple diet of so many campaigns over the last thirty years, from coffee to cosmetics, from cars to chocolates. What we can say is that the 80s has seen an intensification of that process and proliferation of individualities – of the number of 'you's on offer.

These trends were at work in the Levis campaign. The company took their lucrative advertising account not to one of the corporate giants, but to the 'creative' team of Bartle, Bogle and Hegarty. Hailed as a brave step by the industry (a reversal of the trend towards global domination by multinational agency networks), the choice signalled something quite specific. For BBH are self-consciously 'creative', and by creative they mean more than artistic flair. It is a shift from advertising as an informational medium, with the copywriter and rational argument in dominance, to the growing use of 'emotional imagery', resting on the visual skill of the director.[16] For John Hegarty the whole question of how to speak to the youth market was the big issue in handling the Levis account. Establishing mood, atmosphere and the quality of the image was the thing to crack, as much as the brand of product.[17]

Jon McLennan

Market segmentation: mags for the lads, street-wise girls and the just downright curious.

Across different product ranges the same question surfaces time and again. How to tap the youth market? The marketing industry *is* worth listening to here, not only for its own perceptions of the gendered dynamics of youth, but for the way those perceptions relate to young men and women's lived experience. The impact of recession on teenage spending power along with the tapering off of the baby boom teenagers of the early 60s has sharpened up the issues. Closing in on young *men* has been part and parcel of that process – actually now split into at least two market blocs, the 15-19 and the 19-24 year olds. What are now on offer for these young men are a new set of identities, new individualities, partly produced by consumerism. Next yuppies, soul boys, avant-garde stylists, casuals – these echo the continual media reprocessing of women's images since the war. The new man's mother, sister and girlfriend are all too familiar with this endless visual bombardment; it's part of learning the rules of femininity. But for today's young men this is new, and potentially explosive!

For the industry, the holy grail of the new men's market is the search for a successful lifestyle magazine. When Nik Logan of *The Face* started up his quarterly title *Arena* in November 1986 he was the latest in a long line of hopefuls. In fact, *Arena* was a cautious step in a field littered with casualties. Drawing on financial support from *The Face*, and doubling up with the same journalists, it did launch itself as a lifestyle magazine. But the way they were put together in copy, visuals (and soft porn images of women) plumped for the older, affluent and supposedly more stable 25 to 35 year old market. The continued existence of *Arena*, with estimated sales of somewhere around the 70,000 mark, and the appearance of other titles like *Sky*, *Unique* and EMAP's *GQ*, may point ways forward. But successes are often less interesting than failures, in marketing terms at any rate. Flopped products can give us insights into the cultures of consumption – why and how people buy what they do – which are hidden behind the commodity success stories. This was certainly true with the failed magazine, *The Hit*.

IPC's much-hyped title was put out in autumn 1985, with a burst of TV advertising and an estimated print run of around 190,000. *The Hit* aimed at filling 'an archetypal gap for the fifteen to nineteen year old man who has just outgrown *Smash Hits* and *No 1*'.[18] Spurred on by the success of *Just Seventeen*, EMAP's lifestyle magazine for girls, IPC stuck their neck out:

> Never before has there been a magazine, a paper ... so specifically aimed at 15-19 year old males ... Never before has there been anything like *The Hit*. It's the only music magazine to ZAP the core male youth market between the eyes ... Our initial print run is 350,000, with an estimated settle-down of 190,000 and a ... male readership of 485,000.[19]

In reality *The Hit* was more ambitious than a straight music magazine. A month before the launch IPC's chairman, Ron Chilton, was claiming that imprints like his would soon replace music titles such as *Sounds* or *NME*. Put alongside the specialist press it staked out a broader range of stories and visuals. More ambitious still was D C Thomson's one off trial run for *Hero* tested at the same time. *Hero* dealt in a fairly ruptural version of masculinity by magazine standards. 'Style, Looks, Faces'; 'Living On Your Own Without Mum'; 'Life as a Male Model: another pretty face' were some of the features, together with a short story about a young office-boy's crush on an older, dominant woman sales executive!

The almost total failure of *The Hit* after only six issues prompted some hard-hitting comment from within the industry. What went wrong? The nature of the post-mortem reflected anxieties about the sexual politics of consumption for men. After three weeks of plummeting sales, IPC embarked on exhaustive qualitative research to test readers' reactions. Despite shortcomings on coverage and layout, evidence suggested that the lifestyle concept was correct. What surfaced though were reservations about the potential of general magazines to address young men. As they saw it, the problem was 'social and psychological.' Researchers claimed that unlike girls of the same age (and women in general) who identify strongly with a community of women, young men baulked at being spoken to as a community of men: 'they might like BMX bikes, waterskiing and the Jesus and Mary Chain, but they don't like a magazine to suggest that other men within their age group feel the same way as them.'[20] In other words, speaking to young men *as men* is a risky business, because it targets men in gendered terms rather than the norm which defines everything else. Masculinity's best-kept secret is broken open.

In fact the gloomy prognosis of *The Hit* is a conservative, after-the-event analysis of a marketing flop. The point about the new man marketing explosion is precisely that it *does* speak to men *through their gender* – as a community of men. Whether it's Brylcream, 501s or *The Face*, young men are being dissected as a group with their own culture and problems, from unemployment to youthful acne and hair that won't gel up. Teenage girls have always been singled out in this way. For boys it's new and potentially disruptive.

New to men to be spoken to as a community.

Jon McLennan

Just looking – magazine rack at American Retro, Old Compton Street, Soho, London W1.

Which brings me to the crux of what I'm saying about the sexual politics of the marketplace. The images put out by the advertising and marketing industries are important texts where today's youth – and now increasingly young men – learn about sex and gender. But learning about style and masculinity does not happen in a vacuum; consumers are not just blank pages to be written on at will. For the new man ads to catch on they need to tap into where young men are actually at. In other words, they must get listened to by young men's culture on the ground – on the street, in the pub, club, dole queue, etc. So far we have tended to suggest that the rethink about masculinity is all coming from above. There needs to be a more sophisticated way of handling the marketplace, seeing the relation between consumer capitalism and popular

Constructions of gender is a 2 way process.

experience as a two-way dialogue. And it is in that exchange that a sexual politics is in the making.

The Left and Consumption: a love affair with Dracula?

Whenever I've put arguments like this, one classic, critical response has been to put the anti-consumerist case. With variations, it usually goes like this. What is going on with the new man is nothing or less than a coup from above – the ad men are simply onto a new market. It's part of the same old exploitative logic – profit maximisation – with slick images being pulled into the service of capital. And what's new about any of that. Nothing, if this is the model we take of the consumer marketplace. But does consumption work in quite that simple way? It's an issue which is becoming pretty urgent for socialists, given the ongoing success of Tory popular capitalism. If ever the left needed to grasp the nettle of consumption, it is now.

Sometimes I think that socialism's relation to the market is about as tenable as a love affair with Dracula. Keynesianism and post-war thinking about the mixed economy (consumer freedom plus state planning) did something to put the issue on the agenda. But that was revisionism – the tendency we all loved to hate.[21] No, what walks tall within 'true' socialist culture is a moral anti-capitalism. Marxism and theories of surplus value notwithstanding, it's actually experienced as much as a gut reaction as a worked out theory. No accident then that recent rethinks on the left about consumer demand and service delivery have been confined to those politically right on areas of welfare state provision like housing and social services. Those who have raised the spectre of the consumer market are quickly branded as 'designer socialists', middle-class yuppies hypnotised by the glare of Next and Katherine Hamnett.

The block to left thinking here has a number of causes. But it has a lot to do with the way Fabianism mixed with an older, moralising, evangelical tradition got a stranglehold on socialist culture in the early years of this century. Labour's post-war austerity programme – rationing,

coupons, points *and* the black market until well into the 50s
– carved it in granite on the nation's heart. Austerity may
have been a hit with top-down economic planners, but it was
a dismal failure for consumer democracy. Labour's Chan-
cellor at the time, Stafford Cripps, actually said publicly
that he would prefer it if people's desire for fashionable
clothes or jewellery were eliminated altogether, for good![22]
In the 80s, many on the left seem to imagine that the link
between Thatcherism and popular capitalism is natural and
inevitable, rather than something that has been constructed. Three terms of Conservative government have
bought off the popular classes with an orgy of tax cuts and
consumer durables. The result: political tranquilisation. Or
so the argument goes.

When men are thrown into the equation it seems like a
case of double indemnity. How could the market of all
things be into shifting masculinity in a progressive direction? When did a progressive sexual politics ever come out
of consumerism? The answer is of course never, on its own.
But I don't believe that consumption is simply foisted on
gullible populations by marketing hype and the lust for
profit. It doesn't just come from above; from the ad agencies and the marketing men. *The cultures of consumption are
the point where the market meets popular experience and lifestyles
on the ground.* And this is a two-way process. Marketers and
advertisers within the firm have always known this; that's
why they do such detailed consumer research. It is time left
economists and those working in cultural politics grasped it
as well. Popular cultures of consumption are of course
deeply contradictory. They were continually recouped by a
capitalist view of the world. Yet to fail to recognise their
potential, to ignore that they have anything to say about the
state of popular consciousness is to bury our heads in the
sand. Surely everybody can't be in a state of false consciousness?

Blah, Blah – Boy's Talk

The hardest thing of all to crack is what's going on inside
young men's heads. Reading the signs of change from

glossy appearances may be deceptive. Does the take-up of new man images point to more significant changes in male culture, in the way men see themselves, other men and crucially women? Can these public images feed into a different sexual culture and a new settlement between men and women? Getting to grips with the dialogue between the market and young men means moving 'into the field' in some way or other. Listening to the talk of shop boys, barmen, art students, casuals and the like I have been trying to piece together profiles of what it means to be a young man in the late 1980s. The method is something of an experiment, mixing impressionistic forms of looking and listening with pen-portraits, personal narratives and more standard interview techniques. Not quite the quantitative data and questionnaires of market research, nor traditional ethnography either. As a method, I've been struck by how useful literary genres and codes have proved in catching hold of the constructed nature of masculine personas and the 'true confessions' of boy's talk.

Of course, observing people is also about exercising power. Usually, the power relations weigh heavily against those who are on the receiving end of documentary interest – think of the working-class family at the hands of the 'neutral' professional. But there are reversals. Working with young men points up just how powerful some of the discourses of masculinity are, powerful enough to cut against the authority of the interviewer. These structures tend to work behind your back, policing what can be said and what must remain silenced or inviting participation in traditional buddy contact or sexist camaraderie. The point is to be explicit about all this. What also needs foregrounding is the subjectivity of the interviewer; coming clean about the fact that 'participant observation' is not just a one-way transaction. Interviewing young men draws observer and observed into mutual dependencies and obligations, what I call forms of 'male contract', which can tell us a good deal about the social relations of masculinity. Here are some examples.

Chris

Shopping is a good intro for an interview. At *Review* on the

King's Road, London, I fixed up a meet with Chris. *Review* is all matt black and chrome and polished wood floors. Lots of black too on the clothes rails. But it's not intimidating. The lads don't freeze you out like in the élite venues. A clever mix of designer label with street style.

Chris, 21, ex-working class Brummie, started on the rag market in the city centre. What brought him to London? 'The money and a bit more scope for expansion. There's more business and more of everything down south. Birmingham's so limited.' *Review*'s certainly *not* limited; they get their fair share of fashion victims and City spivs, but plenty of lads who come in off the dole. Chris again: 'A lot of people are hard up, but still manage to look good. And it's like a piss-take really of people who have got the money.'

The chat is about this, that and the other. But I've got to get him onto the personal. And the personal is always tricky. Dialogues like this between men are about delicate negotiations. There's a sort of unspoken male contract – a gentleman's agreement – to respect the niceties, not to break the rules. Sex and the personal are breaking the rules. One way in is through fashion and style.

The innocent opener. 'Do you spend much time on the way you dress?' 'No, not really.' (He's in black denims, denim shirt, Doc Martens.) It's the other lad (beret, white polo, sports jacket and loafers) who gives the lead. 'You do Chris, you do.' We all laugh – conspiratorially. Chris: 'Yeah, I think a lot about what I'm going to put on in a morning. Definitely. But like not to the point where it dominates you, you know what I mean.' Both lads are dead clear about what they wouldn't wear. Mid-market style is not on; Next is anathema, 'they just remind me of office workers'. Chris is into 50s originals, rummaging at jumble sales for the real thing. Mix 'n' match with 80s sensibility: 'It's like getting back to a smart era, clean. I suppose it was a time with a lot of money about.'

What does he do when he's not at work. 'Sleeping mainly. Going to clubs – The Wag, Opera House. Getting drunk and sleeping. The London club scene's brilliant at the moment.'

And prospects. He likes working at *Review*, meeting people. 'It's enjoyable.' (The service ethic – almost feminised.) 'Much better than office work.' Does he have ambition? 'Yeah, I want to work in the business myself ... to go back home and set up.' He's even done the figures: '70,000 straight capital outlay, just to get it going. Smart, designer clothes at competitive prices.' He's sharp on the ins and outs of the rag trade. His plan for entrepreneurial success.

And politics. So *is* he the young Thatcherite then? Not at all – very traditional Labour actually. 'Well Labour, 'cos that's the way I've been brought up and I don't see as it should change.' No time for designer socialism though. 'I don't think it should interfere with clothes. Like this Communist designer thing is the worst thing out. It just takes the piss out of everybody, like what true communism stands for. I don't think it should affect clothes at all. It's making money out of something which shouldn't be made money out of.'

And there it stops, 'cos the other staff are getting agitated and it's back to work. You come away pleased with what you've got, but kind of dissatisfied. The personal/sexual thing is still missing – not repressed exactly, but out of discourse. It's interesting too that I (the 'I' of the interviewer) don't have the power to push this one. Male power doesn't accrue if you declare a hand in the personal.

But maybe this isn't the place to track down personal identities. Maybe it's a mistake to think you can get at the personal through the confessional. Unlike girls, lads' competence is low on talk and chat. Maybe it's as much in the non-verbal things – the spaces, gestures, looks and glances – that identities are staked out.

Urban geographers have been telling us for a long time that space is not just a backdrop to real cultural relations. Space is material, not just in physical terms. It carries social meanings which shape identities and the sense we have of ourselves. For young men (and young women) it is the spaces and places of the urban landscape which are throwing up new cultural personas – on the high street, in the clubs, bars, brasseries, even on the terraces. It seems as if young men are now living out quite fractured identities, representing themselves differently, feeling different in different spatial situations. We may not like all of the net result. But there amid the broken glasses and the buddy talk are some distinctly new profiles.

Christmas 1986. In Soho venues like The Spice of Life it's the festive season. Edwardian pub decor – dark and heavy and a bit seedy. Are seediness and the signs of authenticity what pulls the punters? I fix on a gaggle of young men in Saville Row suits, polo necks and loafers. Shoulders square onto each other, feet firmly planted, gripping pints of lager in straight glasses, laying down the law about this and that. The codes seem dead 'straight', no 'progressive' clientèle tonight. But closer scrutiny picks up different nuances. There's a lot of broad grins and loud laughter as these lads playfully jostle and shove each other, rough each other up, going through the motions of camaraderie. There are also, more tellingly, extravagant disclaimers with hands, shoulders and eyebrows as narratives are interrupted and punch lines clinched. Greetings and partings seem particularly formal – a new rhetoric of manners. Hands are shaken firmly, backs are slapped, more giggling. Mutual glances take stock of clothes, hair and shoes.

There's a lot of assing around and buddy contact in clubland tonight. Gestures which I read at first as macho become at moments exaggerated camp. Like the oversize suits and jackets pushed back off the shoulders. Gaucheness with style seems a positive asset. Uncoordinated jerky movements, slouching, lots of mouth, teeth and even saliva deliberately undercut older codes of masculine assurance.

It's there again the following week at The Bell. The dole-style venue for gays (and their friends). Two lads spend the evening playing around with assing around and buddy love. Immaculate 50s lookalikes, they shove at each other, lager cans in hand, knee each other's balls, then giggle and extravagantly embrace, only to bite necks and gob in each others face. At midnight they gallop onto the dancefloor, getting down to hard funk and rock 'n' roll. A choreography of masculine emblems self-consciously replayed as love between men.

Jon McLennan

Jon McLennan

Jon McLennan

Urban topographies for the fashionable and famous: 'What a magnificent spectacle this fashionable boulevard presents… These fashions, these thousand carriages of all shapes and sizes drawn up along the street… the café de Paris and Tortoni's whose open windows display by the light of a thousand chandeliers a crowd of men and women eating cream and iced fruits… these adorable particles which drift from all those dresses and costumes scented ten times a day by the art of Tessier and Chardin'. (August Luchet, *Esquisses dédiées au peuple Parisien*, 1830)

New Man 1988 style: Jeremy at Boy, Soho, London W1.

Conclusion

Progressive texts? And if so, progressive for whom? That
brings us back to the wider issues of sexual politics. At the
outset I posed the question in terms of a new settlement
around sexual relations: a settlement which makes
masculinity self-conscious and in doing so puts the issue of
male power firmly on the agenda. Looking and listening to
the new man we can see at once how partial the changes
are. It is too easy to get utopian here. For in the images, as
on the ground, many of the traditional codes of
masculinity are still in place. The newly sexualised male
body can turn out to be nothing more than the old form of
male exhibitionism. Anyway, in pubs or clubs 'looking
wicked' could be a prelude to: "Ere mate, do you want to

make something of it', as much as a statement about sexual ambiguity. Notice too how often our progressive hero is played off against stereotyped images of women. In the Levis promos it was the sweetheart, the fat lady, the harassed mum and the giggling girls. Freedom for the new man may be the freedom to stand outside conventional masculinity, but it is the freedom to be without/above women – to go it alone like in the standard male romance. So it doesn't follow that the moves now being made by young men are necessarily progressive *for women*. The two things do not move neatly in sync.

Yet before we run to rubbish it all as just another tired re-run of male power – another stylish tune on an old theme – we ought to think about where we ourselves are speaking from. It may just be that young men and women are already renegotiating their personal and sexual relations, renegotiations which have been made via the gains of feminism, but also through the changes in market culture and probably most important of all the impact of AIDS. Old youth is amazingly quick to expose the cultural politics of the 80s as sham and sell-out. Part of that distrust may be genuine. But it also stems from an uneasy feeling of having the ground cut from under your feet, of no longer having things quite on your terms. Style-led sexual politics is a case in point.

So the issues thrown up here are not only about a politics of gender, but one of *generation*. About how sexual and socialist politics listens to and learns from younger men and women whose expectations and life-chances have been put together in Mrs Thatcher's decade. From what we know of the new man, I have more than a hunch that the market is going to have to be in there as part of the left's 'big idea' for socialist renewal.

Thanks to Nicholas Green, Robert Kincaid and second year BA Fashion students at St Martin's School of Art for their helpful comments on this piece.

Notes:

[1] See especially the introduction by Andy Metcalf and Vic Seidler, 'Fear and Intimacy' in Andy Metcalf and Martin Humphries (eds), *The Sexuality of Men*, Pluto, 1985.

[2] 'Bartle Bogle plans record Levis push', *Campaign*, 18 October 1985.

[3] See Ian Penman, 'All Content and No Style'; David Toop, 'Too Much of Everything', Jon Savage, 'The Way We Wore', all in *The Face*, no 94, February 1988, p 58-67.

[4] Janice Winship, 'Back to the Future', *New Socialist*, no 40, Summer 1986. See also her: 'A Girl Needs to Get Street-Wise; Magazines for the 1980s', *Feminist Review*, January 1986, p 25-46.

[5] 'Girls! Is Your Guy A Page 7 Fella?' the *Sun*, 27 March 1986, p 16-17.

[6] 'Chillin' (Not Illin')', *The Face*, no 87, July 1987, p 60; also '1986 The Year In Review', *The Face*, no 81, January 1987, p 68.

[7] Geoffrey Beattie, 'Changing Gear', *The Guardian*, 16 November 1985.

[8] For the most visible signs of 'new man' masculinity in the City, visit the Futures Market opposite the Bank of England in the City of London!

[9] For the impact of postmodernist bricollage on 80s youth culture see Dick Hebdige, 'The Bottom Line on Planet One', *Ten 8*, no 19.

[10] 'Tina, 48, Turns On With Her Toyboy', the *Sun*, 28 November 1986, p 11; also 'The Good Toyboy Guide', the *Sun*, 27 November 1986, p 9.

[11] Janet Street Porter, *South of Watford*, London Weekend TV, 25 March 1988.

[12] For an overview of post-war male consumerism see Jon Savage, 'What's So New About The New Man?' *Arena*, Spring 1988, p 33-39.

[13] 'Retail sales surge to record', *The Times*, 6 August 1985, p 19; 'Sharp rise in retail sales', *The Times*, 17 March 1987, p 21.

[14] 'Designs on the new consumer', *Marketing*, 24 October 1985, p 20.

[15] Stuart Bell, 'Communications Irony that is Killing Off the Copywriter', *Campaign*, 24 April 1987. See also: 'Classifying People – are lifestyles threatening demographies?' *Campaign*, 3 April 1987.

[16] Stuart Bell, *ibid*.

[17] 'How heritage will be used to relaunch a Levis classic', *Campaign*, 29 November 1985, p 39-43.

[18] 'The Hit: Why it failed so miserably to reach its male target',*Campaign*, 15 November 1985, p 15. See also: Steve Taylor, 'Magazines for Men: on the trail of the typical British male', *Campaign*, 29 August 1986, p 41-44.

[19] 'The Hit', *Campaign*, 6 September 1985.

[20] *Campaign*, 15 November 1985, p.15.

[20] For major revisionist statements which discuss consumption as part of the wider economic debate about the mixed economy see: CA Crosland, *The Future of Socialism*, Cape, 1956; Crosland, *The Conservative Enemy*, Cape, 1962; Roy Jenkins, *The Labour Case*, Penguin Special, 1959.

[22] Sir Stafford Cripps, Budget 1949: Budget Speech, 6 April, in Public Record Office, T 171/399.

The Great Pretender: Variations on the New Man Theme

ROWENA CHAPMAN

'I've just met a wonderful man. He's fictional – but you can't have everything'

Mia Farrow in The Purple Rose of Cairo

'He can't help acting on impulse', trills the perfume ad, as a disembodied hand thrusts a posy at an unsuspecting female; all boys are thus characterised the hopeless dupes of romantic fantasy, mere slaves to the caprice of their olfactory systems.

Paco Rabanne man saunters through the park, shrouded in the early morning mist, kicking up the leaves as he goes. A well cut DJ caresses his manly chest, a loose black tie languishes beneath his chiselled jaw; suppressed mirth plays over his face at the memory of last night's romantic assignation. He passes a junk shop and catches up a chair, twirling it round in a playful replay of the previous night's joyous romantic tryst with that special him or her. In the late twentieth century Launcelot has been reborn. Romance and all its attendant retainers has become the prerogative of men as well as women.

Child of our time, the new man is all about us – rising like Venus from the waves or Adonis from the shaving foam, strutting his stuff across posters, calendars, magazines and birthday cards, peering nonchantly down from advertising hoardings, dropping his trousers in

225

the launderette. He is everywhere. In the street, holding babies, pushing prams, collecting children, shopping with the progeny, panting in the ante-natal classes, shuffling sweaty-palmed in maternity rooms, grinning in the Mothercare catalogue, fighting with absentee mums and the vagaries of washing machines in the Persil ad.

His aquiline features and well rounded musculature have become a common denominator of the 80s, a sign of the sexual times. A potent symbol for men and women searching for new images and visions of masculinity in the wake of feminism and the men's movement. The new man is a rebel and an outlaw from hardline masculinity, from the shirt-busting antics of the Incredible Hulk to the jaw busting antics of John Wayne. He is an about-face from that whole fraternity of the Right Stuff, from Eastwood to Stallone, with their staccato utterances and their castellated emotions.

Feminism pathologised masculinity in a way hitherto unprecedented, and lay at its door guilt and responsibility for everything from nuclear war and pollution, to rape, incest and high heels. Its attempt to radically reconstruct femininity meant that the fallout was inevitably registered on the other side of the gender divide. However, whilst the new man may well have provided some useful role models for those redefining their masculinity, he is also the recipient of almost universal obloquy. He is an ideal that even the most liberated men would never lay claim to, except in tones redolent with irony. Women are irredeemably cynical – 'the same old wolf in designer clothing', 'you can't assume that the new man is a feminist man, he's just more narcissistic'.[1] Polly Toynbee, writing in the *Guardian*, offered the most conclusively damning: 'I have heard tell of the new man. For many years now there have been books and articles proclaiming his advent, even his arrival. I have met women who claim that their sons will be he, or that their daughters will marry him. I have met men who claim they are he. False prophets all, the new man is not here, and it does not seem likely that we shall see him in our lifetime.'[2] But why? Why when he seemed to promise so much has he delivered so little?

The Macho and the Wimp

The first thing to say about the new man is that he is a reaction; he presupposes an old man against which he defines himself as other. In this way he is illustrative of the classic dualism which is endemic to patriarchal thinking, providing a masculine counterpoint – the macho and the wimp – to the feminine duo of the madonna and the whore. The Macho is representative of traditional armour-plated masculinity from Bogart to Bronson, a whole panoply of atomised and paranoid manhood wreaking order through destruction; its apotheosis is the figure of Rambo, bare-chested and alone, wading through the Vietcong swamp, with not even a tube of insect repellent for comfort. Give this hard-nosed, hard-headed agenda, the new man was an attempt to resolve some of the obvious contradictions of the Classic Macho, to recognise and make peace with the feminine within itself, in response to feminist critiques.

In the dizzying world of sexual politics it was all stations change on the love train. If women were changing then so were men. Gone was the emotional illiteracy of the past, gone was all that nasty stereotypical role playing. If the old man was characterised by his abhorrence of all things female, the new man was invigorated by his enthusiastic embrace of female roles and qualities. He knew his Borsch from his Brioche, he could dangle junior on his knee while discussing the internecine convolutions of 'our relationship'. Tough but tender, he knew his way around a Futon, and could do more than just spell clitoris. Not for him the Wham-bam-thank-you-mam thrust of the quick fuck. He was all cuddles and protracted arousal, post-penis man incarnate, the doyen of non-penetrative sex. He abandoned a lifetime's belief in the myth of the looroll fairy, did his share of the household chores, ironed tramlines into his own shirts, and could rustle up a chicken chasseur, with an extra portion for that 'surprise' guest, when 'she' brought the Boss home.

He prioritised love and relationships over personal ambitions and promotion. He eschewed egotism, greed and the magnificent seven, in favour of caring and sharing with the partner of his choice. So he could be forgiven for preening himself in front of the mirror, which he passed by more often. And if the bathroom shelf groaned under the weight of his toiletries, that was a small price to pay for his repudiation of the role of the distant patriarch and old-style parenting. There was something charming in his wholehearted acceptance of himself as a sexual object, embracing narcissism with open arms, and just a touch of aftershave. He was the post-modern dandy worrying about the cut of his strides and fretting about the knots in his shoelaces. And he fitted perfectly into an advertising market which was increasingly concerned with lifestyle marketing rather than particular products.

The narcissist and the nurturer

In the 80s this latter manifestation – the narcissist – has come to dominate our perceptions of the new man. Some would argue that he was never more than a gleam in an ad man's eye, just one more nasty con-trick by the mendacious magician of consumer capitalism, an opportunity to exploit the buying power of the pink pound, and the widening recognition of female sexuality.

But there was something deeply suspicious about the enthusiasm with which the new man was taken up by the media, as he cloned and reproduced himself in the pages of glossy magazines and on celluloid. If he was so revolutionary why was he so rapidly assimilated and so easily quantifiable? Images of feminism have not stepped beyond the hostile viragos of tabloid fiction, and have made barely an inroad into conventional advertising stereotypes; 'the feminist', in a society reliant upon heterosexual complementarity is hardly the Belle for Paco Rabanne man's balls.

On the other hand, attempts to pass the new man off as pure media hype simply will not do. Because it is clear that, in stereotypical form at least, he exists – pouting and preening from the pages of men's magazines. And if he exists in the fantasies of ad men he exists in flesh and blood; advertising reacts to social trends, it doesn't create them.

The rise and rise of the new man coincided with developments in advertising which were moving from product-based to lifestyle advertising. More sophisticated market research and advertising techniques were developing in tandem with the search for new markets, and research was uncovering changes in male/female roles. Men were more likely to be single, and as such they were carrying out a whole range of household tasks which had previously been considered the preserve of women.

In the industry, the young male market had always been considered difficult to crack, because shopping and consuming had traditionally been regarded as female activities and thus incompatible with masculinity. Moreover, in order to sell products, advertising had to sell men, to capture them between the covers of designer magazines. And the process of doing that rendered them the recipient of the gaze, passive and therefore female.

Two contemporary developments helped to propagate the new man in his incarnation as consumer, and they were also the genesis of the tensions which were eventually to split him into nurturer and narcissist. One was the emerging discourse around masculinity in the 70s. This was fuelled by feminism, which increasingly characterised masculinity as pathological, and also by the changing patterns in family life. These changes were expressed in the language of the men's movement, with its readiness to engage on female terrain, and its attempt to get men to open up their emotions and to embrace female subject positions. All of this helped to feminise men, which in due course removed some of the obstacles in their path as consumers.

The other development was the rapidly proliferating style culture which codified 'a consensus shorthand male image ... short-haired, polo-necked, be-501d, derived straight from Soho 85 ... disseminated through the pages of such magazines as *i-D* and the *Face*'[3] The style press and the style culture provided an acceptable standard of male representation, which made it easier to target and advertise to. It also legitimated consumption as standard practice for 'right-on' men, and they were not only comfortable with, but positively welcomed its gaze.

The original new man welded together the possibilities of the nurturer and the narcissist into a flawed whole; but in reality the new man was always an uneasy mixture. And the tensions began to emerge with the increasing importance of advertising in propagating the ideal of the new man. With its emphasis on artifice, on style over content, it caused a fragmentation in the image that the new man presented to the world. A narcissistic interpretation of the new man, with its stress upon style and personal consumption, could more easily and more usefully be assimilated into the prevailing consumerist ethos. The fragmentation of the new man highlighted the composite nature of his identity which was the result of the merging of different historical traditions.

The 70s witnessed an explosion of interest in humanist psychology in the US. Led by gurus such as Fritz Perls, it preached a doctrine of growth and self fulfilment which imploded directly on to feminism and the men's movement. This was hardly surprising since all three shared a common language of growth and liberation from constraint, and many of their concerns intersected. Feminism and men's liberation, taking their cue from the new psychology, came to characterise machismo as a form of arrested development, and encouraged men to get in touch with their emotions and the irrational, to cast aside the mask which was masculinity, in search of fulfilment and liberation. The emphasis was on self development and relatedness, men's relationship to their lovers, their children, their friends and other men. The nurturer ideal was the perfect culmination of this discourse.

It was picked up in the mainstream by women's magazines such as *Company*, and *Over 21*. In particular, *Cosmopolitan* provided the ideal nesting ground for the caring/sharing man, with its rhetoric of equality and choice, and its construction around the formula of the career woman. The new man of humanist psychlogy was the perfect partner for ambitious women who needed a wife, not a husband, if they were to survive in the business jungle. After all, what the female executive really wants is 'Men who'll listen and be there at the end of the day. Men who'll soothe, cherish, share the chores, as well as the social and sexual pleasures. They are men who recognise that what women do is as important as what men do.'[4]

The nurturant new man slipped easily into a magazine whose familiar territory has always been sex and the emotions, and which even had its own pop therapist, the cuddly and moustachioed Tom Crabtree. *Cosmopolitan* has done more than any other periodical to disseminate the ideal of the nice new guy to a wider audience, particularly significant since 25% of its 360,000 monthly circulation is male.

The sheer scope of its male readership was an invitation to exploitation, and in 1984 *Cosmopolitan* set about cornering a new market with the launch of its sister publication *Cosmo Man*. Like *Options* and later *Elle* it was to be offered in conjunction with the main title, which would give it a readymade audience from which it was hoped it would expand to become an independent journal. It was also hoped in this way to overcome the problems which had habitually bedevilled attempts to capture the male market in general interest magazines. Similar publications flourished on the continent but floundered in Britain on the familiar rocks of the feminisation of consumption.

In the event *Cosmo Man* failed, but its failure is instructive. Two years later the *Face*'s inspirational and stylish *Arena* had cracked open the market. And there was a significant metamorphosis in the first issues of *Cosmo Man*. The original idea had been to provide a publication which presumed an extension of its existing male readership, ie, emotionally literate and fluent men, who were devoted fathers and lovers. But it rapidly developed an ethos in marked contrast to the prevalent tone and gender assumptions on *Cosmopolitan*. It began to focus more clearly and exclusively on a yuppie male with a substantial disposable income, preoccupied with status and the sterile trappings of success. The nurturant tadpole had become a narcissistic toad.

Arena on the other hand had no such crisis of identity, located firmly in a narcissistic tradition which dates back to the 50s and the inception of *Playboy*. Its success was predicated on a synthesis of the *Playboy* ensemble, updated and informed by modern debates around sexual politics and consumer culture.

A Hefner editorial of 1953 speaks to the same educated and self conscious audience as its latter day counterpart: 'we enjoy mixing up cocktails and an hors d'oeuvre or two, putting a little mood music on the phonograph and inviting a female acquaintance for a quiet discussion of Nietzsche, Jazz and sex'.

Arena is clearly part of a tradition of masculine hedonism, with its emphasis upon conspicuous consumption and life-style, its array of masculine centred commodities, its intelligent and knowing prose, and its delineation of a precise hedonistic etiquette. Not to mention its exclusively boy's own culture, its all male stable of contributors, and its assumption of a young single male audience with an income to dispose of. Nevertheless, it does depart from *Playboy* orthodoxy in two major areas, firstly in addressing itself to debates surrounding consumerism and cultural politics, and secondly in its ambivalent presentation of women. Crude titillation is conspicuous by its absence, yet the advertisements and fashion pages still resort to women as props often in blatantly sexist ways, and as a visual short-hand for heterosexuality. This ambivalence is extended in the text, which performs a delicate balancing act running articles on sexual politics alongside old-style misogyny.

Revolting men

So far I have described these two ideals of the nurturer and the narcissist as distinct and different categories; Barbara Ehrenreich, in her book *The Hearts of Men* suggests a way they can be brought together. She outlines a trajectory of male revolt from the 50s onwards, which materialised in a number of forms, and was to transform masculine identity. She argues boldly and cogently that the 50s male ideal was the breadwinner. Men were encouraged to marry early (average age 23) and to take on the sole support of a wife and family. A whole panoply of professionals were enlisted to persuade men that the breadwinner ethic was the only normal state for an adult male, and that the achievement of maturity necessitated the successful completion of a number of 'life tasks' namely marriage and fatherhood. Failure to complete these tasks was incompatible with adult masculinity; those who failed were characterised as either not fully adult, or not fully masculine. Not surprisingly, this cultivated a climate of rigid conformity and pronounced homophobia.

Hefner's *Playboy* represented a challenge to this ethic, with its propagation of the doctrine of escape from conformity and whole-hearted embrace of hedonism. For *Playboy* was about far more than just the sexual objectification of women. It encompassed and legitimated a whole alternative lifestyle, encouraging a sense of 'membership in a fraternity of male rebels', which was counterposed to the stifling conformity of 50s masculinity.

Its ebullient heterosexuality thus became a tool in the promotion of a litany of hedonistic consumption, a crucial factor in enabling it to rebel against the prevailing ethos of masculinity without being labelled homosexual. At first sight there could be nothing more in line with american culture than to preach a life of pleasurable consumption. However, in the 50s a new consumer ethic was only just beginning to emerge, centred on the nuclear family. Laudable masculinity was organised around an ideal of manhood which promulgated conformity and self-denial. The latter was inherent in the role of breadwinner, denying oneself in order to provide for wife and family. In this scenario men earned, and women spent. Moreover, the breadwinner ethic, constructed on a repressive denial of homosexuality and emotional rigidity, was synonymous with a 'hard' masculinity which was antithetical to consumerism.

By contrast, Hefner advocated a revolt from responsibility and discipline and the support of women and children. In an age dominated by the breadwinner ethic he urged men to enjoy the pleasures that women had to offer without becoming financially involved. *Playboy* outlined a rebellion from marriage and responsibility, and a utopian vision defined by consumer commodities.

In this way Ehrenreich sees it as the first in a long line of male rebellions against the breadwinner role which continued throughout the counterculture of the 60s and the new psychology of the 70s. The cumulative effect of these rebellions was to legitimate a consumerist personality for men. 'What had been understood as masculinity, with its implications of hardness and emotional distance, was at odds with the more feminine traits appropriate to a consumer orientated society; traits such as self indulgence, emotional lability and a soft receptivity to whatever is new or exciting'.[5] In such a critique the 80s new man is a direct descendant of the 50s *Playboy*. In both his manifestations, as the narcissist and the nurturer, he becomes one more rebel incarnate in a male revolt from the breadwinner ethic and hardline masculinity.

'How does he crap?' wonders the boy with the bucket of butterkist. It's a good question which never gets answered. Superheroes do not crap.

(Helen Chapell, reviewing Robo Cop)

I began this piece by suggesting that the new man was a rebel, a sexual law breaker, a tactic of gender insurrection by men and women who desired change. Barbara Ehrenreich's thesis reinforces this position by implying that feminists have common cause with him, because he is on the run from the breadwinner ethic and thus from the manacles of capitalism, social control and traditional masculinity.

However, if consumerism feminised men, we have to ask to what end? If men have liberated themselves from the conformity of the breadwinner role, they have become increasingly entangled in the conformity of consumerism. In reality, the new man has served consumer capitalism very well, and his identity has been manipulated to prioritise those aspects which served it best. This leads me to the conclusion that the new man represents not so much a rebellion but an adaptation in masculinity. Men change, but only in order to hold on to power, not to relinquish it. The combination of feminism and social change may have produced a fragmentation in male identity by questioning its assumptions, but the effect of the emergence of the new man has been to reinforce the existing power structure, by producing a hybrid masculinity which is better able and more suited to retain control.

One of the features of patriarchy is its resilience, its ability to mutate in order to survive, undermining threats to its symbolic order by incorporating their critique, and adjusting its ideology. Gender stereotypes are the bearers of ideology, the channels by which power replicates itself, the means by which behaviour is prescribed. My contention is that the new man ideal is manipulated to become a reactionary figure, co-opted into the service of patriarchy. To illustrate this I would like to examine a number of examples. In themselves they are not the whole case, but they are symptomatic of larger trends.

Soho

Since the Renaissance, western culture has been reticent about male nudity. As men ensured their immunity from criticism, mentally, so also physically they removed themselves from gaze; from the gaze of women and from the gaze of other men. The advent of the new man saw a proliferation of erotic, nude or semi-nude images of men, in part attributable to a dawning recognition of female sexuality. Female desire was now a lucrative business, and this expressed itself in a diverse range of phenomena – from the meteoric rise of a band of male strippers, to a plethora of cards, calendars and posters produced by companies such as Athena.

Sentiment had nothing to do with it. This was merely

sound marketing. Athena's 'L'enfant' poster, which features a seated male, naked to the waist, cradling a young baby, is its largest seller to date, currently coasting effortlessly towards the hundred thousand mark. Its creator Spencer Rowell is unambiguous about the reason for its popularity; 'I was told women go ape-shit when they see a man cradling a child'.[6] Quite why it should cause flutters in female hearts and bowels is another matter. Possibly there's a fatal combo in the association of those virile biceps, granite jaw and the sensitive nurturant qualities implied by the baby. Classic Freudian analysis suggests more subterranean motivations, identifying the baby as representative of a substitute phallus for women; thus his holding the baby/phallus could be read as a classic come on.

Other images, in particular the appearance of male nude calendars in the last two years, are also indices of change. The sexual reversal is obvious, made even more blatant by the following comment from Cindy Palmano about a black male model: 'I think of Tom as a black Bunnygirl, sweet yet totally in control'. The rise of nude male images is also in part due to a thriving gay economy. This has had an influence on heterosexual men, enabling them to treat other men as objects of desire, and to give vent to a suppressed homo-eroticism. At the same time there have been moves to ensure that male models are presented as images of desire for women alone.

Significantly, despite the abundance of homoerotic images, male genitals are largely absent. Sheets, towels and underwear descend provocatively ever lower and lower, but linger just above the danger line. This figurative absence of the penis is replaced by a fetishisation of the phallus. So there are pictures of nude men grasping bottles of champagne between their legs, contents exploding liberally over their thighs; or naked men playing saxophones, or carrying whips in phallic poses.

This illustrates that the inequalities in the social relations between men and women are replicated even in an apparently egalitarian pursuit. On the one hand, the expanding presentation of men in erotic contexts is progressive; men as well as women are objectified, creating a democracy of vision. On the other hand, the unequal presentation of male and female genitalia in these contemporary images, and the moves towards representing men within a specifically heterosexual context (eg, Blues Boys and Girls calendars) undermines this.

Moreover, nudity, and especially nude genitalia, is connected with modesty and privacy, and thus power. Flesh equals vulnerability, regardless of sex, and thus to remove our clothes should render us all equally vulnerable. But this is to deny the reality of power which structures our perceptions, alters what we see, and the manner in which we see it, even the extent of what we are allowed to see. Hence, nude images of women, from advertising to porn, are ubiquitous, whereas men have continued to retain greater privacy and thus greater control, over the exposure of their skin. Mickey Rourke dropping his trousers and flashing his buttocks was a subject of almost universal comment among film reviews of *Angel Heart*. This pays tribute to more than a few homoerotic petticoats slipping, but it is also an illustration of the extent of the protection of male nudity.

In part the absence of male genitalia is a result of the obscenity laws; however, this does not explain the fetishisation of the phallus, which is common currency, symptomatic of the inequality of male nudity. It is as if men have to compensate for the vulnerability engendered by nudity with the strength and power symbolised by phallic substitutes. And the images presented are peopled by paragons of male aesthetics, rippling poems of perfect pectorals and shuddering quads, testimony to current canons of male beauty, but also expressive of action, power and control. Everyone knows you don't get a body like that just by whistling, it requires effort, patience and commitment. Even in passivity it articulates action and potential, identifying the participants as active subjects, not passive objects, controllers rather than the dupes of destiny.

Controllers of destiny tend to be represented in purposive contexts. Hence Hans van Manen's 'Sax', mentioned earlier, depicts a naked young man, legs well spread, eyes closed in concentration, playing a saxophone. The image is suggestive of talent, application and ability. Philip James' 'Victory' shows a man sailing. Gert Weigelt's 'The Whip' figures a side view of the protagonist, clad in thigh high boots and clasping a whip, the handle of which implies an erect phallus, whilst the other hand opens the door. Rowell's 'L'enfant' inspired a whole host of copies which figure men with babies.

Even in more passive positions, power structures our perceptions, so that men can never be represented in the same manner as women. Even nude they are perceived differently, with a tendency towards a greater fetishisation, and concentration on different parts of the body. The subjects are often semi-clad or display only their backs. This is again indicative of a greater capacity for privacy. When horizontal, men, unlike women, are almost exclusively prone – for instance, Mike Owen's 'Narcissus', Naomi Stanley's 'Solitaire' and Spencer Rowell's 'Sensitivity'. Prone positions allow you to obscure and protect your genitals. They are also easier to rise from, and tend to be instinctively perceived as more powerful. Women on the other hand have a monopoly of missionary positions, or ones which arch them back, passive and vulnerable, throats exposed like victims in a lower order.

Grub street

Tabloid newspapers tend to be regarded as the last bastion of reactionary phillistinism, with their exposed mammaries and their rabid and bigoted prose. Nevertheless, the way that the tabloids have taken up the language of sexual politics, in order to subvert the possibility of a new gender order, is intriguing and worth investigating.

The *News of the World* magazine *Sunday*, on 31 January 1988 carried the cover: 'Whose a pretty Wham boy? Frock Shockers'. Inside the exclusive is revealed, Wham stars, George Michael and Andrew Ridgely, dressed in white figure-hugging dresses with sweeping decolletage, complete with earrings, make up and flowers in their hair. The text tells the story: 'Those top of the popsies George Michael and Andrew Ridgely really hit on the perfect way to relax after a gruelling gig – dressing up to lark about in a frock and roll extravaganza!'

The opening sentence suggests that transvestism was a regular feature of Wham tours, yet as the tale progresses it becomes clear that this was an isolated incident. The stars had borrowed dresses from their backing singers, Pepsi and Shirlie, in order to do an impersonation of them at a party in London's Lyceum ballroom. We are told that this was from 'their early days' which immediately distances the reader and renders the incident more palatable, a mere excess of adolescent high spirits. Further, the boys 'were always looking for a way to keep ... the whole mood of the outfit happy' which implies that their motives were strictly altruistic.

Given the pair's reputed homosexuality, the story so far could be mere snide innuendo. However, this interpretation is undermined by the text which persistently constructs them as heterosexual, as in the following comments from Pepsi and Shirlie, who enter the limelight declaring: 'George always told us what to wear on stage'. This positions him in a dominant role; they continue: 'I'm sure he lived out a few fantasies – he once had us wear rubber dresses – but he said he chose our outfits to go with the songs'. This characterises him as masculine by again stressing dominance and decision. It hints at deviance (rubber dresses) but this merrily serves to indicate an unbridled sexuality, something which is again considered peculiarly male. The opening sentences thus establish them as securely male, which is necessary since they are engaged in such unmanly pursuits. As soon as their red blooded masculinity has been established other elements can be brought in, such as the inset photo of Pepsi and Shirlie in the same dresses with the caption 'Who looks best in the same dresses'. Such a comparison could only be invited from a secure subject position. It is symptomatic of a much more advanced view of masculinity, because it suggests that masculinity is not about what you wear, or what you look like, but is something visceral that you possess – you either have it or you don't. If you don't, you're just a Sheila or a Shirlie.

At this juncture, pop psychologist Jane Firbank appears to tell you exactly what it is George and Andrew are revealing in their body language: George is a flirt who is very confident in his sexuality because he's a star, but is less confident with other people, with a tendency towards depression and instability; Andrew shows arrogance, selfishness, an incapacity to flirt, can't relax and finds it difficult to lose himself in the role. Finally his male arrogance is revealed in the position of his hands which draw attention to his crotch.

In case you didn't get the message, there is more over the page, with pictures of Richard Branson wearing suspenders and stockings, Billy Connolly sporting a dress and showing off his legs, Elton John in an outrageous crinoline and headdress, and Derek Randall in stockings and women's underwear.

Despite the fact that several of the above are constructed as gay in the public mind, the text clearly regards them as exemplars of heterosexual manhood, citing them as support for its staunchly hetero bias. This becomes more obvious with 'But Andrew needn't worry, (thus reassuring conservative men everywhere) dressing up as women doesn't mean the Whamsters are any less men – quite the contrary in fact!' And Jane explains why. 'The kind of man who turns up at a party as a woman is usually so confident of his masculinity that he doesn't care what he looks like ...' But there are limits – 'he makes very sure he doesn't look too good as a girl, he would never want another man to fancy him!' The boundaries are made clear; dressing up is ok for boys, as long as they're not convincing.

The article then goes on to explore why 'normal heterosexual men' sometimes feel an overpowering impulse towards stillettos and suspenders. It gives the following reasons: they may be outrageous pop stars; it can be a way of trying to understand women 'Many men are just baffled by women's behaviour'; and 'It's hard work being macho', the natural human state is a female one, 'Men who have been brought up to think that displays of feeling and sensitivity aren't masculine often find this emotional restriction a strain'.

The assumptions are that being female is about what you wear. You put on emotions with a dress, and women are all about emotions and sensitivity: 'If they dress up as women, it isn't because they want to be women, but it lets them release their emotional side'. This is a new and insidious kind of masculinity. It allows men to hijack femininity, to have it when they want it, and dispense with it when they don't. It allows incursions into female spheres – emotions, sensitivity and sexual objectification. Provided that men dissemble as women, they can have access to this subject space. But this masculinity still presupposes an intransigent gender divide, which is what forces them to dissemble in the first place.

The final example is of butch lorry drivers wearing women's panties under their trousers and then being exposed in casualty departments: 'It doesn't mean they're gay, or even bisexual. They just get a thrill out of wearing something that belongs to their wives or girlfriends'. This feature seems to indicate that the dominant culture can absorb what were previously considered deviant forms of behaviour. It constricts possible areas of revolt by placing the dominant masculinity beyond deviancy; it also enlarges the scope of behaviour applicable to men, thus strengthening their position.

An intriguing twist is provided by the 1988 spring edition of *Arena*, with an article entitled 'The single parent fallacy: men are now the weakened sex'. It describes a bleak 'experiment in eugenics and selective lifestyle'. A friend of the author visits an ex-girlfriend abroad. They briefly resume their affair, and he returns to discover that she is pregnant and intends to keep the baby, and look after it on her own. Instead of being applauded for her brave choice, her 'selfishness', and the inhumanity of women in general, becomes the occasion for a woeful misogynist tale. The author first establishes himself in an unassailable position: he is well informed on sexual politics, and ready and willing to concede injustice in the gender divide. This means that from his stance of unquestionable rationality, he can set off fireworks into the feminist arena. He does this by repositioning men as the weakened and vulnerable sex, thus wilfully reversing the power relations between the sexes. Thus he recognises the validity of her own choice – 'She wanted to have his child, but keep her independence'. But at the same time this recognition is undermined by his presentation of his friend, who is portrayed manfully returning to be with her for the birth, and going through a difficult, painful time. In contrast, the woman's desire for independence is about politics, which is somehow different from, and less important than, the realm of the emotions. This disrupts the connection between the personal and the political. Moreover, 'she is guilty of the sort of selfishness that had hitherto been the prerogative of men'. This is in marked contrast to our hero whose emotions are explored in some depth: pride/excitement/ flattery/anger/humiliation/regret/ and acceptance. This encourages our identification with him as the victim.

By a nifty reversal, she is placed in a masculine and thus culpable subject position and he is placed in a feminine and thus innocent one. The rest of the article substantiates this reversal: 'In the transfer of power to women, the hardest blow of all has been to find, despite all their pleading of a higher sensitivity, how readily they abuse it'. This is counterbalanced by a masculine vulnerability and nurturance: 'Men, meanwhile, have had to acknowledge a loss of primacy. They are now the weakened sex'. This movement into a feminine sphere, like all things feminine, is accompanied by a loss of power, and a stoic acceptance of passivity: 'Unlike women we have no choice but to wait. We can take no independent action. We can't have a baby whenever we want'.

A huge sexual transformation is presumed to have occurred, and this is orchestrated so that the author can assume a stance of moral superiority, which is deemed to be feminine. He takes essentialist radical feminist arguments about the nature of gender as the starting point for a militant moralism, which characterises femininity as good and masculinity as bad. But he then disconnects these from their biological association, to exploit them for his own ends. Using the ideology of the new man, and its embrace of the feminine, he circumvents feminist arguments, and absents himself from masculinity and thus for any responsibility for it. The wheel has turned full circle. 'The dynamics of love have altered over the last few decades, probably forever, and new rules have to be found … and so what do you say to the woman who wants to have your child, but not you? Tell her that to be a complete woman she should first learn a bit more about men.' The last lines make it clear – women are incomplete, because of their appropriation of male roles and subject positions. Men who now occupy the high ground of moral superiority, by reason of their more integrated emotions, and their wholehearted embrace of the feminine.

Hollywood

A glance at a clutch of recent films and soaps will help to illustrate how arguments around changing gender relations can be appropriated by men, and used to install a new morality, in men's favour.

Moonlighting is a popular US soap about a detective agency run by a couple of feuding private eyes, Abby and Maddy David. The 1987 Christmas special edition opens with Abby (the middle class career woman) insisting that her staff work on Christmas eve. She then is too busy to visit a favourite aunt who is dying. When the aunt subsequently gasps her last, Abby is thrown into crisis by her own neglect. In a contemporary re-working of the Christmas carol story, a latter day (male) angel turns up to instruct Abby/Scrooge in the error of her ways. He offers her a glimpse into the Christmas Future and Christmas Past; these turn out to be lonely, abandoned and impoverished.

The characterisation of her partner David is intriguing: on one level he is the epitome of the lad, the working class boy made good, by virtue of his wit and charm. He is a rough diamond with a heart of gold, the womaniser in the classic male mould. But his is a humanised masculinity, which takes advantage of new man debates to adopt female subject positions. Thus it is he who argues for sympathy and understanding for their mutual employees. And, though he is no less talented a detective, his abilities are suffused with humour and compassion. Significantly, David's future is shown, as crowned with success, he will be rich, famous, and married to a beautiful woman.

The agency's beloved and daffy secretary is depicted two year's hence having made a spectacular success in business. She has relegated the love of her life to a subordinate role in the firm, but though inferior, he knows the value of love and tries to make her see the error of her ways. She, like Abby, is presented as blighted by success, devoid of human contact, a tyrannical, crazed capitalist automaton. They need to be taught the simple human virtues of kindness and compassion by their empathetic men, who are personified as moral centres, and the focus of true values. It ends like all good fairy stories with Abby reunited with David, and declaring a party for her staff. And the moral of this story is: Abby, the hard-hearted woman, has learnt the error of her ways from the humanised new man.

The Big Easy tells the story of young hot shot DA Ellen Barkin, sent South to investigate corruption in the police force and to nail Dennis Quaid, a worldly lothario and lovable rogue, suspected of corruption. She falls for him, he falls for her, and the rest of the story is about his moral salvation and their capture of the real villain.

So far so good, except that her role as the strong, tough career woman is constantly undermined. Near the beginning, after a date with Quaid, she refuses his attentions to walk home alone. Encountering a mugger attacking another citizen, Barkin lunges in only to be attacked herself. Quaid appears, saves the day and Barkin is shown dishevelled and prostrate. Later, after the first stirrings of mutual attraction, Barkin is presented as decentred by her passion, popping pills and practising her conversation before she picks up the phone. Their first sexual encounter defines her as gauche and inept, destabilised by her femininity and the depth of her desire. Quaid is a gentle and sensitive lover, but her passion is schooled by his. It fits itself to his rhythms, he initiates and she responds. Though Quaid is in many ways the classic lothario, he is also affected by new images of masculinity: his approach to sex is sensitive, he responds caringly to Barkin when she is sick after her first homicide; faced with his own collusion in corruption he breaks down in tears; he secretly finances his kid brother's college education, and he sleeps with a stuffed alligator toy.

This is a masculinity suffused with emotion and warmth, feeling, responsive, caring, vulnerable, and yet playful and competent. There is none of the Ramboesque pirouetting: Quaid is well aware that big guys do cry. Because of this he possesses a masculinity empowered by desire. Centred and ordered by his love for Barkin, he is as at home on the sidewalk as in the bedroom. By comparison, Barkin is neurotic and unstable. She finds herself in love, but only through him. Femininity is yet again unstable and aberrant.

Fatal Attraction is in many ways a moral fable in the age of Aids offering a dire warning to men who put their dicks in the wrong place. Dan Gallagher is a successful yuppie lawyer, married with a young daughter. At a party he meets Alex, they have a weekend affair and he deserts her. She pursues him and it rapidly becomes obvious that Alex is not only pregnant but psychotic, determined to wreak revenge upon Dan for his desertion, and to create havoc in the nuclear family in the process. Alex is the classic femme fatale. She is also aberrant – 36, single, successful, a career woman who is lonely, longing for a child and a relationship with a man. Incomplete and unsatisfied, she desires Dan because he is a paragon of manhood – the good husband, the good father, the good provider, chugging ever upward in his career. He is also emotionally literate, well able to tell the people who matter that he loves them, spending 'prime-time' with his child, weeping at his wife's hospital bedside, expressing warmth and physical affection to his friends, a sensitive and affectionate lover. What's more his behaviour to Alex is impeccable. Raunchily aroused one moment, gently explaining that he has no intention of continuing their liaison the next, he looks after her when she slashes her wrists, and offers to pay for an abortion when he discovers that she is pregnant. He is so darned reasonable, which makes Alex's treatment of him all the more shocking. What, after all, has he done to deserve this?

Alex is aberrant because she won't accept the treatment doled out to her. She is crazy, because she is unable to accept, in her mad feminine way, that a fuck is just a fuck. She wants respect, not a credit card abortion, and an involvement that Dan is not prepared to give. She wants to make him kiss and pay, to accept the seriousness of love and sex. 'I haven't decided yet', she answers decisively, when he asks her if she wants to go to bed. Alex is her own woman; and in a patriarchal value system that is tantamount to insanity. She is determined to assert her own autonomy, whatever the cost. Her pregnancy is her fundamental assertion of female power, of her capacity to be self-defining, to have his child, with or without his consent. Ultimately, it is this that Dan can't face – her visceral assertion of power and creativity.

Alex is a symbol of femininity, unpoliced by men, a femininity linked with neurosis, psychosis and madness. Her reaction to sex is crazy and abnormal; she throws up when she witnesses a happy family scene; she terrifies the daughter when she takes her out. Alex is at one and the same time a personification of the aids virus wreaking havoc on the cosy confines of suburbia, and the fatal consequences of a wild and promiscuous sex instinct. And, because she is mad, everything that is associated with her – her career, her singleness – becomes suspect, expressive of a deviant femininity that must be suppressed. Even Dan's wife Beth is portrayed as destabilised when she loses her child. Unable to cope, she crashes into another car. Women without men don't cope, they disintegrate. Typically, Beth must kill Alex and the femininity she represents. Women are each and everywhere symbolic material, but the only virus is misogyny.

Dan is a pimpleless copy of the new man, and he illustrates perfectly how this image has been hi-jacked by men to strengthen their own position. Alex is impossible and unreasonable; and the sheer terror that she unleashes covers up the fact that Dan – despite all his new moral hardware – is still capable of raunchy weekends on the side, of concealing this from his wife, and resuming relations with his family without turning a hair. But for the fact that Alex refuses to be sent off the field, he would never have cast a glance at the sidelines.

These three examples illustrate a masculinity informed by feminist criticism of masculine shortcomings, which then reforms itself, but only as a ruse to maintain power. The women, Abby, Ellen and Alex are all latter day hysterics destabilised by their own femininity. Everything changes but stays the same. Men are still the standard of normality. Their acceptance of feminine qualities substantiates their personalities, makes them more rational, more sane, not less. They are valorised by virtue of their gender, affirmed in whatever course of action they choose. Their behaviour changes, but their affirmation remains the same – men still write the rules.

'It was absolutely crazy. I never understand men'.
Margaret Thatcher after a recent EEC summit

The new man is many things – a humanist ideal, a triumph of style over content, a legitimation of consumption, a ruse to persuade those that called for change that it has already occurred.

Another more sinister possibility is that he is patriarchal mutation, a redefinition of masculinity in men's favour, a reinforcement of the gender order, representing an expansion of the concept of legitimate masculinity, and thus an extension of its power over women and deviant men. New masculinity, like the old, relies upon a fissure in gender, and an unequal positioning of values.

There is much deploring of feminist essentialism nowadays, but this is to ignore that patriarchy is founded on essentialism, on the assertion of biological difference, and the unequal apportioning of values. It is hardly surprising that in opposing patriarchy, feminism tended towards a position of counterposed essentialism. But as a result of this, male supremacist arguments have been reinforced by a distortion of certain feminist tenets. Essentialist radical feminist arguments erected a moralistic equation around gender: femininity equalled good, masculinity equalled bad. This meant that, in order to lay claim to a stance of moral superiority, men were forced to disavow their masculinity, and to take up a feminine subject position. This process was aided by other developments in socialist feminism which unhitched gender definition from biological sex, claiming that masculinity and femininity were available to both sexes.

Part of the effect of feminism has been to legitimate 'masculine' roles and subject positions for women. If, by some reductionist moralism, masculinity becomes synonymous with evil, this also taints women, for their misbegotten desires; conversely, it elevates men because they are moving towards virtue rather than away from it.

The fundamental problem with these arguments is that they are based on a primary gender divide. If you assert a schematic morality, but don't abandon a cleavage in gender, you merely endlessly reposition men and women around that fissure. Thus New Men can adopt a position of moral superiority as proto-females, and women are characterised as proto-men: whoever is most powerful appropriates the most attractive value system.

There is another reason why it is within men's interests to co-opt femininity. One of the arguments of radical feminism is that the women's movement could be the vanguard of a post-industrial society, the next evolutionary step, 'the key to human survival and transformation'.[7] Futurology suggests that in times to come we will be more influenced by what we regard as feminine characteristics. If what we define as female qualities will be highly valued in our brave new future, then to maintain hegemony it is in men's interests to co-opt femininity. In this case, the future maybe female, but I fear it will still belong to men.

Notes

[1] Lucy Purdy, quoted in Jon Savage 'Vogue Male, three decades of advertising to men', *Arena*, Spring 88.
[2] Polly Toynbee, 'The incredible, shrinking New Man', *Guardian*, 6 April 1987.
[3] Jon Savage, *op. cit.*
[4] Marcelle D'Argy Smith, *Cosmopolitan*, March 1988.
[5] Barbara Ehrenreich, *The Hearts of Men*, Pluto Press, 1983.
[6] Spencer Rowell, quoted by Britan Kennedy and John Lyttle, *City Limits*, Dec 1986.
[7] Robin Morgan, *The Anatomy of Freedom* Martin Robertson, 1982.

Mending the Broken Heart of Socialism

A ROUNDTABLE DISCUSSION

Trade unionists have been making some attempts to accommodate to changing gender relations at work. However the masculine culture of the labour movement is deeply rooted, and the changes are very slow. Here Cynthia Cockburn chairs a discussion reviewing the situation so far. The participants are: Jim Bewsher who worked for twelve years as an area official in NUPE's London division; Jack Dromey who is a National Officer of the Transport and General Workers Union; Inez McCormack who is a fulltime official for NUPE in Belfast; and Jeff Rodriguez who is chair of the Ethnic Minorities Advisory Committee in the National Union of Civil and Public Servants. All are speaking in a personal capacity.

Cynthia The restructuring of the economy seems to be leading to a growth in part-time jobs, characteristically women's jobs. A lot of unions today are waking up to the importance of their women membership, and to the potential for membership in the population of women. How much has trade union practice really changed to serve women's interests better?

Jim I think that certainly the unions are waking up to the idea that there is this part-time membership and it needs to be serviced. But I don't think people have really thought through how they are going to service that membership and what they have got to offer them. In fact, if you look at my own union, NUPE, or any of the public sector unions, they have had women members in their thousands for years and years, but they haven't actually done very much for them. No-one has really come to terms with what this change in the workforce means for the way the union organises. Most unions are run by men, essentially for men.

Jack We are all agreed that the track record of the trade union movement in the past has been an unfortunate one, to say the least. The only time I was ever assaulted in my history as a trade union officer was by a group of women part-timers following a mass meeting at EMI Records in West London, where, because we had won a vote to oppose redundancies, I had my shins kicked off me by a group of angry women who wanted to take redundancy. I then sat down and discussed it with the stewards – in a factory dominated by women, out of 60 shop stewards, half a dozen were women – and heard the vitriol being poured out against the part-timers: 'You can't get them involved in the organisation'; 'We're not surprised that you had the bad experience that you had'. And when I scraped away the surface of that, it became absolutely clear that the part-timers were not, effectively, part of the trade union organisation, and did not share its objectives. But frankly you couldn't blame the part-timers for that – it was the way they had been treated by the dominant minority of male full-timers.

Coming to the present, unions are beginning to wake up. First of all, all unions are having to make calculations about the future, looking at how the labour market is changing, and where the potential is in terms of trade union organisation. And many unions are recognising the enormous potential there is in the organisation of part-timers, in particular part-time women. But it is more than just an organisational calculation about where the growth in the labour market is. Whilst the track record may be an unfortunate one, and whilst we have a long, long way to go, there have been certain real and helpful changes within a number of unions, both in a general awareness of the relationship of the union to its women members, and in terms of some real practical steps that have been taken. For example, in our own union, nationally – and this is mirrored within each of the regions – we have a women's advisory committee. This advisory committee is not just an appendage to the organisation, somewhere you send the women to talk about women's issues, but, crucially, it is linked into the mainstream of the union in a number of ways. You have got to look in very concrete terms at how you link that specific provision for women within the organisation to the mainstream might of the union, so that they can use that platform within the union to influence the direction of the union itself.

Inez The hard reality is that the mainstream of the trade union movement at the grass roots level does not constitute the mainstream at the leadership level. And that is why the trade union movement is facing the question of change. The employers' agenda draws its strength from the lack of value placed by the unions on the organisation of working time for women. From my position of having been involved in battles for a statutory minimum wage, and for part-time workers, in the last ten to fifteen years, I have seen them regarded as peripheral. But the reality is different.

In our movement we have separated the issues of negotiation and organisation. We have been the mirror image of the employers' agenda rather than representing the agenda from our members. The lack of value that has been placed on terms, conditions and organisation of part-time work has, in fact, represented the agenda of our own movement. For example, in the Industrial Relations Act, it was the trade union movement, through the Labour Party, that placed less importance on part-time work in relation to statutory rights. To go from now to the future we need to look at the question of value.

The recognition by the trade union movement of the need to organise part-time workers is a managerial market force reaction. Of course we should allow credit to that – it is a recognition that is necessary for the survival of the trade union movement. But I have yet to hear a voice speaking for the representation of women's needs themselves, and for the movement to be at the service of women, rather than of the movement's need to survive.

We need to ask what has removed women's value within the market, and what has enabled the employers' agenda to transcend and develop, through the simple fact that the agenda organized on behalf of a very large part of the workforce had no meaning for them.

About three or four years ago, we were asked to consult our members about low pay. We asked our activists from service-based committees, organisational structures, nurses, cleaners, all to come together in one room. And we asked them to put themselves in the position of the most invisible member in their branch, and to spell out what they felt the effects of collective bargaining and organisation had been for them in the last ten years. It was very interesting because in many of the branches there were night-cleaners working for five or six hours a week, and home-helps working six hours a week, or whatever. And the reality that showed through was that in low pay we may have done a job for full-time male earnings, but we have not done a job to protect earnings for workers who were not regarded as full time. Any increase accruing to this group out of a pay rise had, largely, been lost either in terms of cuts in hours, or through moving into one section of the poverty trap. And virtually every woman in the room who was working less than eighteen to twenty hours had in fact lost pay every time she'd got a pay rise.

When we asked what the answer was, it wasn't a million pounds a week, it was things like linking flat rate increases to protection of earnings, or re-valuing of the jobs. The men in the room took no time at all to work out that in fact the women's fight was their fight, because two cheap women could be used to replace one of them. They also worked out that many of the arguments the women were making were very important for men too. As one man said to me, 'Because the argument has never been about the basic rate, I work all the hours God sends for overtime and bonus. I go out at five in the morning and go home at seven at night. I never see the weens. And I still can't manage'.

The argument moved to the fact that what had divided the women and men was not themselves, but the mechanism which purported to understand and represent them ... which was our own movement. In other words, these values had not actually represented men either.

I don't think we can change the agenda for this section of the workforce without enabling them to shape an agenda by finding methods of democratising. And that's the problem – to change the structures, you have to change the practices, and that is a very threatening exercise. It is more attractive to change the agenda and demands by deciding what the new demands should be from an analytical exercise, rather than from a democratic exercise. I'm finding that every time I move forward from things that are coming from the members, they demand a re-thinking of me and how I do my job, and that's a very unpleasant discipline. It is a very tiring discipline. You think that you do really understand and then something hits you in the face. It's very tempting to think that you know best.

Cynthia What has to be involved is a change in the bargaining agenda. It is not just a question of an addition of committees and reserved seats. It is a question of a change in the negotiating life of the union. And Inez has suggested that men can see their own advantage in that too, that it is not always a loss to men.

Jack You shouldn't pose the point that I made about the structure against the point about the agenda, because the two are absolutely complementary. I agree with everything that Inez has said in terms of the agenda, but a number of things are crucial to be able to dictate that agenda. One of them is the position in the structure from where you do that.

Jeff The recent growth in part-time working hasn't been as big in my sector as it may have been elsewhere. But there have been part-time workers for a long time, either at very low grades, cleaners, messengers, many of whom are black in the metropolitan areas, or secretaries and typists. And they are all characterised by very similar things, which is that neither management nor unions had ways of making their careers, or their work, any better. For example they were always characterised by immobility.

There were no promotion avenues; to get promoted you moved sideways and then up; there was no way up through part-time work at all. And they were low paid. But my union at the time, and most of our stewards, didn't even recruit part-time workers. They didn't see them as union material. So it's all very well speaking about setting the agenda, but unless the unions actually recruit part-timers in the first place, there is no agenda to set. And at the moment, the trade union movement – a male trade union movement – is trying to come to terms with a growth in female working which it doesn't understand and has never really represented effectively. And it shows no sign of changing its hierarchy to do so now. It changes its policies – because most unions now have positive action policies – but that is not reflected in the hierarchy.

Jim The Thatcherite project has changed people's expectations. For many people there isn't really that expectation of permanent employment any more. And that has very strong implications for the sort of trade unionism you are going to have. Somehow you have to find a form of trade unionism that can link into people's experiences, and can offer them something when their relationship with work is fairly tenuous. If you look at a lot of people in part-time work, if you look in schools for example, a lot of those part-time workers are not people with young kids who are doing it because it's the only job they can do, they are doing it because it suits them. And so their relationship with employment and their relationship with the union is much more tenuous. And in a way that goes against everything the left and progressive forces have stood for – that you have to be, if you're a trade unionist, 190 per cent committed, you have to be going to meetings all the time. It is almost impossible, as an activist, by the very nature of the term, to be someone who takes a little interest in the union, and does a little bit, because of the way our present structures organise themselves.

It is very noticeable that if you look at branches run by women, their approach is completely different. Instead of having the classic meetings above the pub, people are having coffee mornings, and meeting in small groups. In schools it's very obvious. Traditionally, when I joined the union ten years ago, nearly all the schools branches met on Sunday mornings, because it was a time when the caretakers didn't have their lettings, their overtime, so they would adjust things to suit them. Of course most women were involved at that time in cooking and other things, and couldn't come along. And you'll find now that when women have got control of the branch the whole system just falls away, and there is much more openness about trying to take the union to people, and to take on board issues which historically have not been the mainstream of the union, but may be the mainstream of what the women membership of the union want to take on board.

Cynthia Is that happening in other unions? Is there space being made for women to do things their way, for instance in your union Jeff?

Jeff No, I don't think so. In the last eight or nine years there has been a much higher profile for women in my union. But it has been a very difficult and painful process. We now have, for example, a much higher profile for 'women's issues': it is more featured in our union journals, our sections journals, it is something we have trade union schools about, women-only schools, etc – all of which are very important. We have glossy papers that go into the Trades Union Congress and look good. But there is no substantial increase of women in the hierarchy of the union. We seem to have a change in the union's policies, but not a change in its structures, its priorities, its orders, or its culture.

I heard recently that even management are adopting strategies for incorporating more women into their policies for, for example, equal opportunities. On our promotion boards now it has been insisted that there be at least one woman, out of the three members. But just having women on a promotion board, in itself, isn't enough, if they are operating within a framework of a male culture, if they carry male values. Because they may have the same expectations of our members and staff as men do. So this whole issue of policies, by itself, is actually a con. We have to talk about feminism as well as just women.

Jack I referred earlier to some of the structural changes that we've been undertaking in the union. Bluntly, these were strongly resisted from within some sections. And I have to say that some of that resistance came from the queen bees within the union, the people who had made it despite the traditional dominant male ethos, the people who used to get up and say, 'If I made it then so too can others'. There was this fascinating alliance between the old macho die-hards and the queen bees; they were ranged up against some outstanding women within the organisation, supported by progressive forces.

I don't want the discussion to be one which is too pessimistic. We are only in the infancy of these developments. I'd like to give some examples of progress. One was last year, the 86-87 review of the grading structure for local government. Now, although it has not resolved all the problems in local government in terms of earnings or equality of opportunity, significant progress was made. And to make that progress it required unions, and particularly my own union, which has traditionally been a sort of praetorian guard of drivers, dustmen, roadworkers, to go and have the argument with the members as to why it was right that the structure should change and take account of equal value and caring skills. And it was not easy in all circumstances, but, frankly, neither was it that difficult, if the argument was put.

Another example is our union's 'Link-up' campaign. We have been analysing developments in the two-tier labour system, and the growing army of people in part-time work or casual employment, and seeking to organise in those areas. There are other unions doing the same thing.

And some of the most interesting experiences I've had, in terms of imagination of approach towards the organisation of workplace, or branch life, have come from groups of women. For example I remember dealing with a company out in Greenford where the branch meeting used to consist of a dozen die-hards in a cold room. A couple of outstanding women from the workplace decided that this had to change. And to cut a long story short, they organised a semi-social event, semi-branch meeting which took place quarterly, not every month. They arranged childcare facilities, had a film or a speaker along, out of the branch funds bought some booze and some bread and cheese, and the result was that you used to get 150 or 200 women coming along.

So I don't think we should paint too negative an image, because I am in favour of welcoming the tentative steps being taken. Not least, that's very important to encourage further steps to be taken in the right direction.

Jeff That model you cited of women being backed up by progressive forces in the union, I find very problematic. On what issues are these forces progressive? They are progressive on traditional left issues, all the big miners' strikes, all the things that the trade union movement gets excited about, but are they progressive on women? I wonder about that because I think that one of the centres of male power is in the broad lefts. They only identify with women's liberation on their terms, on male terms. It's a women's rights approach rather than a feminist approach. They don't read anything about feminism, it isn't part of their language, their thinking and talking. They don't understand the theories of feminism like they would do the theories of Marx, or Trotsky or whatever. It isn't central to their thinking at all. There is no feminist literature on broad left bookstalls. In terms of women's rights – that is in defining women in relation to production – yes, they can do that because Marx did that didn't he? They see women's oppression in terms of women's relationship to production and work, not in terms of women's relationship with men, which changes the issue completely and fundamentally.

Inez I suppose it is not always right to generalise from your personal and bitter experience, but allow me to try. I'm speaking as a woman who was involved in the fight for change within a very unreconstructed Irish trade union movement ten years ago when there wasn't much support for the issue around. And I remember the left-wing men who stood off the issue when it was unpopular; and the brutal fights of which I still bear the scars, when you were the bitch, or when you were magic until you said 'I'm not accepting the position for myself, I want change as a whole'. My experience of left men has been of them waiting until the unpopular fight was over, and then asserting that the women's issue was a real one. I certainly wasn't flooded around with left support ten or twelve years ago.

I remember getting elected on to the All-Ireland Executive, where I was the first northern woman ever on it. I was elected with a fairly massive majority, against all the odds. And this left-wing bloke came up to me afterwards – who hadn't lifted a finger in the fight – and he said to me 'Do you realise you could get two of us on next year Inez?' And I said 'Who's the "us" brother?' Suddenly I had become a progressive force.

There's a coldness in me because it seems that the women's issue becomes a progressive issue when it is of use to the progressive forces, rather than when it is serving the needs of women.

What are women's objectives? In my experience, if women are interested in anything they are interested in responsibility as opposed to power, and men are interested in power. This may be too much of a stereotype, but in my experience, while some men may be interested in responsibility, it isn't an overwhelming characteristic. And this difference leads to different kinds of demands, but they have no voice within the movement. I'm thinking of women who work six hours a week, like home-helps – how do you represent them, how do you take the initiative? They are not interested in being represented in terms of taking power, what they want represented is the responsibility of what they do, and who they look after. And it is not a question of finding ways to represent an agenda for them, the issue is to find ways of giving them confidence. But the trade union movement is not, ultimately, about giving people confidence, it is about giving importance, and positions, and roles. It is not about giving confidence in value, and this is reflected in the fact that the women I know would not have been interested in holding branch office until we reorganised the branch in such a way that branch office was the least important thing, when it became a matter of spending an evening to carry forward certain things that were important.

You can't go in to represent the value of a woman cleaner without first of all, organisationally, taking on the task of making her assert her own value. My experience is that unless your value is asserted organisationally you can't assert it representationally. So then the cleaners always come out at the bottom. If cleaners in the health service, for example, are represented in terms of the importance of hygiene and the provision of medicine, they become as important as doctors. But you don't get that confidence, that assertion of value, unless you perform the organisational task first.

Those issues of confidence, together with value, conflict with the present structures of organisation within the trade union movement. It is not a question of being pessimistic, it is a question of being realistic. The value of confidence amongst our members is being realised in issues like the nurses' dispute, where you can see the value of members being able to speak for themselves. But that was because of the politics of the trade union movement, which was drawing back, not wanting to be seen as the bad people organising the strike. It hasn't happened from the positive recognition. But there's nothing more powerful than seeing a home help speaking about the old person she loves and works for. And it's not sentimentality. That power that is there has begun to be recognised now, but it is as something that is going on out there, it has not been seen as constituting the agenda.

Cynthia Inez is speaking out of the experience of being in a branch which is women-led, woman-centred in a sense. Is this kind of thinking coming out of any unions or branches that are male-centred, or male-led, today? Why is it that within the unions it is the women who are always having to do the pushing? Is there no way in which men are beginning to take responsibility themselves for dealing with other men's masculine approach?

Jim I think the root of that problem is culture. If you ask what is a trade union official, everyone knows that a trade union official is a forty-year old man in a grey suit;

it's not a mother with two kids. That culture runs very strong. I'll give you an example from my own union. There was a move among some of the officials in London to get a policy of being able to job-share, because there were people coming to an age where they were likely to be responsible for kids. And this would seem perfectly possible and practical. But although this idea was accepted by some people, others saw it as almost a full frontal assault on what the concept of an official was. The idea that you could actually share your work with somebody was a complete challenge to the notion of the official – the man in the white Escort that comes in and solves people's problems. And if you ask really top-ranking women activists whether they are going to put in to be an official, the answer is usually no. And it's not necessarily that they don't have the confidence; it's people saying that they don't want to be in that form of lifestyle, and that type of approach. And we have to look at ways not of trying to get people involved in the structures, but of making the structure something very different, offering a different set of values. We need an approach that takes account of mainstream issues for our women members, which are often completely different from those of men; and a lot of those are about the relationship with children.

Inez Let me tell you about something I saw happen that I have never ever seen before. We ran a course a couple of weeks ago on stress, for lay officials. And we put on some of our senior activists, about fourteen of them, of whom about eight were men. And for the first time ever I heard men speak in front of other men, in a trade union environment, about being vulnerable. And it was magic, there was an enormous strength in the room. The issues which were talked about made it possible, in a way that the women's movement has done for women, to talk to each other openly; for the first time this gave men a reason to talk about things which they felt. The lack of defensiveness in the room was extraordinary.

Jeff I am worried by Cynthia's question about men taking responsibility on these issues. It seems to me that the reason that these changes are taking place is that

women have forced these questions on the agenda, not
because men have. And the bottom line is that there is a
need for women to be in the organisation, in powerful
positions, to change the agenda and to make the challenge,
supported by men. But I don't think there is any evidence
to show that men are willing to change their practices
substantially enough to allow those changes to take place.

Cynthia That's exactly what I'm saying. You're being
rather gentlemanly about this, and saying that it is only the
women who can act on their own interests. But we're
saying that there is a big problem in the trade union
movement as a whole, as there is in the world, which you
could sum up in the word masculinity, the kind of persona
that men feel they have to carry around with them, a very
burdensome persona. If women are going to have to be
the ones always breaking their heads against that persona
of masculinity, our energy will be just bleeding away the
whole time. Whereas if men could take responsibility for
this themselves, we might be able to see some change. Now
these men, who in Inez's workshop were able to show some
vulnerability, would they be totally unoperational in the
trade union movement at large, if they maintained that
openness to their feelings and to each other's feelings?

Inez They would be unoperational in the trade union
movement. They would not be unoperational in terms of
their ability to represent their members to the boss. And
that's a hell of an indictment of the movement.

Jack Of course everyone here would agree that women
should be the engine of their own liberation. But having
said that, it does not mean that men haven't got a role to
play. Now it would be supreme arrogance for me, or any
other man, to say 'Well, alright girls, this is the way you do
it'. But it is critical that men come out in certain ways.
What does 'come out' mean? Perhaps this is not the best
example I can think of, but, for example, I used to feel
embarrassed, about four or five years ago, admitting that
the reason I had to get away from a meeting was to go and
take over the kids. And I realised in the end that this was
nonsense. Now I don't feel embarrassed. And people's
reaction to this is interesting. Three or four years ago

there would have been a nudge in the ribs, 'are you a man or a mouse?', that kind of stuff. But now the occasional silly fool makes a comment, but people ask how they are, and start talking to one another again, men start talking to one another about their kids. But it's more than that, it's more than just coming out that you are going home to take over your kids. We will not make fundamental progress until such time as men come to terms with the fact that they are going to have to give up power.

Jeff I think there is a complacency behind the assumption that somehow if men are more vulnerable – and I think it's good that they should be, or that they should talk about it – and if, somehow, they can bring their personal lives into a public domain, that that will necessarily mean that they will hand over power. That's a gross simplification of masculinity, because men are perfectly capable of taking on and dealing with these softer issues, while still retaining the power they have. The assumption is that somehow there is a link between being vulnerable and giving up power. Well there isn't. I think masculinity is much more complex than that.

Inez I think the connection is when, as in the women's movement, the personal becomes political. Men have got to relate the courage to be vulnerable with the practice of democracy. Those men who expressed vulnerability in the workshop would not be able to be operational in the trade union movement.

Cynthia I was going to ask whether the realities of bargaining with the government and with the employer are such that a de-masculinised man could operate as a trade unionist. But you're saying that he might actually be able to operate better vis-a-vis the employer, in certain circumstances; but it's our own movement which is keeping men in their macho straitjackets.

Inez The unreality in which men live is removed from the responsibility of daily living, removed from taking responsibility for the effect of what they do in the public domain. Therefore someone who becomes more in touch with reality is better enabled to have the confidence of his members, to represent them better, because he under-

stands them better. He's much more able in dealing with
the boss because, simply, he's got the imagination to move.
Democraticisation produces flexibility, of movement,
thought and action. We have one branch secretary who's
very unusual. He's a very, very tough rough guy, but he is
one of the most democratic individuals I've ever met. He's
capable of some of the most crass sexist remarks, but more
women have come through this branch than any other
branch. And what characterises him is his democracy
within the movement. He's the best negotiator I've ever
been in with. And that's what I'm talking about – what is it
that makes you effective in there with the boss? It's not the
politics of position, it's not the politics of ego, or of power –
any manager can deal with that; you can buy them off or
you can find ways of co-opting people. That is why in the
old days the shop steward who was in negotiating
happened to be in the top grades. But if you have a
democratic branch secretary, the grade represented will
not be only the grade in the room; the invisible grade
outside will be represented too. The next trick is to make
sure that the invisible grade is in the room as well.

Cynthia One of the things we want is for men to
explore their own feelings and each other's feelings, and
to shed some of the carapace of masculinity. But Jeff is
saying that that doesn't actually lead to a relinquishing of
power. What then do we need to enable men to let go
power, if we're not just going to bring armies to bear on
them in the way that men have brought armies to bear on
each other all these years? We are not going to do that. We
are not going to 'man' our barricade. What is the
mechanism for getting men to relinquish power within a
movement like the trade union movement?

Jeff This question comes from a model of change which
has come from the women's movement, where the
intersection of the personal and the political occurs in a
particular sort of way – confidence building, particular
sorts of behaviour to each other, etc. I'm not sure that this
model applies to men in the same way. An opening up of
men's softness can co-exist with their position of power; we
have strategies of doing that which don't fit into the model

that you may be coming from, in the women's movement. There are ways of changing but I think they are the big ways, not the little ones. First of all we need to tackle the theoretical level. Underpinning much of the left's view of this issue is the notion that women's oppression is purely a class-based thing. It is to do with them being workers – being in production and part of the working class. And they naturally assume therefore that to be pro-women is to be pro-socialist. But I don't think that's true at all. They think that there is some basic alliance between women and the workers' movement. I don't think there is. So I think that at a theoretical level left men, with their marxist tradition, need to question this view in a fundamental way, and to recognise that they aren't going to hitch up women to the workers' movement unless they really try, unless they change their structures completely. For many left wingers this could be a motivating force, because politics motivates them.

Cynthia So, if you're talking about people who are influenced by ideas, how do you get them to read the shelves full of stuff written by feminists in the last twenty years, which are making exactly these points?

Inez Solitary confinement.

Cynthia How do you get at these men through their marxist ideology? Where have they got it from, their mother's milk?

Jeff They have got it because they grow up in it. I'm not talking only about left men, but about men who are in any way 'progressive'. They have grown up in a culture, a labour movement culture, which reproduces itself and its ideas. When I use the word theory I don't mean theory as a well worked out thing, I mean a set of common sense ideas, which people pick up: 'Well obviously women's oppression is to do with class'.

Cynthia Are men actually going to change the common sense of the left, or the common sense of trade unionism?

Jim Doesn't that come right back to the changes we were talking about at the beginning? If you look at the various campaigns there are to recruit more part-time women, then, partly, it is a cynical survival move. When people lose huge numbers of members it's quite natural that they will look to see where they can get new sources of survival for the organisation. But for that to be effective people have to start to change, or else they won't succeed. If you recruit all these people, but you don't have any changed ways of working, then you won't be able to offer anything to them and they won't stay. So I see it as an organic process.

Within NUPE, there was an ideological move in terms of positive action, women's advisories, women's seats, at a national level, and that has now started to develop some life of its own. Once you get past a certain point, it's difficult to go back. There's a demand that the organisation start to reflect more the needs of the mass membership. People are suddenly saying 'We need all these part-time workers to keep our Escorts on the road'. And if then you can't hold those new members, and if you haven't got anything to offer them, people will start to think again. I don't think anyone gives up power, and it's not in the tradition for men to give up power out of the goodness of their hearts. There will only be change where it is forced on people.

Inez I agree with you that need will be the motivating force. In fact I see that those who hold power recognise the need to adapt and amend their forms of organisation, but I don't see any sign that it has occurred to them to give up their power. As one of our women officers said to me 'But do they not understand. If they just got out of the way we're on to a winner'. And that's actually right: there's a huge social force that's on the move. But the reality is that men are not going to walk away. The utility of need will be a motivating force. The question is how can women ensure that that utility of need becomes a utility at their service.

Jack I agree with Inez that when it comes to impressing an employer it's not just a question of banging on the table, or how loud you can shout. Ultimately it's about collective strength, and how you go about representing the members. And my experience, my bitter experience, is that an organisation that is unrepresentative of its members is a weak organisation that is not properly taken account of by the employer.

Cynthia We haven't touched on the question of separate

organisation by women. There are a lot of women who have got tired enough of wasting their energies in dealing with men to have felt that we need a separate branch, or at least we need a caucus, maybe we need a separate union. That is the logical conclusion if men don't, in some sense, voluntarily give up power, because women are not going to be able to take it forcibly from men. What do you feel about that?

Jeff I suppose the difference between gender oppression and capitalist oppression, in a sense, is that, with gender, the oppressor is split and divided, and there is some common interest between the oppressed and the oppressor. There is a fundamental underlying, not unity, but commonness that you can find. I'm not saying it's always there, but it is different. The issue of separatism comes up occasionally in the black movement; but it's suicide for black workers because there aren't enough of us – we aren't a majority, we're a real minority. And I'm not expressing a view either way, but I'm not frightened by gender based unions because you're talking about a large number of workers who can organise across a whole range of industries, whereas with black people you can't do that.

Inez I work in a gender based union, in that it is dominated by the representation of men. But you are very conditioned by your own experience so that, perhaps, you lose the power to envisage the courage of deciding 'That's it boys, you're on your own'. I'm not sure whether I lack the imagination, or whether I'm trying to go for the reality of where I think my members are. The majority of the women I work for live with men, and that's part of their reality.

But they love the space their union gives them to be together. Love is the right word, they enjoy the warmth of it, they enjoy the humour of it, they enjoy the challenge of it. And the types of struggle coming from them are extraordinary. But I don't see from them their wish to organise separately. I see the absolute impatience with a movement that simply isn't moving with them. And the job of anyone who's interested in the class and gender ever taking power in this society is to enable them to be on the move.

Jim I'd just like to pick up that thing that Inez talked about, which I always find amazing, and I've heard it from other women officials, about the relationship between the women in the union, and the space and warmth that there is. I've heard it from numbers of women officials talking about how when they go into meetings, women come up to them and say, 'How nice it is to see a woman representing us'. And that feeling – not of comradeship but of some word like it – is something that I don't think I've ever really experienced. It's as if there's something completely different going on in the organisation.

I'm not really interested in discussing a union where women have withdrawn, because I don't think it's part of the agenda. I'm much more interested in how things change, and how will unions change. I was discussing with some of our women officials before I came here what it was that would make the change, how it would happen. And one of the points that was put forward was that at some stage a particular union would have an identity where it was seen to be representing the interests of women, to be somehow capturing that feeling that Inez has referred to. And then women would flock to that organisation in very large numbers. I certainly don't believe that that kind of change will come from the top.

Inez This reminds me of a very beloved friend of mine who would describe it as 'mending the broken heart of socialism'.

Cynthia What would you feel as men working in a union from which the feminists have withdrawn? Would that still be a progressive union with hopeful movement within it? Or is it feminism which is giving it a lot of feeling of progressiveness to the unions that you're in?

Jeff I don't think it's just feminism, because I think that the whole debate around equal opportunity potentially brings in an enormous wealth of experience and renewal to the union. And I wish I'd had time to take up the question of democraticisation. From the point of view of black workers as well, it's exactly right. Black workers are a very small percentage of the population, it is a minority issue, but the key to these issues opens a door to a massive space. The issues raised by women and black workers, and other so-called minorities, are pushing at a door which leads into a very big space; and this space is a union which is truly democratic and can represent all its workers. The failure of the union to represent black people, and women, is also the failure of the union to represent ordinary workers, rank-and-file workers, ordinary male workers as well. But to answer your question in particular, without feminists in the union, and without women in the union, it would be a hopeless union – in that one of the major motives for change would have gone somewhere else. And it would be a very sad day.

Jim It's fascinating asking that question now. I have very odd feelings about it, because I feel that this is almost a question from a different time, of that period in the 70s when there were men's groups, and all those things. And somehow it seems that that whole debate is just nowhere on the agenda now, and that the world has moved into a different, much harsher, environment. Now you can immediately come back and say 'Ah, you forget all those issues when it comes down to the serious business of the class struggle'. I'm not saying that. I just find that whole line of questioning very difficult. It just did seem like something ...

Cynthia ... from another world?

Jim Yes, from another world.

Inez But for you it's important to recognise, on a very simple level, what it is like for a woman to live in your world. To take one of my own memories again: a country, rural area, which had only had an organised union for a few years; a middle-aged woman who came to a women's event which was largely organised by young gay women; she'd never seen gay women in her life, and a couple of them were necking in front of her that night. I said to her 'Is this upsetting you?' – the word lesbian was a word she hadn't heard until three days before, she hadn't known what a lesbian was; and she said something which stuck in my mind for its absolute sensitivity and analysis: 'They live on the edge of my world all the time, it's quite right that I live on the edge of theirs for tonight'. That's what I'm talking about: the capacity to understand that you have a responsibility to put yourself in the other person's position. Actually the thing was upsetting her, she couldn't cope with it very well, but she had the self discipline. Now, would that men could have that self discipline when women are on the move, or act in a way that's perhaps not acceptable, or a bit silly.

Jeff I completely sympathise with what you're saying, but I think there's a slight complacency here and a tendency towards essentialism – women are intrinsically good, and men are intrinsically bad. If you look at English literature, there's one thing that characterises the way black people are portrayed in all those novels I read when I was a kid, things like *Prester John* and *Four Years Before the Mast* and all that stuff, and even more modern things like *Mandingo*: if you look at the writing, the most powerful thing that comes across is the sense of the black as the other, as something outside you, as something alien and difficult to understand. So I really do sympathise with what you are saying about the way men respond to issues that are in the world of women. But women also can appear to look at people as other. White women can look at black people as other. You only need to take white women's attitude, and feminism's attitude, to black male sexuality, to see what the other is. So I think you're absolutely right, I sympathise with you, but I think it's difficult to argue this on a pure gender basis.

Cynthia Shall I say more about what's behind the question. I think it's my feeling that women's struggle is two things, not one. It's not just a struggle for the expression of women's needs, and giving a voice to women's needs, and getting what we need. It's a struggle about the world and about masculinity, and about how men are suffering in the straitjacket of masculinity, and what it's doing to society. And so it's difficult for us sometimes to separate out those struggles because both of them are a lot of effort, and exhausting. And it's interesting to try to separate the struggles for a moment and say 'Supposing women stopped trying to wage the world's struggle and just thought about our own, women's issues, or women's interests, what does that leave?' It leaves the world's struggle, which is actually about men, for men to handle. And maybe we can pass on a little bit of the struggle to men, and ask them whether there isn't something, a struggle there, that they can begin.

Jeff As long as we accept your premiss – that men are victims as well as oppressors.

Cynthia Yes. I think you're victims of your own internalised oppression.

Jeff I'm not sure that I accept that that is equally important. I'm reluctant to accept your model of thinking which almost seems to say 'You poor lads, you suffer because you're males'. Whereas I think there is a hierarchy and in the hierarchy the male oppressor is a much more important actor than the male as sufferer. I find it very difficult to accept your model of questioning.

Jack Aren't we posing the two things unnecessarily against each other? To use the phrase again: the engine of women's liberation comes from the women themselves. But I don't believe it can succeed without men then playing a certain role. Now what does that role mean? Part of it is responding to the agenda as it has been dictated by women; but part of it is also taking responsibility amongst men, for criticising attitudes and the way we do things. I'm not quite sure why you're posing one against the other.

Inez What is the engine of men's liberation? I mean I agree that men are oppressors rather than victims, that there's a hierarchy. But I know an awful lot of men who don't have much joy or warmth. And I'm thinking of what sustains me, how you see the possibilities of solidarity when you go into that warmth. And you can go to a meeting of good decent men, and there'll be a friendly feeling, but there won't be that warmth and solidarity.

Jeff I think the question is really problematic because you assume that men have a common interest with women. I find the whole model of questioning one which just doesn't match with mine. I'm not sure whether it's because it's from a feminist perspective, or whether it's from a model of political thinking that I'm not in sympathy with or familiar with, which I think is more likely to be the case. I don't think an oppressed group has a great deal of common interest with the oppressing group in the way you're posing it. For example when you ask what is the motor of change for women, there is a common interest – liberation. It's not the same with men. All I can say, as a socialist, and as a revolutionary, is what the motor is of my movement's change. Now that I can answer. What I want to do is to build a united, strong revolutionary class. And there can be no strong united revolutionary class without those oppressions, of women and black people, being completely marginalised and disappeared. For me that's the motor.

Cynthia I am coming to it from a different direction. I'm thinking about gender as a cultural thing, in terms of masculinity and femininity, this complementariness we are caught up in. And I think it is generally accepted that masculinity is deeply implicated in a lot of the things that your revolutionary struggle is against – fascism, militarism, the state. So that men's struggle against those things can't be waged without having some resolution to the problem of masculinity.

Fathering, Authority and Masculinity

VICTOR J SEIDLER

Fathering and Authority

The visions of authority which we inherit within Western culture are tied up with conceptions of the father. Both Judaism and Christianity have learnt to think in terms of God The Father, though they have different conceptions of this relationship. Within a more secular culture the way that these visions continue to order our conceptions of identity, power and experience can be harder to grasp. Since the Enlightenment in the 17th century we have been encouraged to believe that all forms of authority can be legitimated in terms of reason alone.

Within a patriarchal society our understanding of the nature of political authority has been tied up with our sense of the position of the father within the family. But the Enlightenment has provided an ambivalent[1] inheritance. Reason as an independent and autonomous faculty replaced traditional religious authority, while at the same time being identified with a transformed sense of masculinity. Morality was henceforth to find its source in reason alone. Liberal conceptions of freedom and equality were to be based on a conception of the person as a rational agent, which helped to create the conditions for a liberal conception of citizenship defined in terms of universal legal and political rights. For Kant freedom and reason are interdependent, so he is able to declare in his famous essay 'What is Enlightenment?', 'For enlightenment of this kind, all that is needed is *Freedom*. And the freedom in question is the most innocuous form of all – freedom to make public use of one's reason in all matters'.[2] It is the strength of Kant's vision of freedom that it cannot simply be handed to people on a plate as a set of discrete rights but also involves a process of individual change and transformation.

But this insight was part of the early challenge of Kant's formulation of a liberal moral theory. It has been lost as the bourgeoisie has consolidated its power. Freedom was no longer conceived as a process of individual and collective transformation but increasingly, within liberal theory, as a set of legal and political rights that could be guaranteed to people regardless of their position within the social relations of power and subordination. This renders invisible Kant's insight that 'it is difficult for each separate individual to work his way out of the immaturity which has become second nature to him. He has even grown fond of it and is really incapable for the time being of using his own understanding because he was never allowed to make the attempt'.[3]

In this essay at least Kant was prepared to acknowledge that the Guardians who have taken upon themselves the work of supervision will soon see to it 'that by far the largest part of mankind (including the entire fair sex) should consider the step forward to maturity not only as difficult but also as highly dangerous'.[4] This carries its own resonance in Thatcher's Britain where the Guardians have assumed a new confidence, having been allowed to appropriate the language of freedom as if it were their own. Kant's ethical theory has embodied the authority of reason within liberal moral culture. For Kant it was because reason was to be uniquely identified with masculinity that men were to have authority in relation to women and children. It was only in association with men that women who would otherwise be governed by emotions, feelings and desires – gathered together by Kant as 'inclinations' – can learn to order their behaviour by reason. So it was that men, as fathers, were to have authority in relation to their children, and it was only in relation to men that women and children were to enjoy freedom. This can help us illuminate particular flaws in the liberal conception of freedom. It reveals the shallowness of its claims to universality.[5] This was also part of a feminist challenge as women came to recognise that if freedom and equality were to be understood solely in terms of rights it meant accepting the terms already established by men. Women sought the freedom to define their own reality, whether this was a matter of work, domestic life or sexuality.

Within an Enlightenment tradition reason is set in fundamental opposition to nature – our emotions, feelings and desires. In the family the father is to be the source of reason. He is also to be the source of discipline for, as Kant says in the introduction to *Education* 'Discipline changes animal nature into human nature'.[6] It is only as rational agents that we can exercise our freedom and autonomy. This has profoundly influenced liberal conceptions of authority and shows how circumscribed is its vision of freedom. Freedom remains a threat. As Kant acknowledges, 'The love of freedom is naturally so strong in man, that when once he has grown accustomed to freedom, he will sacrifice everything for its sake. For this very reason discipline must be brought into play very early ... Undisciplined men are apt to follow every caprice'.[7] So it is that children should 'accustom themselves early to yield to the commands of reason'.

Kant is convinced that in the first period of childhood 'the child must learn submission and passive obedience. In the next stage he should be allowed to think for himself, and to enjoy a certain amount of freedom, although still obliged to follow certain rules'.[8] For Kant education is fundamentally a matter of preparing children to exercise their freedom and autonomy. But this is conceived in fundamentally rationalist terms for there is no grasp that our autonomy and independence might also be grounded in our feelings and emotions. For Kant these are essentially forms of our unfreedom, determining our behaviour externally as they seek to influence us. So that even though Kant recognises that 'one of the greatest problems of education is how to unite submission to the necessary *restraint* with the child's capability of exercising his *freewill*,[9] he can only respond by saying that 'we must prove to him that restraint is only laid upon him that he may learn in time to use his liberty aright, and that his mind is being cultivated so that one day he may be free; that is, independent of the help of others'. But he also recognises that 'This is the last thing a child will come to understand'.[10]

These liberal ideals are set within a framework that views children as needing to be trained for 'It is discipline which prevents man from being turned aside by his animal impulses'.[11] The task of discipline is 'merely negative, its action being to counteract men's natural unruliness'; and for Kant it is clear that 'Unruliness consists in independence of law'.[12] So it is that 'By discipline men are placed in subjection to the laws of mankind, and brought to feel their constraint. This, however, must be accomplished early. Children, for instance, are first sent to school, not so much with the object of their learning something, but rather that they may become used to sitting still and doing exactly what they are told'.[13] This is important for Kant so that 'in later life they should not wish to put actually and instantly into practice anything that strikes them'.[14] In truth what Kant seems to be protecting himself against is the early 'love of freedom'.

Feminism has claimed emotional life as a source of dignity and self-respect. In this way it has challenged an enlightenment inheritance and the liberal conceptions of freedom, equality and human dignity that have emerged from it. We have inherited a rationalist tradition which is bereft of a moral language which can validate and honour our emotional lives. Within a Kantian tradition there is little space to draw meaningful distinctions between the different levels of our emotional experience. In contrast to reason these tend to get lumped together as 'inclinations' and treated as caprice. So it is that parents and teachers are warned that 'Undisciplined men are apt to follow every caprice'.[15] This is reinforced in a way that shows how a European tradition of dignity and human rights is tied in its inception to a disdain of other peoples. For, as Kant says 'We see this also among savage nations, who, though they may discharge functions for some time like Europeans, yet can never become accustomed to European manners. With them, however, it is not the noble love of freedom which Rousseau and others imagine, but a kind of barbarism – the animal, so to speak, not having yet developed its human nature'.[15]

So it is that within the family paternal authority is based on the capacity of men to discern what is morally right. In this sense Kant gives a secular form to a Protestant tradition which separates radically what our reason discerns as 'right' or 'wrong' and what our feelings and emotions might lead us to discern. We learn to distrust our own feelings and perceptions. As Kant says 'Men should therefore accustom themselves early to yield to the commands of reason'.[16] We learn to accept the authority of our fathers without question. The question then is posed as to what extent this discourages children in their own insight and understanding, so making it hard for them to trust their own knowledge. In part feminism has made us sensitive to these processes of *invalidation* and the ways it can leave people feeling worthless. It encourages us to think that within a modernist culture formed in the images of the Enlightenment we have inherited a false rationalist conception of human action and the relationship of thought to feeling.

For Kant morality has also to be universal and impartial. Fathers have to learn to be impartial in their discipline. Supposedly, if they are not to show favouritism or partiality, they have to punish their children as they would anyone else who did something similar. As men learn to identify themselves with this position of authority, fearing any emotion as a sign of weakness, it can encourage them to be *distant* and *removed*. So with the Enlightenment we already have impersonal aspects as defining the character of paternal authority. Discipline is impersonal because authority is no longer visibly embodied in individual persons: individuals are judged impersonally before the moral law. The law exists in a realm of its own, even though the faculty of reason gives us the possibility of knowing its dictates. It is crucial for liberalism that we accept a vision of freedom in which we legislate for ourselves as we come to accept the dictates of reason. So it is that authority is supposedly not external but has its source within ourselves. This is the way that liberalism seeks to reconcile freedom with authority.

Critical Theory: Authority and Reason

The Frankfurt school[17] developed critical theory in the 20s and 30s; it sought to synthesise the analyses of Marx and Freud, in order to connect the categories of individual psychic development – psychoanalysis – with the changing forms of familial authority. In part this was an ongoing attempt to restore the historical character of psychoanalytic conceptions that would otherwise present themselves as universal. They were seeking to transform Marxist forms of ideological analysis through an appreciation of the mediating role of the family. It isn't that we internalise an ideology as individuals but that we become the kind of individuals that we are through the relationships that we have experienced in the family. So it is that individuality can no longer be assumed in its autonomy and integrity as it was within classical social theory. It was fundamentally Freud's contribution to provide us with a language capable of illuminating the precarious character of individuality. The strength of critical theory, in contrast to structuralist appropriations of psychoanalysis, is that it is seeking a way of acknowledging the autonomy of our inner lives without disconnecting them from the experience we live in relationships.

Critical theory pointed to a change in the character of fathering as part of grasping the changing character of authority within capitalist societies. They drew attention to a transition in the character of familial authority. This work drew on both Simmel and Weber who had in their different ways studied a shift away from more *personal* forms of authority towards more *impersonal* and bureaucratic forms of authority.[18] For Weber this was part of the process of rationalisation that characterised industrialisation. A form of instrumental rationality was reorganising personal and social relations as people were encouraged to think increasingly in terms of means to realise pre-given ends. There was less concern with fundamental values, as efficiency and rationalisation became ends in themselves. This fosters a particular form of moral education. The Frankfurt school understood that the move towards an increasingly bureaucratic form of work fostered a change in the character of prevailing masculinities.

The Frankfurt School significantly connected an understanding of individual psychic development with the critique of instrumental reason. Influenced by Weber, they came to recognise the dominance of this form of rationality and the ways that it subverted any experience of intrinsic value. But unlike Weber they did not see this as an inevitable process, but as tied to the reification of capitalist social relations, in which relationships between people increasingly take on the form of a relationship between things.[19] They identified a loss in the father's moral authority owing to the growing powerlessness of individuals within monopoly capitalism. With the deskilling of work many men had lost control at work and the power to ensure a skilled job to their sons. With the bureaucratisation of many middle-class jobs men had learnt to identify themselves with the rules of the organisations for which they worked.

This has led to a transformation in the authority and presence that many men have within the contemporary family. Children have often not experienced their fathers as powerful and dominating figures, but as absent and withdrawn. This has led Alexander Mitscherlich, a psychoanalyst who in part continues a Frankfurt tradition of bringing psychoanalysis to bear upon an analysis of modern society, to use the term 'fatherless society' in his influential work *Society Without the Father*.[20] The Frankfurt School had already argued that paternal authority is replaced by bureaucratic state institutions, and the moral image of the father by images provided by the media, education and science. This means that the form of domination that characterises recent capitalist societies does not express itself directly as authority; instead, as Jessica Benjamin describes, it operates: 'indirectly as the transformation of all relationships and activity into objective, instrumental, depersonalised forms'.[21] For Max Horkheimer,[22] this change was important because it fosters a change in personality type, no longer based on the internalisation of authority, but instead on conformity to external standards. This means that resistance to the social order is being subverted as people learn to love their own chains.

Critical theory, as Horkheimer came to define the theoretical work the Frankfurt School was developing, in opposition to the traditional theory of positivism, accepted the idea that internalisation of authority, and the conscience that it creates, is the only basis upon which authority can be later challenged. This was a reassertion of the notion of a conscience based on reason. However, as instrumental reason comes to dominance, rationality becomes unconcerned with the ends and values it serves; and this leads to a weakening of reflection and critical consciousness; questions of morality and politics are no longer experienced as, fundamentally, issues of values. We learn to identify happiness with individual success and achievement in existing society, and are no longer able to explore our fundamental values and beliefs. We are encouraged to take up an instrumental attitude towards the self, learning to think that we must be happy because we have achieved in the eyes of others. Feminism provided a challenge to this form of reality, identifying an oppression that had been rendered invisible within a liberal moral theory. So it was feminism that developed an understanding of critical consciousness that was at odds with the particular rationalisation of the Frankfurt school. Women, out of sharing their felt experience with others, learnt to identify their subordination within a supposedly equal relationship. They learnt to identify their own vision of freedom and autonomy.

An important part of an Enlightenment inheritance has led men to identify themselves with work. As Weber explains, this has become an end in itself. We learn as men to identify our well-being with our material possessions. As Weber says in *The Protestant Ethic and the Spirit of Capitalism*, which in many ways can be read as a study of masculinity, 'Man is dominated by the making of money, by acquisition as the ultimate purpose of his life. Economic acquisition is no longer subordinated to man as the means for the satisfaction of his material needs'.[23] Weber echoes the insight of Marx, that this is essentially irrational because it means that instead of working in order to live we seem to be living in order to work. It is crucial that we accept this as quite natural and do not recognise it as the irrationality that it is. As Weber says 'The reversal of what we should call the natural relationship, so irrational from a naive point of view, is evidently as definitely a leading principle of capitalism as it is foreign to all peoples not under capitalist influence'.[24]

Within this world of men it becomes difficult to listen to claims that are being made by partners and children. It is also difficult for men to value their relationships – to give time and attention to them. Even though men will often say that their families are the most important thing for them since this is what they are working so hard for, women will often experience it quite differently. It is difficult for men to break with an instrumentality that has come to dominate so much of life. It is as if men are often not *available* in relationships, their thoughts constantly drifting off. Real life and real work exist elsewhere, so that it can be hard for men to put their energies into relationships. Often we arrive home too exhausted, drained and used up. Our best energies have been used up at work and we rarely hold ourselves back so that we have something to give when we get back. In this state it is difficult to face challenges from our partners. It is hardly surprising that so many men seem so shocked when their relationships break down, assuming that it must be because of another relationship. It will be easier to blame others than take any responsibility ourselves. Sadly it is as if we have never learnt to appreciate what is involved emotionally in taking responsibility in our relationships.

Nor do we seem to have a language to explore what has gone wrong.

The Frankfurt school understood it as a feature of modern culture that our capacity for determining our individual and collective ends and values has been diminished. As men we are trapped into feeling that we have to constantly prove our masculinity. We have to be constantly on our guard against being put down by others. Without self-esteem established in this way, it can be hard to make space for relationships in our lives. Learning to be independent and self-sufficient means that we tend to discount our needs. Men learn to pride themselves on the fact that they do not have emotional needs, but can be relied upon as a firm shoulder for others. But at an unconscious level this can leave men feeling tense and uneasy, unsure that they are really achieving anything. It is as if men want to have their emotional needs recognised by women in heterosexual relationships, without having to own up to them. But as men learn to assume an instrumental relationship to themselves it becomes difficult to listen and respond to their partners.

With the Enlightenment we have learnt to identify progress with the domination of nature. This has formed our masculine sense of self-control as the domination of our inner nature, our feelings, emotions and desires. As Jessica Benjamin puts it, following Horkheimer, 'The victory of instrumental reason is a victory *against nature*. The world of objects becomes simply a field of resistance or an empty reflection of the subject's will to dominate. As nature is increasingly subordinated to the principle of instrumentality, it ceases to have a life of its own. The reality of the outer world disappears for the subject'.[25] So in relationship to men's bodies we learn to treat them as instruments that should respond to our will. We become deaf to the needs and life of the body. Similarly we are deaf to the sufferings of a wider nature that we have learnt to use for our own ends. In learning to assert our dignity as superior to nature, we diminish our humanity.

For critical theory it is the decline in familial solidarity, related in turn to the changing character of the father's authority, that brings the instrumental side of rationality to the fore. The children supposedly no longer identify with the father whose position has been undermined. He is no longer idealised, and his authority is no longer internalised. Conformity takes its place, as impersonal, extra-familial forms of authority in the school, surgery and media take his place. Denied a childhood experience of authority, the ego is supposedly weakened because it has grown without much struggle against paternal authority. This means that children no longer develop a critical consciousness able to defy and question authority. Rather, with the impact of mass media, education and professional guidance, people are now manipulated into an unthinking conformity. This leads to an acceptance of the rationality of the status quo. This tempts Horkheimer to regret the passing of the era of personal, paternal authority as the only firm basis for the development of a critical consciousness.

Horkheimer helps us understand the appeal to individual self-interest that has been so developed within Thatcherite politics. He is clear that self-interest can be a sufficient basis of an authority relationship. He demonstrates that reason takes the form of accommodation rather than critical insight into social relations. Individuals are encouraged to focus themselves on freedom as a matter of individual choices, giving up the claim to determine intentions or authorise actions and relations which transcend the single individual and her/his interest. The individual learns to conceive of herself or himself as a self-contained reality who affects no-one and is affected by no-one. Freedom is strictly a matter of individual opinion and choice, disconnected from any sense of effective control or power in social relations. Society exists as something quite independent, as the opposition between individual and society is raised to a fact of nature. Society, like nature, is organised according to its own laws. Reason seeks to grasp its laws, secure in its conviction that society can only be understood not changed. We have to learn about society so that we can accommodate ourselves to it, as we do with nature. As Horkheimer has it social relations 'appear to be a self-contained reality, another principle confronting the knowing and acting subject ... When it attempts to bridge the gap between the self and the world by means of thought it is already acknowledging reality as a principle in its own right ... which reflects the incompleteness of his freedom: the impotence of the single individual in an anarchic, contradictory inhuman reality'.[26]

So it is that we learn to identify reason with the calculation of self-interest. This becomes the basis of our compliance to existing relations of power and subordination. As men we learn to accept responsibility for our individual fate.

The Protestant work ethic, which has played such a powerful role in defining western conceptions of masculinity, is based upon the seeming consistency between individual effort and success. So it is that competitive capitalist social relations encourage individuals to feel that they are masters of their own destiny only able to blame themselves for the position they have achieved in the larger society. In the modern era we have also lost any conviction in the relation between effort and reward. This has further undermined paternal authority as it subverts the father's insistence that the child take blame and responsibility for actions. The father is unable to guarantee his children any future, let alone secure employment. Authority has generally lost any semblance of legitimacy and therefore no-one expects it to act according to legitimate principles. People have come to feel that politicians serve only their own interests. Their words carry no conviction. In this context a Thatcherite politics can develop, for people expect no more than a self-interested form of politics and they have learnt to suspect those who stand for anything else. In this respect the experience of Labour governments in power has prepared the ground for the deeper crisis in socialist theory and practice.

In part the current disenchantment with politics expresses itself in a developing interest in psychology. In order to break with the instrumentalism in contemporary social life people come to feel that they can only trust their own experience. It is a big enough struggle for people to reach some honesty with themselves. Sexual politics recognises the workings of power in personal relationships so that the relationship between the personal and the political has to be radically reformulated. It establishes a different starting point, for it shows the difficulties of men and women exploring their needs and wants within a single relationship. It is not, as critical theory had it, that our needs have been totally instrumentalised, but that it can be difficult for us to explore what we want out of relationships and how to be ourselves in the context of a relationship. This places questions of ethics, values and beliefs at the heart of our politics. If socialism involves the insight that what sustains people in their lives is not simply the substitute gratification of accumulation but the quality of their relationships, then these issues have to be crucial.

Horkheimer's early arguments rested on the supposition that the plausibility of bourgeois social relations worked because they really appeared rational from the point of view of individual self-interest. This has become apparent again with Thatcherism. Somehow the market vision of freedom has been made compatible with a cynically instrumental vision of authority. Domination works through the direct manipulation of the subject whose approval and agency is no longer required. At least for a time it seemed as if changes in the labour process meant the workers no longer had to identify with and feel loyalty to their work. The assembly-line could enforce its own discipline and regulation. In part this has meant that workers do not expect the same kind of satisfaction from work which is more nakedly conceived as simply a way of earning. But at another level work remains important for giving men a sense of control over their lives. Even in the midst of acute domestic crisis few men seem to take much time off from work.

Authority, Masculinity and Emotional Life

In Horkheimer's reconsideration of the relationship of family to authority in his 1949 essay 'Authority and the

Family Today', he looks favourably to the past and stresses the moral, rather than the formally rational element in paternal authority. He talks of earlier times in which 'a loving imitation of the self-reliant prudent man, devoted to his duty, was the source of moral autonomy in the individual'.[27] As Jessica Benjamin has characterised this, he 'inaugurates an era of nostalgic romanticisation of paternal authority in the age of reason which has not yet ended'.[28] As if shocked by the Holocaust, which the Frankfurt School were slow to acknowledge, Horkheimer had returned to the safer ground provided by Kantian ethics.

Benjamin also helps identify a serious problem in Horkheimer's thought in his insistence, shared in part by Freud, on the link between the identification with the father, internalisation, and the independent conscience. Freud's idea of internalisation argues for the creation of a super-ego or conscience which embodies the external prohibitions of morality. It is partly through the oedipus complex that boys learn to identify themselves with their fathers and so identify their masculinity with a rejection of feelings and emotions that are tied to an early relationship with the mother. This is the path through which we learn discipline and self-control. There is a tension here because Freud also understood that we can be too rigidly and tightly controlled.

Psychoanalysis partly works to shift the burdens of responsibility. We learn to accept that it is natural for us to have sexual feelings or a sense of anger. We learn to distinguish between acknowledging these feelings and acting upon them. In part we learn to reinstate the value of our emotional lives against a utilitarian culture which would denigrate them. This can help us recognise our need and capacity for love and mutual recognition. As we learn to deny these needs they are not extinguished but take on an objective form which is opposed to, yet depends on the original need or capacity. Thus Benjamin points out that our need and capacity for mutual recognition 'become alienated into objective forms of instrumental culture which imprison and distort them'.[29] A structuralist tradition which would seem to dispense with a language of alienation would be left with an instrumental attitude, in its assumption that subjects are socially and historically constituted.

If we assume, as a structuralist tradition tends to, that the active nature of subjectivity is only brought into being by external pressure, or through particular discourses, then it will be something that can be extinguished. This implies that the child has no inner spontaneous desire to individuate or to become independent. It also implies that the mother has no desire to encourage independence and autonomy so that the father is required to save civilisation from regression. In part this shows a continuity between Kant and Freud, for both assume that civilisation is to be identified with reason and share a conception of autonomy grounded in the notion of the rational self. Freud knew that it was no longer plausible for the rational self to assert its autonomy through the domination of our feelings and desires, but somehow had to find a path through coming to terms with them.

The idea that the father is required for individuation, according to Benjamin, is based upon a confusion of gender identification with separation-individuation from the mother. It seems as if the child can only leave the mother by identifying with the father, whose masculinity consists in part in the repudiation of maternal dependency. Not only does this deny the possibility of a relationship with the mother that actually encourages autonomy, but it fosters the Kantian idea that autonomy consists in the denial of the need for the other. This is an undialectical understanding of autonomy and independence which defines it in opposition to feelings, emotions and dependency. In traditional masculinist terms we can only strive for independence through releasing ourselves from all forms of dependency. This makes it difficult for men to acknowledge their emotions and needs without feeling that their masculinity is somehow being brought into question.

But the emotional needs of men do not disappear, even when they are consciously denied. It is as if we learn to expect these needs to be identified and met by our partners without their having to be named in language. It is because critical theory saw the subject as largely constituted by the idea of critical reflection that its vision remains within a masculine framework. They lament the decline of nurturant activity but their conception of psychic nature cannot include the need for recognition of self in other and other in self that is indispensable for it. They lacked any developed sense of intersubjectivity and sense of the need for people to be recognised and confirmed in their abilities and capacities in their relationships with others. So in asserting that authority has become depersonalised they neglect the fact, as Benjamin has it, 'that personal strivings toward activity and recognition continue to underline the fetishised appearances. Were it not so, we would need not a theory of alienation but only a theory of manipulation which presupposes that the subject is infinitely malleable'.[30]

Critical theory was trapped by its image of revolt as a critical consciousness formed in the image of the just and moral father. For Adorno and Horkheimer, in the *Dialectic of Englightenment*, the father whose 'responsibility for wife and children (was) so carefully nurtured by bourgeois civilisation ... (whose) conscience consisted in the devotion of the ego to the substantial outside world, in the ability to take into account the true interests of others',[31] is the father who teaches the sons to revolt. The sons first internalise the father's principles and prohibitions and then challenge him for his failure to live up to them. This legitimates their revolt against him. But as Marcuse recognised in *Eros and Civilisation*[32], on Freud's story of the primal horde it is difficult to distinguish revolt from restoration. It is difficult to grasp how boys, let alone girls, come to define themselves in relation to their fathers. As Chodorow has pointed out in *The Reproduction of Mothering*[33] children tend to have a more abstract and impersonal relationship to their fathers. Divorced from the day to day care it can mean that fathers become unreal and idealised figures who only enter the family as authorities or else to ensure separation.

Feminism has challenged men to reconsider the character of fathering and their involvement with children. It has fostered an image of revolt quite different from the model of critical consciousness based upon the father ideal, his discipline and rationality. As Benjamin has described it, 'contemporary feminism has articulated an image of revolt based upon identification with others stemming from awareness of one's own suffering and oppression. The knowledge which is based upon paying attention to one's feelings and denied aspirations implies, ultimately, a different view of human nature and the civilising process as well'.[34]

But this is a conception of human nature that is difficult for men to appreciate. It involves a challenge to our inherited conception of the rational self. It talks of a knowledge that is grounded in feelings and a sharing with others that men have learnt to fear because it threatens a precarious sense of self-worth that other men are bound to belittle and challenge. If this gives us a way of rejecting the alternatives of internalised authority versus seamless conformity it opens up a terrifying and unfamiliar path. It teaches men to acknowledge and respect their emotions and feelings as integral aspects of the self, rather than to conceal and denigrate them. So it is a matter of the quality of the relationship that I have with my father, not simply whether he is strong or weak in the social world. It raises as a crucial question the ways we were recognised and affirmed by our fathers, and the difference this makes to the ways that we might be able to affirm our children. The language of internalisation fails to illuminate these issues, caught up as it is with seeing others as the projection of the self. Its rationalism denies the importance of intimacy and relationship.

Because Freud tied the formation of super-ego or conscience to castration anxiety, he considered women to be deprived by nature of the impetus for a clear-cut Oedipal resolution. This meant that women's super-ego was compromised since it could never separate itself from its emotional origins. This was central because Freud had accepted Kant's identification of morality with an independent and autonomous conception of reason. This allowed Freud to conclude that women showed less sense of justice since 'they are more often influenced in their judgements by feelings or affection or hostility'.[35]

Writing against the masculine bias of psychoanalytic theory Nancy Chodorow replaces Freud's negative description of female psychology with a positive sense that 'girls emerge from this period with a basis for 'empathy' built into their primary definition of self in a way that boys do not'. As she describes it, 'Girls emerge with a stronger basis for experiencing another's needs or feelings as one's own'.[36]

In contrast boys, in defining themselves as masculine, separate themselves from their mothers, thus separating themselves from their primary love and sense of empathy. Feelings of need and dependency are eschewed as they are identified with the soft and the female. So it is for boys and men that separation and individuation are critically tied to gender identity since separation from the mother is presumed essential to the development of masculinity. This helps explain why male gender identity is threatened by intimacy and why regression to pre-oedipal relational modes is a basic threat to the male ego. This also helps explain the difficulties that men can have in redefining a less distant and impersonal form of fathering. Relationships with infants and small children can remind men of an intimacy and closeness that they have long disowned. It can be painful to be reminded of the costs of manhood. Men can be deeply jealous of the relationship that mother and child can establish. They can respond violently to exclusion as this awakens deep feelings of rejection.

Since the 1960s, in the radical movements concerned with sexual politics, there has been a sharp move against thinking of 'fathering' and 'mothering' as unique and distinct activities and towards thinking in terms of shared parenting. The degendering and depersonalising of authority has allowed members of both sexes to play the roles formerly restricted to one. For a time in the 70s this led some people to think that, for instance, breast feeding,

which threatened to bring an inequality into the relationship that parents could have with their babies and infants,
was to be regretted. There was confusion revealed in our
conceptions of equality and rights. We tended to think of
equality in terms of sameness, and the dominance of
structuralist theory encouraged people to deny the
significance of natural differences as if they are all equally
socially constructed. Reflecting upon some of these
changes in our conceptions of parenting illuminates
central questions in our understanding of change, equality
and social transformation.

Men, Feminism and Fathering

Feminism has challenged men to develop more involved
and personal relationships with their children. This can be
difficult to achieve if we have learnt from our own fathers
that we care through being a distant and respected figure.
It can be hard to care in more personally sensitive ways
because we have learnt to be quite insensitive to our own
emotions and feelings. If we have learnt, partly through
work, to take on a more instrumental attitude towards
ourselves then this will shape our relationships with our
partners and children. It can be even more frustrating if
we feel that we cannot respond in the way we would want
to. We learn as men that we can do anything if we put our
minds to it and show will and determination. It can annoy
us to discover this does not work in our personal relations
for this is the only rationality that we know. It can
encourage men to pressure their partners to organise
childcare as if it can simply be a routinised activity. This
will allow greater male participation without men having
to face the difficulties they have in relating more
personally and intuitively to the needs of an infant or
child.

Horkheimer also identifies a decline in maternal
nurturance as an important cause of change. He thought
that the professionalisation of motherhood so that it is
modelled according to new principles of social hygiene
and efficiency had led to a lack of real emotional

relationship between mother and child. Women had been dispossessed of their own insight and understanding as they were taught that the experts knew best. They were encouraged to discount their own intuitive knowledge as 'subjective' or 'emotional'. In this way mothers were often disempowered. For a period breast feeding was discouraged. Childcare was a matter of rational control rather than a matter of responding to the needs of the infant. This understanding was slow to develop. Mothers were taught to assert control – to show who was boss – even before the baby had left the maternity ward. Instrumental rationality had extended to the sphere of mothering. Even birth had been redefined. It was no longer a natural event in a woman's life but it was a technological event in which a woman's body was seen as an 'interference' in the medical problem of 'getting the baby out'. But the 1980s saw a move against these forms of instrumental rationality. Women refused to accept the passivity that medicine had imposed and insisted on an active birth. What is more, birth became an experience within a relationship in which men were learning to participate, rather than a medical event from which they were excluded as passive observers. Attendance at birth has been a powerful experience for many men.

The Frankfurt school was significant in encouraging us to consider changes in the nature of men's authority within the family. This shows that patriarchal authority is not a given structure of power but is socially and historically transformed. Rather than thinking in structuralist terms of the ways that capitalism and patriarchy, as given structures of power, are to be related to each other, we can identify shifts in the character of power and authority. In this way we escape the central tension between acknowledging that masculinity is 'socially and historically constituted' and the identification of masculinity with 'male power' which blocks any possibility of change. This fixes masculinity into a stable ontological category, a condition that is inescapable for men.[37] It becomes pointless to explore the historical forms of masculinities, for the differences between them are assumed, in advance, to lack significance. Paradoxically men are let off the theoretical hook as these issues can safely be left to feminists alone. How is it that we are to bring into relationship mens' power and work and their experiences at home? Traditional sociology has treated these as distinct realms that have to be analysed in their own terms. Structuralist and post-structuralist work does little better, for it tends to think of the tensions and contradictions in peoples' experience as the outcome of 'subjects' being organised, 'constituted' or 'articulated' through the different discourses of 'work' and 'home'. It is as if subjectivities are organised according to these varying discourses. Crudely we have to dispense with the category of 'experience' for this is assumed to imply an appeal to a non-discursive form of practice. So it is that the contradictions in our lived experience, central to Gramsci's understanding of Marxism in the *Prison Notebooks*, are presented as contradictions between the prevailing discourses.

This grows out of the confusions that surround what we mean by the phrase 'socially and historically constituted'. It derives its meaning from implicit opposition to an 'essentialism', for our 'subjectivity' is itself constituted or brought into existence through these discourses. It is important to identify this way of thinking because it has become so widespread that it is uncritically taken for granted as the only starting-point for theoretical work. Sadly it has meant difficulty in learning from the insights of Gramsci, since his work is so often explained within this framework.[39] In truth he provides a powerful challenge to it, for he wants to keep open the theoretical possibility of a *tension* between who men are expected to be at work, and who they are striving, however tentatively, to be or become. This is foreclosed if we simply identify 'men' with 'male power'.

At least if we recognise that there is a 'frustration' that is built into the humiliations of work, of being treated and experiencing oneself as being no more than an appendage to a machine in the modern factory, then we are forced to explore how it is that people learn to cope with the stress, tension and frustration. In part this is what makes Marx's language of alienation as a material relation tied to a particular organisation of the labour process still indispensable. To treat Marx's analysis as 'humanist' or 'essentialist' to be replaced by a theory of history and politics has been to injure our understanding of significant historical and cultural changes.

This is part of giving substance to the notion of a 'hierarchy of powers', learning from Simone Weil's neglected writing in *Oppression and Liberty* that it is part of the *workings* of relationships of power and subordination that people in a relative position of power can take out their frustrations and hostilities on those who are beneath them.[40] Working people who are constantly told that they are paid to take orders and that 'if they don't like it they know what they can do' often have to take their resentment and frustration home with them. This is a reality of class relations of power that shows itself in the increasing incidence of domestic violence and child abuse. Only if we learn to make connections with the increasing intensity and tensions of work can we appreciate the forms in which a 'crisis in masculinity' fosters violence and brutality.

So much post-structuralist work is bereft of a moral language that could illuminate the tensions and indignities of work. To treat morality as simply one discourse among others is to reproduce a crude scientism. As Weil understood, if people are mistreated they will take out their suffering on others, for this works as a way of relieving the self. So it is that we might connect what Braverman has called the 'degradation of work' with an intensification of frustration and tension.[41] It is children who are often at the bottom of the 'hierarchy' with few rights of their own. Children often resent the silent tensions that can fill the house when their father comes back from work. They learn to keep out of his way. Sometimes they are already expected to be in bed, so they don't even see him.

The Frankfurt school recognised transformations in forms of male power. With a change in men's position

within the labour process their position of power within
the family was also undermined. But they did not explore
the dimension of men being under pressure to act out a
power within the family they have lost within work. They
tended to assume that men had somehow been 'tamed'
through the bureaucratisation of work and so had been
reconciled to a loss of authority at work. It could be that if
men feel they no longer have dignity and self-respect at
work that they will demand this more intensely from
partners and children.

In Philip Slater's *The Pursuit of Loneliness*[12] there is an
appreciation of the shock to the sense of freedom and
independence people have learnt to take for granted when
they have a child. It awakens feelings and needs that
people are not prepared for, especially when they have
assumed that after a few weeks life will return to normal.
Traditionally these difficulties have been left for women to
cope with as men have taken refuge at work.

The myth that many men still share that mothering is
'natural' to women makes it that much harder for them to
appreciate the difficulties and frustrations in say, learning
to breast feed. If women are left feeling that they must
hide the anxieties and difficulties involved in these
difficult weeks and months of learning, distance and
resentment will take deep roots. The fact that resentments
are not expressed does not mean that they go away. They
can produce an unwanted distance and coldness as
partners find communication gradually being blocked
between them.

Without a fundamental restructuring of the nature of
capitalist work relations it is difficult to actualise more
equal forms of childcare. Slater argues that the isolation
and loneliness that both working-class and middle-class
mothers often feel would make the mother both more
dependent on the child and loath to allow it autonomy, as
well as making her more demanding that the child
perform according to reified standards. Separation
between mother and child becomes a critical issue when
the mother has learnt to gain emotional support from her
child, because of difficulties in communicating openly and

honestly with her partner. It is often difficulties in the relationship between the adults which are reflected as difficulties with the child. In this sense it is often the youngest child which carries the tensions and difficulties in the family. Within an instrumental culture we learn to treat our infants in instrumental ways. We learn that we are foolish if we do not organise our childcare according to our needs as parents. We have to get babies adapting to our patterns so that they learn to eat and sleep not when they are hungry or tired, but when it suits us. It is part of an instrumental culture to deny the autonomy and agency of babies and children. It eradicates the tension that exists between learning to acknowledge and affirm the rhythms and needs of even newly born babies and the needs that parents themselves have.

This is to argue that the striving for recognition and self activity are basic to establishing a relationship of trust. If a baby's cry is responded to in the early days, weeks and months, she will learn that she does not have to cry incessantly to be responded to. She will trust that a response will come. But if it is immediately presented as a 'battle of wills' in which the baby has to learn to wait, it will soon learn to silence its own needs or else learn to bawl its head off. Unfortunately Horkheimer follows Freud in assuming that like the active and synthesising functions of the ego, these capacities for activity and authorship seem only to emerge in response to outside pressure. This pressure towards activity was provided by the father and then internalised. Against this I think Jessica Benjamin is right to argue the opposite, 'that these capacities are distorted and take on the appearance of secondary, derivative phenomena because their growth is thwarted by instrumental culture. Critical theory misses the active intersubjective process which creates this culture, although it identified so clearly the loss of agency authorship which prevail in and through it'.[43]

So it is that critical theory, in asserting that authority has become depersonalised or cultural forms reified, neglects the fact that personal strivings towards activity and

recognition continue to underlie the fetishised appearances. It is in this context that we can grasp some of the
challenges of sexual politics since the early 1970s. Though
neglected in the early years of the women's movement
when motherhood was sometimes regarded as a trap that
should be avoided at all costs, there has been a serious
reconsideration. There was a challenge that the tasks of
parenting should be equally shared. This raised the crucial
issue of what it was that men were learning to do. Were
they being asked to do what was traditionally done by
mothers or were they being challenged to redefine the
nature and character of fathering. For a period at least it
seemed as if there was nothing specific in the nature of
fathering. It was simply a matter of sharing the tasks.

If we learn to develop closer more personal
relationships with our children it is very painful to think of
life without everyday contact. This reworking of the
nature of fathering involved a different conception of
respect and authority. It has less to do with teaching
abstract moral principles and maintaining a due distance
than it has with serving as examples for our children. We
can no longer say 'do what I say, not what I do', for we
have to embody our morality in the character of the
relationships that we establish. This is not because morality
is learnt through imitation but because we establish values
in the quality of the relationships we have. In part this
involves being clear about one's own needs as adults and
establishing clear boundaries for children. This is a
different vision of parental authority.

Psychological theories of the 1940s and 50s talked about
fathering in terms of roles and serving as a role model for
your children. It had a sense that fathers had something
distinctive to offer as role models for their children. This
led many women who were left alone with children to feel
incapable of bringing up children on their own. Often it
meant they felt they had to seek new husbands so that they
could provide a father for their children. It was feared
that without the influence of a father to model themselves
on boys would be less likely to develop heterosexual
relationships. So it was that mothers were undermined. At

the same time fathers learnt that they were not to be involved with their children for otherwise they would not be able to sustain their authority as fathers. They would threaten the respect that was due to them as fathers. So it was that psychology served to normalise a particular form of paternal authority. Little in the way of every day personal involvement and relationship was expected. It was in preserving distance that fathers supposedly offered us what we needed as children.

So it was that fathers learnt that they would be failing in their duties towards their children if they got more involved with them. They had to curb their own inclinations so that they could maintain the respect of their children. This vision is clearly represented in Kant's *Education*. It is because children are seen as natural and instinctive beings who are controlled by their feelings that they require the external restraint of adult reason. This defined the duties of fathering as educating children into accepting rational principles of behaviour. So it is that fathers learn not to listen to what their children have to say, for this is not the voice of reason. Children have to learn that 'silence is golden'. They have to show respect to adults by waiting until they are spoken to. So it is that children learn to distrust speech as a means of expression, learning to speak when they have discovered something 'worthwhile' to say. It is this pattern which is reinforced within so many schools as children learn to accept that knowledge exists externally in the control of their teachers.

Childhood is conceived as a movement from nature to reason. This goes along with movement from dependency to independence. This vision of childhood development as a movement towards separateness leaves us feeling in Freud's work that forms of attachment are impediments to development. This has led many psychologists, including Piaget and Kohlberg to regard male behaviour as the norm, and female behaviour as some kind of deviation from that norm. As Carol Gilligan has described it in *In A Different Voice*, the disparity between women's experience and the representation of human development, noted throughout the psychological literature, has generally been seen to signify a problem in women's development'.[42] She prefers to think that it shows a limitation in 'the conception of the human condition, an omission of certain truths about life'. These truths concern the importance of relationships and attachment in our lives. It is because separation from the mother is essential for the development of masculinity that issues of separation and individualisation are critically tied to gender identity for boys. Male gender identity is threatened by intimacy, so that men tend to have difficulties with relationships while women tend to have problems with individualisation.

In part we inherit a false conception of autonomy within a liberal moral culture. It leaves no space for dependency, relationship or feeling. These are stages that we are supposed to have left behind us as we take this linear path towards adulthood within a Kantian tradition.

Within a Kantian tradition we learn to achieve autonomy at the expense of our emotions and feelings. It is through dominating our emotional lives that we assert our autonomy which is a feature of reason alone. In challenging traditional conceptions of fathering we bring into question this taken for granted framework. We look towards different relationships of authority and discipline as we bring forward different understandings of childhood. We sensitise ourselves to the ways children can be hurt and abused through not being heard or recognised for who they are. We can help displace false polarities as they learn to be both dependent and independent, emotional as well as rational, tender as well as strong. This helps us rework central concerns in our inherited social and political theory.

This is part of a larger study of fathering and authority. I would like to thank the Masculinity Research Group at Goldsmiths College, University of London, as well as Paul Atkinson, Paul Morrison and John Tosh who were all part of the session on Fathers and Children at the Breaking Out Event.

Notes

¹ With the Enlightenment we have the idea that society be organised according to the principles of reason, and that traditional forms of religious and autocratic authority rely on tradition and habit. An age of reason was to bring light into what had been a period of darkness. Immanuel Kant provided an important statement of this vision in 'An Answer to the Question: What is Enlightenment?', in *Kant's Political Writings*, edited by Hans Reiss, Cambridge University Press, 1970. It has been a central essay in the discussion of modernism and postmodernism. See, for instance, the essays by Foucault and Habermas in *Foucault: A Critical Reader* edited by David Hoy, Basil Blackwell, 1986.

² *Kant's Political Writings*, edited by Hans Reiss, p 55, Cambridge University Press, 1970

³ *Ibid.* p 55

⁴ *Ibid.* p 54. The issues relating to conceptions of autonomy and dependence inherited from Kant within liberal moral theory are discussed in Victor J Seidler *Kant, Respect and Injustice: The Limits of Liberal Moral Theory*, Routledge and Kegan Paul, 1986

⁵ The difficulties which a universalistic moral theory has in illuminating the particularities of women's moral experience has been raised by Carol Gilligan, *In a Different Voice*, Harvard University Press, 1982. She draws out how women have been judged by standards not of their own making. Some of the difficulties which a Kantian tradition has in dealing with altruistic feelings, care and responsibility in relationships is also raised by Lawrence Blum, *Friendship, Altruism and Morality*, Routledge and Kegan Paul, 1980.

⁵ Immanuel Kant *Education* p 2 University of Michigan Press, 1960. Kant's distinction between reason and nature has significant resonance within contemporary social theory for it provides the philosophical grounds for the pervasive structuralist distinction between culture and nature.

⁷ Kant *Education*, p 4

⁸ *Ibid.* p 26

⁹ *Ibid.* p 27

¹⁰ *Ibid.* p 28

¹¹ *Ibid.* p 3

¹² *Ibid.* p 3

¹³ *Ibid.* p 3

¹⁴ *Ibid.* p 4

¹⁵ *Ibid.* p 4. The Enlightenment prepared the terms for the identification of civilisation with reason and science. It was to legitimate colonialism as it allowed a predominantly white and christian culture to assume an automatic superiority. Europe had science, culture, reason and freedom while the others had only nature. Sadly the degradation of nature and feeling is written into the rationalism we inherit within a structuralist tradition. A useful challenge is provided by Susan Griffin, *Women and Nature*, Womens Press, 1984.

[16] Kant *Education*, p 4

[17] The Frankfurt School whose members included Max Horkheimer, Theodor W. Adorno, Walter Benjamin, Erich Fromm, Leo Lowenthal & Herbert Marcuse, developed a form of critical theory that included the influence of both Marx and Freud in its analysis. Martin Jay in *The Dialectical Innovation: A History of the Frankfurt School and the Institute of Social Research, 1923-50*, Heinemann Educational Books, 1973, focussed on the 1930s and 1940s which were Horkheimer's most productive years before the Institute moved to New York with the rise of Nazism. Susan Buck-Morss, in *The Origin of the Negative Dialectic* focuses on the relationship of Adorno and Benjamin to the Frankfurt Institute (Harvester Press, 1977).

[18] Both Weber and Simmel, as part of an earlier generation of German social theorists, had been an influence on the Frankfurt school. A useful introduction to Max Weber is provided by Donald Macrae, *Max Weber*, Fontana. While for Simmel there is David Frisby's *Sociological Impressionism*, Heinemann, 1981.

[19] Georg Lukacs' theory of reification was a powerful influence on the Frankfurt School. Lukacs was a student and friend of Max Weber, who studied with him in Heidelberg, before he broke with Weber and became influenced by Hegel and Marx. The theory of reification was his break with orthodox Marxism and his continuing appreciation of the importance of Hegel's conception of the dialectic for any understanding of revolutionary Marxism. His understanding of reification, that still bears the influence of Weber's conception of rationalisation, is developed in Georg Lukacs *History and Class Consciousness*, Merlin Press, 1971. His insights have often been lost within an Althusserian tradition that derided his work as 'humanist'.

[20] Alexander Mitscherlich is a psychoanalyst who has attempted, as director of the Sigmund Freud Institute in Frankfurt, to bring a modified Freudian psychology to bear upon issues of authority in *Society Without The Father*, Schocken, 1970. There are certain common themes with the Frankfurt school, but their concern with authority was more clearly within a Marxist tradition.

[21] Jessica Benjamin has worked to bring feminist theory and the Frankfurt school into critical relationship to each other. In part it provides a challenge to the structuralist emphasis within much feminist theory, which threatens to marginalise some of the central insights of feminism. See, for instance 'Authority and the Family Revisited: Or, A World Without Fathers?', which is a critical revision of Max Horkheimer's influential writing on the family and authority. *New German Critique* Winter 1978 (p 35).

[22] Max Horkheimer was partly responsible for the focus upon issues of family, authority and culture within the early work of the Frankfurt School. Both Erich Fromm and Herbert Marcuse contributed studies to this work. For Horkheimer's essay 'Authority and the Family', see *Critical Theory: Selected Essays*, Seabury Press, 1972.

[23] Max Weber *The Protestant Ethic and The Spirit of Capitalism*, p 53.

George Allen and Unwin, 1930.

[24] *Ibid*, p. 53

[25] Jessica Benjamin, *op. cit.*, p 40.

[26] Max Horkheimer, *op. cit.*, p 79.

[27] Horkheimer's reconsideration of the issues of authority and family in the post-war context tended to accept the view that internalisation of authority is the only basis for the later rejection of authority. See his essay 'Authority and the Family Today' in *The Family: Its Function and Destiny*, R Anshen, New York 1949, p 365.

[28] Jessica Benjamin *op. cit.* p 48.

[29] *Ibid.* p 43.

[30] *Ibid.* p 55.

[31] Max Horkheimer and Theodor W. Adorno *Dialectic of Enlightenment*, Allen Lane, 1973.

[32] Herbert Marcuse, *Eros and Civilization*, Beacon Press, Boston, 1955. Without talking scientifically about masculinity, Marcuse recognises that 'As the scientific rationality of Western civilisation began to bear its full fruit, it became increasingly conscious of its psychical implications. The ego which undertook the rational transformation of the human and natural environment reveals itself as an essentially aggressive, offensive subject, whose thoughts and actions were designed for mastering objects. It was a subject *against* an object ... nature (its own as well as the external world) was 'given' to the ego as something that had to be fought, conquered and even violated – such was the precondition for self-preservation and self-development', p 110.

[33] Nancy Chodorow, *The Reproduction of Mothering*, University of California Press, 1978.

[34] Jessica Benjamin, *op. cit.*, p 56.

[35] Freud, *Some Psychical Consequences of the Anatomical Distinction between the Sexes*, Standard Edition, Vol 19 Hogarth Press, 1925.

[36] Chodorow, *op. cit.*, p 166 and 167.

[37] The historical formation of masculinity in relation to Foucault's post-structuralist analysis is further discussed by Victor Seidler in 'Reason, Desire and Male Sexuality' in *The Cultural Construction of Sexuality*, edited by Pat Caplan, Tavistock Publications, 1987.

[38] The relationship of structuralist Marxism to the category of experience is carefully explored by E P Thompson in *The Poverty of Theory and Other Essays*, Merlin Press, 1978. See also Victor J Seidler 'Trusting Ourselves: Marxism, Human Needs and Sexual Politics' in *One Dimensional Marxism*, Simon Clare, Terry Lovell, Kevin McDonnel and Victor J. Seidler (eds), Allison and Busby, 1980.

[39] See, for instance A Gramsci, 'The Study of Philosophy' in *The Prison Notebooks*, Lawrence and Wishart, 1971. Attempts to rethink his work in terms of structuralist categories on 'economy' and 'ideology' fail to illuminate the connections that are crucial for him in developing a counter-hegemonic relationship.

[40] Simone Weil *Oppression and Liberty*, Routledge and Kegan Paul, 1958. For an assessment of these themes see Lawrence Blum & Victor Seidler.

A Truer Liberty: Simone Weil and Marxism, Routledge, 1988 (forthcoming).

41 Harry Braverman, *Labour and Monopoly Capitalism*, Monthly Review Press, 1975.

42 Philip Slater, *The Pursuit of Loneliness*, Beacon Books, 1970

43 Benjamin, *op. cit.*, p 56.

44 Carol Gilligan, *In a Different Voice*, Harvard University Press, 1982, p 2.

Masculinity the Left, and Feminism

CYNTHIA COCKBURN

In some countries of Europe one finds few women today who will describe themselves as socialist feminists, or even as marxist feminists. This is not because such women are liberal, bourgeois or rightwards inclined. Far from it. Feminism in Greece and Spain for example was born as part of the struggle against fascism and it retains that stance today. It is rather because the bitterness of the experiences of many women in the communist parties and other left groups in the course of such struggles has driven them out of the organised left. In some cases it has amounted to a purge of feminism. A notorious instance is the sacking in 1982 of the feminist editorial group of the trade union women's journal *Antoinette* by the leadership of the French Confédération Générale du Travail. For such feminists, now separatist in their politics if not always or necessarily in their personal lives, the parties have no longer a claim to be the progressives.

In Britain there is still (just) a socialist feminist current, though the title is less readily adopted by women than it was in the days of mass Socialist Feminist Conferences in the 1970s. There is of course a problem of meaning and definition. Some teachers, researchers and writers attempting to wed feminist theory to marxist and post-marxist theory call themselves socialist feminist, as does the journal *Feminist Review*. The current exists, often without carrying the name, among the thousands of women who continue to be active as feminists within the

Labour Party, the Communist Party, other left groups and
the trade union movement. Besides, many women who do
not think of themselves as socialist feminists and who are
active mainly on 'women's issues' such as reproductive
rights and women's health, rather than in the (mixed sex)
left, also maintain a class analysis and a critique of
capitalism. Indeed many women would claim that 'the left'
doesn't always mean what many left men think it does.

This chapter aims to explore ground that lies between
'radical feminism' and 'socialist feminism' and to
strengthen the links between feminisms inside and outside
'the left' as presently defined. My aim is to contribute to a
debate that I sense exists within socialist feminism.

There is a tension amounting almost to an impossibility
in the lives of feminists within the left. The equation is
simply: the more aware you are of women's subordination
and the scope of the transformations posited by feminism,
the more you come into conflict with your corner of the
left (union hierarchy, Labour Party branch) and the more
rapidly you become burned out in dual struggles – against
the right and against men. There is a latent tendency
within the British left parallel to the situation I have
described as existing in some other European countries:
feminists who are 'in' the left are rapidly impelled 'in and
against' the left and ultimately forced to consider
themselves 'beyond' the left.

A new manner of being men?

The one belief a feminist needs as a prerequisite for
staying in-and-against the left is that 'men are capable of
change', indeed that 'men are *demonstrating* change' in
their relationship to women and to each other. It is this
optimism that characterises socialist feminist theory. It is
on the one hand an enabling optimism that has sustained
many practical struggles by women. On the other hand, I
want to argue, optimism has at times substituted for a
much needed reformulation of feminist theory and
practice on the left.

In piecing together this argument I want to refer to the

work of three socialist feminists whose thinking has been important enough to women working in the mixed-sex left organisations to warrant, by now, calling it a 'tradition'. They differ from each other of course, but they also have something in common. They came together in 1979 in producing the book *Beyond the Fragments: Feminism and the Making of Socialism*,[1] which provided a focus for a good deal of socialist feminist debate at the time. Sheila Rowbotham, Lynne Segal and Hilary Wainwright made a bid, in *BTF*, to bring together the more open and exploratory social movements surrounding left politics in the 70s and to feminise socialism in the process. They argued for a redefinition of priorities on the left, a new approach to socialist theory and consciousness, and for an open and searching examination of past and present forms of socialist organisation.

The book in many ways echoed the faith expressed six years earlier by one of its authors, Sheila Rowbotham, in the ability of men and women to work together.

> We are moving towards a new world together, but development is an uneven and painful process. We must be honest and help one another until they (ie, men) find a new way to express and organize themselves towards us. The generalisations of our consciousness of our own subord-ination enables them to discover a new manner of being men.[2]

A more recent book by Hilary Wainwright is an analysis of the Labour Party in 1987. *Labour: A Tale of Two Parties* tells the sorry story of the betrayals of socialism by the Labour leadership and the Parliamentary Party. But also sketched in are the dim outlines of the radical left that Hilary Wainwright's optimism affirms to be not only a theoretical possibility but an actual reality – what she calls a 'party in waiting' within Labour.[3] This is a left that is as much concerned with transforming social relations as it is with seizing control of the means of production. It is committed to electoral reform, to environmentalism, to peace and internationalism. It is a left that puts energy into grassroots movements rather than merely using them to harvest votes. And, being in favour of women's sections and black sections, it is reputedly responsive to feminism.

Finally, the third *BTF* author, Lynne Segal, recently published an important book that was originally sub-titled 'arguments for socialist feminism'. *Is the Future Female?* is a complex book and one that lends itself to diverse readings, but to some women (of whom I'm one) it reads as a fierce indictment of separatist 'radical feminism', seen as the dominant tendency within feminism in Britain in the 80s, and a restatement of faith in the project of working with men for socialism.[4]

In *Is the Future Female?* Lynne Segal casts back to the origins of the contemporary wave of feminism, to the early 70s when she suggests

> ... masculine and feminine identities were seen as neither fixed nor monolithic. Feminism, it was hoped, would give birth to new women and to new men. Indeed an attachment to gender stereotypes, or to any idea of a 'natural' difference underlying them, was criticised for causing women's oppression.

By contrast Lynne Segal is disturbed by the popular feminism of the 1980s which she characterises as celebrating an 'essentially different' women's culture and women's values, castigating men and men's 'innate rapacity and violence'. She feels feminism 'gave up on men just when more men appeared more willing to embrace its ideas. Many feminists began losing hope for any real change, just when some men began to look to feminists as a source of change'. She feels we should acknowledge that 'things emphatically *have* changed for women' and that men too are showing signs of change. 'Watching childbirth, pushing prams, putting children to bed, many men now relate sensitively to women and children in ways unthinkable to their fathers.'

Perceptions of male violence

Lynne Segal's book is an appeal to feminists in the autonomous middle-ground not to be lured by the siren-song of women's 'difference' but to recommit themselves to the socialist project and to stress anew 'the social and economic disadvantages of women and seek to change and improve women's immediate circumstances, not just in the area of paid work and family life but by providing funding for women's cultural projects, increasing women's safety in the streets or meeting the special needs of particular groups of women'.

Here I have a rather different group of women in mind, those already within the left, and with a rather different message. The difference is indeed small, because I share most of the analysis of the socialist feminists referred to above. Over the years I have learned a lot of my politics from them. But the difference of perspective, small as it may be, is I think significant for practice.

Among the (highly material) disadvantages and fears of ordinary women today, among 'the details of objective conditions' to use Lynne Segal's phrase, is, I would argue, a pervasive and well-justified fear of men and masculinity. Women are afraid for their own safety at the hands of men. They are afraid of what men may do to their sons: part of their experience is the passion of some lads to own a gun, drive a fast motorcycle or join the army. And they are afraid of what men may do to their daughters: the daily news of raped and murdered girls (and boys) screws up the pitch of women's fear for their own children and anxiety whenever they are out of sight. Women worry among themselves about men in the same way they worry about unemployment, poverty and ill-health. In their dreams surely such women imagine a world in which gender, as well as the control of production and distribution, is ordered differently. It is time that 'material' and 'materialist' extended to include this objective condition of the lives of working class and other women.

It was not until 1978 that the women's movement acquired its seventh demand, which dealt with sexuality and violence. Lynne Segal sees the late 70s as a turning point at which feminism began to go astray, giving explanatory primacy to male violence. I see it as a productive moment when the foregoing history of the women's movement brought home to women that 'equality' was an unachievable, indeed an undesirable goal, that equality could not be achieved by women as we are, with men as they are, or in the world as it is – and that 'difference' was the name of the game.

For 'difference' does not always or only mean an essential or natural difference between women and men. It is not necessarily idealist. It does not deny differences *between* women. Nor does it refer to the difference of that femininity in which we are stuck, the 'compensations of the power-less'. It evokes, most usefully in my view, a differing cultural and historical experience on the part of women and men and a positive valuation of women, on the very material basis of our part in the sexual division of labour. For that has given to women the most necessary and productive economic and social tasks – childcare, food production, clothing, health and shelter – while men have specialised in accumulation, war and the exercise of state power.

For me, then, the perceptions of feminism concerning male violence and issues of sexuality do not mark a wrong route taken but offer the chance of a strengthening and changing of socialist feminism by the insights of radical feminism.

For as socialist feminists we have tended to maintain our workable position within the left at a cost of sticking to a 'politics of equality', in contrast to what left feminists on the continent of Europe are happy to call a 'politics of difference'. The issues that signify difference, the ruder politics of the body and the emotions (violence, sexuality, desire, feeling) remain to stalk and sometimes destroy our personal lives while in public and on the left we represent women's needs as issues that do not jar too outrageously the equilibrium of a trade union or branch agenda.

As a result many socialist feminists have been obliged to live two lives. A radical and angry feminist is kicking within them, but it gets little expression in their political work. For them, too, insights like 'the myth of the vaginal orgasm', and 'the personal is political' were mind-shattering and life-changing. They too enjoy the creative space opened up for women by the separatism of

Greenham Common and the women's peace movement that flowed from there. They do not take seriously, perhaps, the excesses of 'womanism' in radical feminism, though enjoying to the full its affirmation of women. They don't number themselves among Mary Daly's Gnostic Nag-Nation of Dreamers. They don't believe in an *essential* womanliness. But they do feel that somehow women's long march through history has given us, broadly speaking, a *gender-specific set of values.* They aren't averse to thinking that 'womanly times' might make a good rough approximation to a socialist future. And why not?

Why not is because to go too far in this direction, to listen too much to one's feelings as a woman, makes one very angry with men of the left, acutely aware of misogyny, and this in turn leads one to intemperate and colourful words and actions that are resented and ridiculed by men (and some women) with whom one is committed to work. The problem is obviously worse for such women if they are, say, members of the Socialist Workers Party than if they are active in, say, a leftish constituency Labour Party or in a woman-frequented branch of NUPE. But everywhere there is that risk of being no longer a credible comrade.

Our socialist feminism in practice is thus very often a culturally self-policed and edited version of feminism. It is a feminism that concurs in dealing with the left within the left's own terms of reference – terms which exclude 'difference', body politics, sexuality and feelings. Not all, but most, men of the left prefer to think that the struggle for social change is essentially class struggle, the struggle for control of the means of production or of the state. Though many would disagree with Trotskyist analysis of class and conjuncture they would nonetheless endorse Tony Cliff's *Class Struggle and Women's Liberation* in defining the woman problem as originating in class exploitation.[5] Even men whose analysis takes in patriarchy do not necessarily see masculinity – and their own part in expressions of masculinity – as a problem that male socialists have to confront in the name of socialism.

Yet stark evidence exists that an integral part of what

the left conceives itself as struggling *against* – capitalism, imperialism, militarism – is precisely the nightmare world of sex and gender as we have come to live these things. We were told so by Wilhelm Reich long ago in *The Mass Psychology of Fascism.*[6] And we have been told again more recently in Klaus Theweleit's *Male Fantasies*. A brief account of this work will help clarify what I mean.

The dread of women

Theweleit analyses the novels and memoirs of a number of young German proto-fascists of the early 1920s. They were men who, embittered by the defeat of the Reich in 1918, continued to maintain illegal military organisation in the Freikorps, the private volunteer armies that roamed Germany, dedicated to the elimination of proletarian and left-wing movements. These men were killers. Some became the Hitler vanguard of the 1930s. Yet they were idealists and they wrote novels.

The special value of Theweleit's book lies in the fact that he asks first and foremost: what are women in these men's lives? Only in the light of that does he then look for an understanding of their relationship to the Fatherland, to Jews, Reds, to fighting, killing and death. And what these soldier-males manifest above all else is a dread of women. In a sense their never-ending war is a never-ending flight from woman.

In their writings woman is represented in three ways. There is the wife or lover, who is characteristically unnamed, is absent, distant, the one from whom they walk away. For love-making weakens a man; succumbing to the love of woman is incompatible with love of country and the bearing of arms. There is secondly the chaste, white woman who appears in the soldier-males' world as sister – his own, or his fellow soldier's sister, a nursing sister or a pure mother. It is she who is the true love object of these men, but she is portrayed as smooth, inactive, pale as death. The love is never activated. The only good woman is so still as to be dead. One is reminded of Andrea Dworkin's analysis of the fairy-tale representation of woman. 'When she is good, she is soon dead. In fact, when she is good, she is so passive in life that death must be only more of the same.'[8]

Third in the fascist ontology there is the Red Woman, the rifle-woman of the proletarian uprisings with which the Freikorps were in hand-to-hand battle. She is equated with the whore. She is the woman most feared and most loathed. She awakens in these men the terror that is expressed in their characteristic metaphors: flood, blood, mass, filth. Communism, like womanhood, represents for these men a terrifying melting of the upright and defended posture of the fighting man, a promiscuous mixing, a relaxing of both psychic and national boundaries. It is flowing and various, the supreme danger.

Many of the women of this third category meet their death in the course of these narratives (as they were killed by the authors and others in reality) by explosion, by bayoneting, by gunshot. Of an account by soldier-males of the killing of red women Theweleit concludes,

> It is as if two male compulsions were tearing at the women with equal strength. One is trying to push them away, to keep them at arm's length (defense); the other wants to penetrate them, to have them very near. Both compulsions seem to find satisfaction in the act of killing, where the man pushes the woman far away (takes her life) and gets very close to her (penetrates her with a bullet, a stab wound, club, etc). The closeness is made possible by robbing the woman of her identity as an object with concrete dimensions and a unique name.

The dread of women emerges as a terror men feel regarding the precise location and integrity of their self-boundaries, and their identification of woman with what lies outside those boundaries and threatens to overwhelm them.

The historic struggle of the European left, its chief responsibility in the twentieth century, has been to understand, contain and resist an organised right – often armed, often wielding state power. The Theweleit material throws light on this project: the contradictions inherent in contemporary European masculinity are highly dangerous to humankind and they are central to fascism. How can masculinity not be a central concern, then, of socialism?

Male Fantasies ought to be a warning to socialist feminists never to be satisfied with feminist demands that remain at the customary level of politics, located only on the familiar marxist terrain of labour, the economy and the state. Whatever we envision socialism to be, it has to involve for men a genuine resolution of the contradictions of masculinity, a restructuring of male subjectivity, that is emotionally realistic and that both defines and satisfies desire in a positive way. Fascism after all offers, as we can see, a workable if extreme way out of the contradictions thrown up by men's dread of strong women: kill them.

Femininity in fascism and socialism

It is important to add here, of course, that masculinity cannot be considered as distinct from femininity: gender is a relation and the genders always mirror one another. For every form taken by masculinity there is a corresponding form of femininity. Fascism therefore can be seen as offering accommodation of an extreme kind also to the contradictions experienced by women. As Maria Antonietta-Macciocchi points out, there is a problem that is often overlooked by feminists: the problem of women's active consent to fascism.

In an analysis of Mussolini's Italy she suggests that the fascist community is comprised of homo-erotic males (she says 'homosexual', but I would suggest that we leave open the question of the precise nature of such men's regard for each other), who exclude women and valorise Mother-hood.[9] Fascism depends to a large degree on the consent of women, their positive response to a very precise appellation: as asexual, as extremely differentiated from men, and as essentially mothers. Women all too readily deal with the contradictions of femininity, with the experience of 'weakness', by giving power to men and to male leaders and by seeking power exclusively through men.

Analysing a less extreme expression of right-wing culture, Beatrix Campbell finds among Conservative women in contemporary Britain a similar active accommodation by women to the subordination of their daily experience.[10] She says, 'the Conservative Party is about nothing if not about power: the power of men. Their power has been nursed by the most powerful courts, clubs and corporations in Britain – and by women; it is through the work of women that men have secured their popular base'. And women are to some extent rewarded for this loyalty. They are afforded influence. There is in many ways a more welcoming space for women within the Conservative Party than within Labourism. The price (as in fascism) is an acceptance of second place, valued but role-bound, and a distinct differentiating gender culture. 'Their femininity is reasserted in the frock.' Beneath this tip of course lies the invisible iceberg of the organization of sexuality and desire in the culture that right-wing women inhabit.

We have to recognise of course that right-wing accommodation of the contradictions of femininity does not amount to any real resolution or transcendence of them. 'What works for women in the Conservative family ideology is the sense that women are important to society because they are important to the family ... But women live their relationship to the family always in the tension between power and powerlessness, passion and pain, self-realisation and self-denial.'

Theweleit's narrative on the soldier-males of the Freikorps finds the key to their political positioning in their relationship to women. Surely the task of the left today must be to attempt the same process, in reverse, for socialism. We have to ask what would men's relationship to women be that could create, enable, or respond to a radically new politics in men with regard to nation, mode of production, militarism, nature. It has always been assumed rhetorically that if *this* is fascism, women giving their wedding rings to Mussolini, then socialism by natural contrast is a project in which women are 'liberated'. If women are liberated then the gender order among socialists must somehow be a revolutionary one. Yet socialist ideology, the practices of the left and certainly men's desires have never by any means actuated that. And until they do, nothing much else about socialism will change.

The history of 'socialism' to date shows a movement only part-way to its potential. Theweleit in fact traces the representation of women among left poets and writers, the counterparts of his fascist authors. They include Cesaire, Lorca, Brecht, Mayakovsky, Guillen, Neruda. It is striking that the imagery used negatively by the fascists is found in the work of these men too. Now it is used positively: wave, flood, stream, flow, desire. But for both right and left these are metaphors for women, and woman herself is, for left as for right, metaphorical material.

A reading of Bertolt Brecht is a case in point. I can remember my own bitter disappointment when I moved on from those few political verses of his that had been so central to our movement in the 60s and 70s to read a collection of all his poems.[11] Woman and women for Brecht are symbolic material. To read this work and fully 'get Brecht's message' I had to read *as a man*, with a man's aesthetic concerning woman. I myself (it seemed) was written out of Brecht's own project, the European socialist project with which I had always identified myself.

I understood Theweleit therefore when he wrote of these socialist poets that for them, while they do not share the fascist's terror of women, women nonetheless remain symbolic.[12]

> In a certain sense desire always flows *through* women, in relation to the image of woman ... Women it seems to me were subjugated and exploited ... put to use mainly by themselves having to absorb the productive force of men belonging to the subjugated classes of their era – all to the benefit of the dominant class.

This, for a socialist feminist, is the most devastating conclusion. Fascist men, with luck, we can keep at a distance. Socialist men we have to work with. How can we work with men for whom we are not comparable people at all, just symbolic matter? Yet how, on the other hand, can we relinquish the socialist project, the tranformation of systems of wealth, production and government, to men?

The invisible problem

A condition of working on the left, for women, is that whatever our perceptions of masculinity we must normally behave 'as though' it were possible to work with men. Similarly our theory has often steered clear of problematic issues that might throw doubt on our ability to do so. How can we build into our understanding of patriarchal capitalism (or whatever we might want to call it) a perception of masculinity and its baleful part in politics of both left and right? How can we understand the reproduction of gendering?

Freudian and post-Freudian psychoanalysis of course does explore the sexual and gendered side of human behaviour. There are socialist feminist schools of thought that do build on Freud and deal with the unconscious. Klaus Theweleit and R W Connell (whom I cite below) both choose to explain the reproduction of gender and gender differences by means of psychoanalytic theory.

Many feminists have, however, for a number of reasons, been reluctant to take that path. One reason has been its reliance on inborn instincts, with the biological determinism that implies. Another is the emphasis on the phallus, such that women (contrary to our own experience) appear as physically incomplete creatures characterised principally by a lack – of a penis. A third reason has been the individual and unpolitical nature of the Freudian cure – psychoanalysis – and the unequal social relations it involves. But perhaps more than anything we have doubted psychoanalysis for its exclusive preoccupation with infancy: experience seems to show us that our subjectivity is not fixed forever by the age of five.

Having doubts about psychoanalysis however has sometimes meant we have under-played the depth of the problem represented by masculinity. Lynne Segal's *Is the*

Future Female? may again serve as an example. She discusses the (widely acknowledged) 'gender fragility' of masculinity as it is constructed within the mother-present, father-absent family. But concludes 'a study of men's sexual fantasies and obsessions ... should lead us more to puzzle over how it is still possible for men to retain control over women *despite* their sexuality, not because of it'.[13] Feminists, she says, used to poke fun at the prick, and ridicule was the right response. Now the fun has been eroded by the rage of radical feminism. Andrea Dworkin's perception that 'sex and murder are fused in male consciousness' she dismisses as 'terrorising rhetoric', 'false and alarmingly unhelpful'.

Yet to me it seems that the fragility of masculinity is not laughable. It is expressed in the most dangerous things we live with: nuclear arsenals, uniformed men, husbands and lovers who batter and kill. And as we have seen, sex and murder are indeed fused in male consciousness, in a form of masculinity that has at periods in this century been hegemonic at state level in Europe. It is significant too as a sub-theme in the dominant form taken by masculinity in Britain today. Pornography does not seem to me, as it does to Lynne, a 'pathetic weakness', 'the last bark of a stag at bay', but rather a contemporary and very effective reassertion of men's collective project of dominating women.

Gender and oppression

Causing the blindspot in some of our socialist feminist theory and practice, it seems to me, even now is a confusion of 'sex' and 'gender'. We rightly wish to be generous to men, as individuals, and to acknowledge men who support us. And we fail to recognise that that need not hold us back from a profound anger towards *masculinity*, as we experience it today, and from challenging it with all the resources at our command. To express that anger is to do men as a sex nothing but kindness, since our culture cruelly constrains them, in varying degree, to be the bearers of a gender identity that deforms and harms them as much as it damages women. After all, feminists have recognised the same in femininity and much of the energy of the women's liberation movement has been spent on breaking out of our half of the mould.

A second problem however is that when we do affirm that sex is not destiny, that men are not jack rabbits (even when jackbooted) and that a woman is not a doe, we assume too readily that it can therefore be changed simply by wishing it changed. In actual fact, today, it might well prove easier to modify men's sexual nature (a simple hormone injection) than to remodel their gender character. The social is the truly intractable material.

We have to understand the extent of the oppression and pain inflicted on boy babies, little boys and young men, so that it is capable, internalised and shut in, of producing adult males who are equipped to participate in our violent culture as a man among men. A counsellor in the Re-evaluation Counselling movement sometimes tries to bring home to women the extent of the damage inflicted on young males by saying: 'Try to imagine what would have to have been done to you that you would grow up believing that you must be prepared to kill other women to prove yourself a woman'.[14] If we believe in the social construction of gender, that is surely the way we have to understand it. But undoing such experiences, both retrospectively by transforming our own consciousness, and for the next generation by transforming our practice, can only occur through *work* on our subjectivity – collective work and political commitment of intention, time and resources.

Structures and practices

We should ask, then, first what is the relationship between the individual and her or his history and culture? How far can we suppose that a person, the product of a particular childhood, locked into a given culture and carrying a burden of internalised oppression, is free to think and do the unexpected? And if she or he through collective effort does open up, shed the distress and shrug off the gender straitjacket – how possible is it for her or for him to transform in turn the surrounding culture? We need a way of thinking the relationship between 'me' and 'it', between the subject and society, that neither evades issues of sexuality and desire nor forecloses on the kind of transformations we have evidence can, if with difficulty, occur.

A recent analysis by R W Connell is helpful in this respect. In *Gender and Power* Connell identifies three important and enduring structures of relationship between women and men.[15]

> One has to do with the division of labour: the organization of housework and childcare, the division between unpaid and paid work, the segregation of labour markets and the creation of 'men's jobs' and 'women's jobs', discrimination in training and promotion, unequal wages and unequal exchange.
>
> The second has to do with authority, control and coercion: the hierarchies of the state and business, institutional and interpersonal violence, sexual regulation and surveillance, domestic authority and its contestation.

In outlining these two structures Connell is on ground that should be familiar and reassuring to socialists. Labour and power are after all what we know about, even if we often forget about the domestic side of labour and the male face of power. Importantly, however, Connell adds,

> There seems to be a third major structure. It has to do with the patterning of object-choice, desire and desirability; with the production of heterosexuality and homosexuality and the relationship between them; with the socially structured antagonisms of gender (woman-hating, man-hating, self-hatred); with trust and distrust, jealousy and solidarity in marriages and other relationships; and with the emotional relationships involved in rearing children.

In this third structure, the structure of cathexis, we are in new space for socialism and it is into precisely this area, I would argue, we need to carry it. Importantly, cathexis is not defined here as exclusively sexual. It is what is desired – and that may mean the love of children or the lust to kill.

Connell proceeds on the assumption that these three – labour, power and desire – while not totally exhausting the field are nonetheless the major structures within which gender relations are formed and acted out. But how can change occur? We have to suppose that a dialectical relationship links the individual subject with such cultural structures. Our practice acts on the material we are given. It negates and transforms it.

Our relationship to the 'natural' for instance is neither so tight as some feminists portray it nor so loose as others hope. 'The social practices that construct gender relations do not express natural patterns, nor do they ignore natural patterns; rather, they negate them in a practical transformation. This practical transformation is a continuing historical process. Its materials are the social as well as the biological products of previous practice – new situations and new people.'[16]

It is social practice after all that has constituted the very categories of 'men' and 'women', two groups with common identities and interests. As Gayle Rubin wrote 'Far from being an expression of natural differences, exclusive gender identity is the suppression of natural similarities'.[17] Men have been contrasted in a particular way and set at a particular distance from women, without intervening categories, not as a reflection of but as a negation of biology.

The individual too is always working on the material given – in her or his life history and in the culture. As Connell puts it, 'the personal world *is* relational ... personality has to be seen as social practice'. But individuals cohere in movements. Interests are constituted in particular categories and around these identity and action may be organised: masculinism and male dominance for instance. But new practices on old ground can cause categories and identities to splinter, giving rise to new sets of interests (contemporary gay men, for example). If a formation of interests coincides with crisis tendencies occurring at certain points in history, then resistance and struggle may be effective in bringing about change.

Thus for Connell structure is simply the intractability of the social world. It is not negligible (as some socialist feminist theory too often has it), nor is it immutable (as some 'radical feminism' sometimes suggests). The world yields, just a little, to the pull and shove of practice. Some of the practice in which we are gendered occurs in parenting and infancy. But gender, regendering and ungendering – these are lifelong projects.

Uncoupling the couple

An important component of Connell's analysis has been his notion of the multiplicity of masculinities and femininities. This makes sense if we think of the differing expressions of masculinity and femininity in different social classes, races and cultures. In a given society at a given time one form will be dominant while others may contest it. The fascist masculinity of the Freikorps is not, for the moment, dominant in our culture. Neither however can it simply be dismissed as psychotic. It is active among some men and similarities to it exist in the masculinity that is hegemonic in Britain today.

Connell's analysis however fails to take account of a key mechanism contributing both to domination by one sex of another and the reproduction of that domination over time. It is heterosexual *complementarity*. Gender is essentially a relation. A male may very well be able to exist momentarily without a female, if we are talking about biological individuals of the species. But masculinity by definition cannot be thought even for a moment without femininity. Femininity is formed *as and only as* a complement to masculinity. It has no other meaning. Any given femininity is coiled around 'its' masculinity like *yin* around *yang*, two matching, necessary, but asymmetric and unequally weighted parts of the unitary whole: the couple.[18]

This doesn't mean of course that women's and men's actual needs are complementary. Femininity may for

example specify 'helplessness' and masculinity a complementary 'chivalry'. Women are not well served by being
helpless. Men likewise may benefit little from being
obliged to be chivalrous – but the cost to them of this
gender prescription is clearly less serious than its cost to
women and its compensation is power. Neither does
observing complementarity lead necessarily to understanding between women and men. On the contrary, it is
riven with contradictions that emerge in the course of
daily practice. Complementarity exists as a rigid substruc-
ture of institutional gender regimes and societal gender
orders. In work we have a complementary sexual division
of labour: he sets it up, she does it. At home we have the
man-and-wife. In romance we have Romeo-and-Juliet.
Even the media's New Man seems to have his complement
in the Single Working Woman. Gender complementarity
is an artefact and underpinning of male power and
multiple masculinities have a linking thread: the 'otherness' of women.

We can of course assume rupture and change among
masculinities and femininities to involve momentary or
partial mismatches. But so long as heterosexual relations
inhere, such contradictions represent a crisis in the sexual,
domestic and working accommodation made between
women and men. They cannot for long be lived by
individuals in close contiguity – in bed, at home, at work,
in political struggle – without resolution. In the long run
the pressure in the gender order is for femininity to
conform to, to be adequate to, the hegemonic masculinity.
Since male power is not merely ideological but also based
in wealth, social organisation and physical might,
femininity has had little power of its own to force
adaptations in its complementary oppressor. The initiative
normally lies with masculinity. That is what is so startling
about feminism, and why our project so often seems
unlikely to succeed.

The womanhood (for we can no longer call it
femininity) to which socialist masculinity will be called to
respond and to match up will involve, tendentially and in
general outline: strong, active, inventive women, as

oriented towards women as towards men, autonomous in their values, economically independent, politically distinct, sexually various, intimate and expressive, with and without children. These women will not play dead or stay pure to please men. They will not invite or serve a sexual desire organised around a fetish rather than a person. They will 'look' all kinds of ways. They will be no-one's symbolic material, unless their own.

Women like this are emerging. But today's dominant masculinity reacts to such a person with distaste and aggression. A reconstituting masculinity might seek to find some complementary mode – a flight towards the feminine perhaps. This is hardly desirable (who wants to be feminine?) but neither is it likely since this woman is not masculine. She is complete without a complement. A change of cathectic structure is therefore called for. And it has to involve a restructuring of desire at all levels. For it is not simply that men have to be able to work politically with such women. Their relationship with *woman* has to change. It cannot be a world in which socialist men stand shoulder to shoulder with new-woman comrades, while keeping a traditionally 'attractive' and compliant wife or lover in the wings.

The implication is of course an end to complementarity in the gender order. This will do more than fragment gender into yet more multiple masculinities and femininities. It will obscure the meaning of masculinity and femininity, and indeed of gender, entirely. We are anyway probably doomed as a civilisation if we do not learn to constitute men who are similar to, not contrasted with, the women described above. Men as lovers and partners of strong women, men who are not afraid of 'mother' nor afraid 'to mother', and men for whom other men are as likely to fill the need for emotional support and softness of touch as women are. Noël Greig sees something of this when he says

> If the brave path to the future is carved out by the finger-wagging men, then sure as hell the gender system will remain intact, managed by men with whom I cannot be

tactile, whose fear of their own femininity makes them lash out with tongue or with fist.[19]

Our practice somehow has to make use of the multiplicity and transformability of the two genders in order to negate and transcend the dichotomy between masculine and feminine itself. It is not enough to bring into existence some amiable New Man, if he in turn is viable only in relation to a contrasted, fixed and responsive – albeit a touch more independent – form of femininity. The whole gender order has to be deconstructed and non-complementary female and male subjectivities made available. What we think of as socialism has to be predicated on that and on nothing less. If the 1980s is the decade of 'rethinking socialism', this should be taxing our minds.

A woman's socialism

Meanwhile, what do we have? We have Thatcher's government not only attempting to restructure the economy in the interests of capital and to subdue the working class by destroying its organisations and its 'rights', but also making inroads into our lives in the interests of intensified patriarchal domination. The scene of those thousands of flag-waving, sun-drenched families along the quay at Portsmouth welcoming home the Falklands Task Force on the aircraft carrier *Hermes* lives in my memory as a supremely successful updating and reaffirmation by the right of a gender order in which men are heroes and women love them, in which men go to war and women serve by suffering at home, in which father is absent and the child awaits him. The Conservative government's invoking of the invulnerability of the nation against a threat by an external enemy, its insistence on the acquisition of the phallic Trident missile, ring with a classic British masculinism.

Meanwhile, however, changes in capitalism are in practical ways transforming women's lives. The new flexible economy depends on proportionately more women than in the past being in paid work. While 'men's work' declines, the great majority of new jobs are clearly designed to be 'women's work' – low paid, part-time, temporary posts involving polyvalent unskilled activities. Discourses of law and the media therefore are struggling to constitute an adequate femininity for the new conjuncture. Housework and care of children, the sick and the old are reasserted as woman's first responsibility, but they must be combined with earning. 'Equal opportunities' are therefore invoked to iron out the contradictions occurring in the workplace: training for women, 'return to work' schemes for mothers. But loopholes to freedom are being stopped: abortion rights to be trimmed; the new law on embryo research to make it illegal for women to inseminate themselves with donated sperm.

The transformation of gender structure by individual and collective practice then is not only possible. It is inevitable. The right is achieving it all the time. Whether or not socialism should enter this terrain is not really the question of choice we take it to be. To be fully effective it has to.

The Labour Party's response in the 1987 general election was interesting for involving a certain apparent femininity in contrast to the Tories' assertion of masculine grit. There was the slender red rose of the public relations image. There was the emphasis on care and concern. A Ministry for Women was proposed. The unilateral nuclear disarmament policy to which the party was (narrowly) committed risked looking wimpish to a people so long exposed to Conservative militarism. That this risk was recognised by Labour was clear from its anxious affirmation of more spending on conventional military men and machines.

How conscious was the gender politics of the Labour Party campaign? Women were pushing hard for it within the Party. And some gender significance may have been visible to the voter. There was a swing of 6 per cent by women towards Labour between the 1983 and 1987 elections, as against a 2 per cent swing by men. Yet it seemed as though somehow the Labour Party were sleepwalking onto gendered terrain, led there by the Conservatives.

Meanwhile the Labour left, together with socialists outside the Labour Party, organised in October 1987 their own response to Labour's response to the Tories: a two-thousand strong conference in Chesterfield. Many women went, some of them hoping that here if anywhere would be found Hilary Wainwright's 'party in waiting'. Here the regendering of the left might become a conscious project.

But what met us there? A left that had learned not a jot from two decades of women's struggle. The platform was swathed in the scarlet satin of Labour's historic march: the banners of male-dominated trade unions. They proclaimed a return to socialist fundamentalism and a political style to match. The barracking and heckling began before the first speaker had said a word. Interrupters from Militant forcibly grabbed the microphone and were as forcibly ejected. Visitors from the Soviet Union were shouted down and mobbed by Trotskyists. The chair(man) proclaimed 'I am a physically moderate man', while flexing his muscles for the show-down. Many workshops that had been designed to enable discussion became instead platforms for a string of Socialist Workers Party plants – of appropriate sex for the topic in hand.

In such a milieu only those with the deepest and most carrying voices were heard. Only the most rehearsed interventions by the most hardened speakers got uttered from start to finish. The most simplistic arguments inevitably carried most weight. Doubts, tentative suggestions, the exploring of contradictions, for which many women (and no doubt some men) had wanted to make space – these were stifled and silenced.

It was a reminder how much the left, supposedly committed to anti-militarism, is itself militaristic in its ideology. We fight. We campaign. We form a vanguard. We hold our ground. Hugh Gaitskell's response to the party's decision on unlitateralism in the 1960s was 'I will fight, fight and fight again' to bring the party back to

sanity. Sanity and socialism will never be won by fighting.
Socialism, probably, will not even be 'built'. It is more likely
to come about by living, breathing and loving it into
existence.

The Chesterfield conference confirmed in me many of
these nascent thoughts about masculinity, women and the
left. It seemed to demonstrate that there is really still no
left in which masculinity is problematised and with which
women can productively work. The situation is critical for
us. Yet women do have a particular need of socialism and a
sex-specific interest in bringing it into being. Women's
work is often super-exploited and calls even more perhaps
than men's work for labour organisation. Women have a
characteristic conflict with the state too because so many
policies are targetted on the family. Women, as mothers,
wives and carers, are clearly designed into social provision
as unpaid workers. The Thatcher regime has its own
scenario for women, and it's not sweet freedom. So women
cannot opt out of the socialist project. Yet *our* struggle in
that project is often overlooked, misrepresented or
subverted by the men who have defined and appropriated
worker organisation and socialist politics.

A commitment to work on it

Lynne Segal harks back to 1970, to the early days of
contemporary feminism, to a time before radical feminism
had, as she sees it, misrouted the movement with its
concept of women's 'difference'.[20] I would look back to
those days too, but with another purpose. There was a
material reason for the growth of difference-politics. It
was a response to women's lived experience in the 1970s of
struggling with men's response to feminism. We *felt*
different. Not some essential or biological difference but
an empowering difference born of our centuries-long
experience as the subordinated half of the heterosexual
couple. Our history *had* given us different values. Why
should we want, in the name of equality, to be like men? As
a different kind of people we could make a different
world. And the feeling was consonant with Leftism. A

strong expression of 'difference' for instance erupted among Italian women trade unionists in 1975, angered by the failure of equality politics.

We may need, besides, to recover a number of other insights from the early days of the movement. For instance – that if the personal is political, the political is embarrassingly personal. We need to address men's masculinity, personally as women, politically as feminists, *as part of the socialist agenda.* But even more, we need to see socialist men address it themselves.

We need to remember the days of the CR group too. It was thousands of small women's affinity groups that questioned thousands of marriages, took issue with gender and gendering and gave such an impetus to the women's liberation movement. It is difficult to imagine what else could do it. In those days we expected that we would have to *work* on our consciousness if our minds were to change. That kind of work is never done once for all, or once for all succeeding generations, since the culture around us is gendering us all the time.

The logic of this analysis is of course much more separatism in socialist feminism. I do not suggest this because men are incapable of changing. Quite the contrary. It may only now be feasible, precisely because some men have begun to worry about gender for themselves and sense that it is feminism that has been giving the left whatever sense of renewal it has. Until women break complementarity, stop playing the female to the political male, stop being the token woman on the committee, progressive men will not face any necessity to be the ones to raise the gender issue and do the CR work they need to do with other men. It is possible that 'being the feminist' in the mixed group is the latest twist in the feminine gender role. It certainly ensures that women's energies continue to bleed away into the left.

Socialist feminism has been afraid of separatism. It has been seen as relevant, if at all, only on matters clearly definable as 'women's issues'. Yet peace is a universal issue and the autonomous women's peace movement has been powerful. Through a productive (if tension-ridden)

alliance between radical, anarchist, socialist and other
kinds of feminism, it has come up over a period of six or
seven years with insights about the relationship between
masculinity and militarism, and a brilliant political
expressiveness, that could not have emerged from a
mixed-sex movement alone.

There are structures where separatism may seem
self-defeating and where a pushy internal autonomy may
seem better: the Labour Party, the unions. But even in
these cases I believe it is still correct to wonder whether the
only significant effect can be had from within. It is
arguable that in the long run the lesbians who absailed
down the visitors' balcony in the House of Lords in
February 1988 may have more impact on gay rights than
the women who watched them from the chamber below.

Women could be independently active, with all those
flashes of imagination we have learned to use, on any
number of 'socialist' issues: civil liberties; anti-racism;
against privatisation; for education; international solidarity. We will never know the shape and scope of a woman's
socialism until we take the space to be inventive of it – not
on a limited range of concerns that men are happy to leave
to us, but *on socialist terrain*.

Many of us are after all part-radical, part-socialist
feminist (whatever those names in the end mean) and the
radical within us is saying: we either have to go it alone or
set far more rigorous terms for any continuing
engagement – 'alliance' may be premature – with men on
the left. Our struggle with the right has to include a
conscious struggle with its gender ideology, and it is
impossible for that struggle to happen until we are actually
living a new gender politics on the left.

So our terms might include for instance making it a
condition that any mixed group we are in should engage
the help of a counsellor to increase awareness of the
gender, race and class dynamics, and work to improve
them. Or we might only agree to join with men on the left
so long as those men themselves are committed
simultaneously to meeting and working with each other on
issues concerning their own masculinity and the quality of

their relationship with each other and with women. More – on what those perceptions mean for a socialist agenda. Gender ideology and practice aren't transformed by simply deciding to do it. They are only changed by hard graft, collective and sustained. A policy commitment in left organisations to that kind of work, led by men rather than pushed by women, would be a real beginning to rethinking socialism.

I would like to thank a number of women friends, including Lynne Segal, for their critical but patient engagement with me in developing these ideas.

Notes

[1] Sheila Rowbotham, Lynne Segal and Hilary Wainwright, *Beyond the Fragments: Feminism and the Making of Socialism*, Merlin Press, 1979.

[2] Sheila Rowbotham, *Woman's Consciousness, Man's World*, Penguin, 1973

[3] Hilary Wainwright, *Labour: a Tale of Two Parties*, The Hogarth Press, 1987

[4] Lynne Segal, *Is the Future Female? Troubled Thoughts on Contemporary Feminism*, Virago Press, 1987.

[5] Tony Cliff, *Class Struggle and Women's Liberation*, Bookmarks, 1984

[6] Wilhelm Reich, *The Mass Psychology of Fascism*, Penguin, 1980

[7] Kalus Theweleit, *Male Fantasies*, Polity Press, 1987.

[8] Andrea Dworkin, *Woman Hating*, E P Dutton (New York), 1974.

[9] Maria-Antonietta Macciocchi, 'Female Sexuality in Fascist Ideology', *Feminist Review*, no 1, 1979.

[10] Beatrix Campbell, *The Iron Ladies: Why Do Women Vote Tory?*, Virago Press, 1987.

[11] Bertolt Brecht, *Poems 1913–1956*, Methuen, 1976.

[12] Klaus Theweleit, *op. cit.*

[13] Lynne Segal, *op. cit.*

[14] Personal communication.

[15] R.W. Connell, *Gender and Power*, Polity Press, 1987.

[16] *Ibid.*

[17] Gayle Rubin, 'The traffic in women: notes on the political economy of sex', in Rayna R Reiter, ed, *Towards an Anthropology of Women*, Monthly Review Press, 1975.

[18] Cynthia Cockburn, *Brothers: Male Dominance and Technological Change*, Pluto Press, 1983; and *Machinery of Dominance: Women, Men and Technical Knowhow*, Pluto Press, 1985.

[19] Noël Greig, 'The Body Electric', in Eileen Phillips (ed) *The Left and the Erotic*, Lawrence and Wishart, 1983.

[20] Lynne Segal, *op. cit.*